Marketing Mayhem

Why Marketing Isn't Producing The Way It Used To

- † The Symptoms
- † The Antidotes

HERSCHELL GORDON LEWIS

© 2001 Herschell Gordon Lewis

Published by

Racom Communications
815 Ridge Ave.
Evanston, IL 60202 U.S.A.

And

DIRECT Magazine
11 River Bend Drive South
Stamford, CT 06907 U.S.A.
DIRECT is a trademark of Primedia Business.

All rights reserved. No part of this book may be reproduced, stored in a retrieval system, or transmitted in any form or by any means, electric, mechanical, photocopying, recording, or otherwise, without the prior written permission of the Publisher.

Catalog-in-Publication data available from the Library of Congress.

Printed in the United States of America
ISBN: 0-9704515-3-9

Contents

Acknowledgments   7

Preface   9

Introduction   11

I.   Imaginative Sterility   15

The Jamie Lee Curtis Syndrome   17

Nike and Mike . . . John Paul, The Frito Bandito, Pierce . . .
     and Almost Everybody Else   21

Lee Iacocca, Look What You Did   23

Hara-kiri: 21st-Century Style   26

"Please Stay on the Line for a Self-serving Message"   30

Reader's In-Digest-ion   34

Where Does an Alien Go to Register?   37

Idiots' Delight   41

New Uses for Software Campaigns:
     A Limp 3½-inch Floppy   44

Hit-and-Run Appeals to Fragments   50

The Peanut Gallery: A Digestive Directive   58

Our Version of the Boston Tea Party   61

It Ain't Necessarily So: Ten Creative "Myths"   64

II.   Process/Technology Abuse   79

Marquis de Sade, Author of Owner's Manuals   83

Invasion of the Term-Throwers, Part 1   86

Invasion of the Term-Throwers, Part 2   90

Invasion of the Term-Throwers, Part 3   96

What a Surprise: Nobody Is Responsible   100

Before We Had "CRM," We Actually Had
    Customer Relationships   104

CRM by the Pound   107

Darwin Was Right: The Evolution of Motivators   110

Will the Real Sax Lewis Please Stand Up . . . ?   114

Some Attitudes Just Don't Compute:
    Smart Uses of Smarter Tools   117

They'll Never Know the Difference"   120

Sweet Sue!   125

A Really Simple Way to Connect with Your Customers:
    Shipping and Handling   129

Some Really Dumb Uses of Really Smart Tools   133

III. Language Abuse   137

Basically, I'd Like to Define This as a Paradigm Shift 139

Cell-Phone Phonies   142

But Wait, There's More!   146

L.O.L.: Take Out the Periods and It's Short
    for Lollygagging   150

A Blockbuster of a Marketing Mistake   153

The Importance of Saying "Important"   156

Free at Last? Well, Sort of . . . Except . . .   164

An Embarrassment of Riches   167

When It Comes to Award-Winning Artists,
    We Mean Business. Let's Shake on It   170

If Your Caddy Zigs, Does Your Jaguar Jag? Does Your
    Saab Sob? And How about a Pap Test for Your Volvo?   174

Rocket and Roadmaster, Where Are You?   178

Lawyers on Skateboards   181

Aw, Come On, You Know Better than to Use These Words 184

I Admire You, You Rascal, You 187

If John Caples Were Alive Today, He'd Be
    Turning over in His Grave 192

Standing on Our Heads, Riding the Tsunami 195

Let's Be More Niggardly with Our Euphemisms 199

New and Improved: A Good Old-fashioned
    Home-made Original 203

IV. Customer Abuse 207

Service with a Snile 209

Get Out of My Face! 212

Your Call Is Important to Us. Please Rot on the Line. 216

"And How Are You Today?" "Terrible, Thanks." 219

The Decline and Fall of Telephone Manners 223

Au Revoir to an Old Friend 227

Latest Online Service: Customer Elimination Department 231

Retail Riddance 234

High Tech, Low Tech. The Breitling Chronicles 238

The Large Type Giveth & the Small Type Taketh Away:
    That *$%#@*Asterisk Strikes Again 241

Is It Any Wonder They're Skeptical? 248

Where Is Ed McMahon Now That We Need Him? 253

Vee Know Where You Liff! 257

Here's Your Official Survey: We Need Your Opinion
    on Latvian Flag Design 261

Post Mortem 267

Index 271

Acknowledgments

That this wild and blasphemous book appears in print is due to the wisdom and foresight—no, make that the courage—of Richard Hagle, who survived being my editor at another publishing company and now runs Racom Books. Rich, my supreme thanks.

My thanks, too, to Ray Schultz, the editor of the magazine *Direct*, in whose pages some of these comments have appeared in a different form. Ray's combination of editorial grit, patience, and indefatigable sense of humor have to be unique in the world of editorial judgment.

My son Bob, quoted often in these pages, supplied some of the nasty examples. More to the point, he has inherited my malevolent view of inept communications and is my co-sponsor of National Boycott Stupidity Day.

Carol Nelson and Peggy Nelson, who probably are embarrassed to acknowledge their relationship to me, both contributed some of the episodes in this weird collection.

But as usual, the principal motivator, the principal source of both information and inspiration, and the principal reason I still can lay claim to a modicum of sanity is my wife and life-partner Margo . . . who, as you'll see in these pages, not only buys me wristwatches but also brews a mean cup of coffee. (Off the point: Nobody makes better fried chicken.)

Without these folks, the book you're holding in your hands

would still be wood-pulp. Maybe you'll think that would have been better. Or maybe you like, as I do, to stick it to people who deserve getting stuck.

—Herschell Gordon Lewis

Preface

"You attack just about everybody in advertising and marketing, in this book."

That comment, made by a friend who read the manuscript, is unfair. I don't attack everybody. I attack three types: (1) Those who run on tracks; (2) Those who perpetuate clichés; (3) Those who come up with, execute, and then defend stupid and/or transparently venal ideas.

It's that last group who are the most infuriating. Coming up with a stupid idea is no creative crime . . . if someone with even a dollop of common sense squashes it before it sees daylight. Even executing a stupid idea doesn't have to confirm that the brain stem comes to a dead end. But defending a stupid idea? Or selling out your common sense to greed? That deserves being drummed out of the corps.

You may conclude that the whole notion of this book is outside the pale of fair comment, a wasted effort. You know what? You may be right. Proof will be whether one person—*one* person, who might be on the cusp of giving a car a ridiculous name . . . or adding to the dull and hackneyed pile of "You've been pre-approved" mailings . . . or sending an "Invitation" that includes a self-defeating "Application" . . . or putting together a cell-phone ad loaded with disclaimer-asterisks . . . might be deterred and re-tracked. If we accomplish that, then it hasn't been a wasted effort after all.

On the positive side, if you have a sense of humor I think you'll like this book. If you object to television commercials that leave you wondering, "What was that all about?" I think you'll like this book. If you object to celebrity endorsers who obviously don't have a clue about what they're endorsing but are simply collecting money for the use of their names, I think you'll like this book. If you object to class-action suit lawyers, you'll like this book.

So why not join me as we take a good-natured swipe at the poseurs, the posturers, the no-talents, the copycats and imitators . . . and everybody else who doesn't think the way we do?

HGL

Introduction

In the Preface to this book I said I want you to enjoy a laugh at the expense of the impostors and poseurs.

My reputation may precede me. If you've read any of my previous books or articles, you'll recognize some of my criticisms and complaints. Please say you were entertained. That was part of the objective, as is true for this book. I'm confident you'll be agreeing with me when I ask, "Who pseudo-created that piece of silliness? Even more disastrous, who approved it?" And if you laugh at some of my comments, you're my kind of cynic.

But please don't misunderstand. This is a deadly serious book about a deadly serious subject: money—yours, your company's or your client's . . . which in the 21st century means it's about profitability and survival. It's about the "Marketing Mayhem" that has been going on for the last batch of years, ever since the "Look how clever I am" school took over so much of the rocky world of force-communication. It's about the chaos and financial bloodletting caused by thoughtless and ill-considered approaches to communicating with one's markets.

We have new and sophisticated technology and marketing capabilities—on a level people only dreamed about a decade ago. Yet response rates have plummeted to catastrophic levels. Marketing costs and expenses are up. You know what that means: Profitability is down.

And no one seems to know why. Huh? Sorry, folks. In this era of advanced term-throwing, the management types—armed with their statistical models and advanced computer applications—don't *not* know what they're talking about. They just "lack visibility." Despite all the talk about the importance of "branding," customer skepticism about products and the marketers who sell them is at an all-time high. In short, we seem to have more means of communicating with customers and we're using all those channels to do a more dismal job than ever. And no one knows why.

Aw, come on. Make that no one *admits to knowing* why.

Skeptical curmudgeon that I am, I think I do know why . . . or at least I've identified the symptoms and some basic antidotes. The mayhem of our Marketing Apocalypse, like its biblical counterpart, has four parts:

- Imaginative Sterility
- Process/Technology Abuse
- Language Abuse
- Customer Abuse

I've organized this book around these four symptoms of the current problem with marketing.

It may be ironic, but over the course of the past twenty years, there has been an exponential increase in the number of books devoted to creativity and innovation . . . and a corresponding *decrease* in actual productive creative output (at least the only kind that counts . . . the kind measured in sales and profitability).

I won't arbitrarily disagree with any individual system for organizing one's thoughts (oh, all right, I probably will). But systems are mechanical. The greatest faults are in areas requiring salesmanship: emphasis and application. I certainly believe in rules (God knows, I've written book after book devoted to rules), but they're rules to be applied with intelligence and sensitivity. Unfortunately, would-be marketers, like gambling addicts on a losing streak at Las Vegas, look for a magic system that will do the job for them. No thinking required; just, as the statisticians say about statistical software, "plug and chug."

They look everywhere . . . except at the obvious place, the customer. Once you have a picture of the customer—and we have a plethora of tools for getting a photorealistic picture—you need to replicate the image of that person. Not just a bunch of statistics, a picture of an actual human being with real motivations and wants and aspirations. *That's* the person you're selling to. Once you have that picture, you can speak to that person in language and terminology that matter to him . . . you can sell him without lying or bullying or speaking down . . . and you've achieved the beginning of a genuine customer relationship, not just the by-rote repetition of the already-clichéd acronym CRM. That's how the world of marketing can avoid Apocalypse . . . now and later.

Notice, please: I didn't number these four symptoms 1,2,3,4. I can't know what the sequence or relationship is, or should be, for any specific marketing program. These are more like a continuous thread. Imaginative sterility might cause a desperate marketer to abuse his process or technology or language. Or it might start with term-throwing or overreliance on production effects that eventually degenerate into imaginative sterility. I don't know, and if you waste your time and energy on that exercise, you'll have missed the point.

And what's the point? Any of these symptoms spells trouble. They're like the creeping blight. One eventually leads to the presence of all . . . and plop! Into the trash-can goes marketing that uses the best of the wonderful new processes and technology, creates customer rapport by speaking in language that matters to the prospect, and forges links creating strong customer relationships.

Consider the happy alternative: Eliminating one diminishes the effect of all . . . and improves the productivity and profitability of your marketing.

You're in command. Which choice do you make?

Imaginative Sterility

Those who pay others to "create" advertising, Web sites, e-mail, and direct mail should ask themselves two questions:

1. What does my creative source offer, that will convince the reader, viewer, or listener to do business with me?

2. Am I qualified to judge whether the person or company I'm paying for this creative work is competent?

The second question is at least as important as the first . . . possibly more so. Oh, yes, we see so much mediocre, unconvincing, unprofessional, downright amateurish creative work appearing in expensive campaigns that our quick and natural reaction is, "What idiot wrote that? What moron art-directed it?"

Coincidentally, we should be asking, "What idiot approved that ridiculously unprofessional, non-motivating message? What moron said, 'Go ahead and run it'"?

Who is the more guilty party, the marketing murderer-for-hire hitman who pulls the trigger or the hidden puppet-master who pays for the hit?

We see a nondescript campaign. We shrug.

Then we see the campaign elements repeated. Again we shrug.

When we realize that whoever is pulling the strings doesn't know when to stop a runaway train of mediocrity, our shrug turns to a sneer of contempt.

We see advertising and, increasingly, Web sites in which the creative team has tried to cover imaginative sterility with a bunch of mechanical tricks. Overuse of color replaces simple use of imagination. Whirs and flashes replace simple salesmanship. Should we be impressed . . . or *de*pressed, because others outside our own orbit have to recognize, sooner or later, what we (as cold-hearted internal critics) immediately recognize?

And on we go, to a technique that's such an obvious crutch it's painful—dependence on a "celebrity" to have that celebrity's notoriety bleed over onto our product or service.

What is most frustrating about these current practices is their melding of the nasty elements of ignorance and cynicism. Oh, Watsonian Behaviorism—the "bulk" theory of multiple impressions hammering down the walls of buyer resistance—still has a minor effect in The Age of Skepticism. So what happens? The perpetrator overproduces a television spot or spends a ton of money on an advertising campaign or dresses up his Web site like a Kabuki performer or sends half a million semi-effective e-mails.

And of course *some* action results. And of course those involved crow, "It pulled." Ah, did it? Do they have the remotest clue how much better it might have pulled if attention to human motivation and simple targeting had been more thoughtful and more effective?

The epidemic of dot.com demises was (is?) due as much to arrogance as to stupidity. Oh, yes, those two character traits often travel in tandem. Oh, yes, the maniacal need to show off too often overrides any fragment of good judgment that may try vainly to prevent the inevitable waste . . . and then disaster . . . that have to attend the implementation of promotional plans founded on the loose sands of arrogance and stupidity instead of the solid rock of sound, ego-less business judgment.

With that imprecation, take a look at some case histories:

The Jamie Lee Curtis Syndrome

If you've seen those incomprehensible television commercials displaying the actress Jamie Lee Curtis strutting around with that annoying swagger she affects, I have three questions:

1. Do the commercials make any sense at all?

2. Can you remember the name of the misguided phone company that for some insane reason is paying her to smirk at the camera, both on TV and in those silly space ads?

3. Haven't you, over years of exposure to nonsensical celebrity "endorsements" (whatever happened to William Shatner?), become cynical about the sincerity of these for-pay spokespeople?

REBUILDING FIRESTONE WITH MATCHSTICKS

I bring this up not only because I find the Jamie Lee Curtis Syndrome an indication of the imaginative sterility so many advertisers and their agencies seem to share, but also because of Firestone's naive blurting in the advertising trade publications that it would be seeking out a celebrity endorser to help rebuild its tarnished image.

Note, please: Firestone didn't announce any changes in production or quality control. Instead, the company carved the standard crude crutch that substitutes attention for salesmanship: We'll hire some actor and let his own image rub off on us. He gets a lot of money, which makes him happy, and we don't have to struggle to come up with salesworthy ideas, which makes us happy.

Years and years ago, Firestone made a deal with the highly respected actor James Stewart. I'm not defending the late Mr. Stewart, but circumstances were different. He was a sort of interlocutor, a sincere-looking introducer, not a winged savior. For a company to crow with pride about a decision to coattail ride on an actor's ego-rich image, assuming that temporary rapport is optimal advertising . . . well, that speaks too well about the decline of the magical marketing "cocktail"—the easy blend of rapport with sanity and aggressiveness.

WHERE'S YOUR WATCH, ANNA?

Now we have saturation advertising by a wristwatch. Do we see a watch? No, we see tennis glamour girl Anna Kournikova, *not* wearing a watch. Uh . . . what's the name of the watch? For that matter, when was the last time Anna Kournikova won a tournament?

Winner or not, if she were hawking tennis wear or sporting goods, or even if she were just wearing the watch, we could qualify the advertising as advertising. But no, we have to add this to the Firestone stack—mindless dependence on a celebrity.

Now, wait. Is she replacing Cindy Crawford, who is just coming into full flower hormonally and is becoming a senior citizen as a model? Cindy Crawford also has been in these watch ads, never wearing a watch. Aah, who cares, except the celebrity endorsers and their agents? I'll tell you who *should* care: Whoever is paying for these ads.

Jack Nicklaus is reported to be switching from Maxfli golf balls to Nike. I suppose it's his right, as he approaches his dotage . . . and who cares that Maxfli balls flew through the air so wondrously during his peak playing years?

Venus Williams is in sync, collecting her $40 million from Nike. There's a bit of Nicklaus-type irony here, since Venus Williams had a contract with Reebok when she shot to fame.

Typical one-upmanship, generic to contemporary sports endorsers: Nike made a $25 million deal with Monica Seles. So Martina Hingis had to get $30 million. Venus Williams needed a sweeter bottom-line, didn't she? (I'd better get off this tack. I play a respectable game of tennis, and Nike won't even give me a tee shirt.)

Understand, please: Despite the obscene amounts of money involved, I'm not criticizing Nike for paying Venus Williams and also dishing out—what is it, another $40 million?—to Tiger Woods. Tiger Woods is the ultimate endorser—bright, affable, literate, and probably the best golfer ever. He wears their swoosh. Michael Jordan still has his name on Nike basketball shoes. Buick's deal with Tiger Woods? More questionable, because endorsing two high-profile products smacks of the kind of commercial insincerity we identify with Arnold Palmer and Bill Cosby (although with Tiger Woods' charisma, he might have saved Oldsmobile).

Nor am I criticizing Kyle Maclachlan for Ermenegildo Zegna men's fashions. He is nothing more than a model here, a tailor's dummy for men's fashions. And maybe he'll make enough money to buy a comb.

Jerry Seinfeld's pitches for the American Express card always made me itchy. I felt it was a mismatch—too proletarian a pitch for AmEx and a weak attempt to promote Seinfeld as a comedian. In no way did this campaign have the verisimilitude of ancient but credible Karl Malden and his still-remembered "Don't leave home without it." Malden was totally in character and had instant credibility as he moved from a recent role as a street-smart, straight-down-the-line honest cop from a popular contemporary TV show.

AND, BY THE WAY, WHAT WAS THE POINT?

Did Jonathan Pryce abandon Infiniti or was it the reverse? Regardless, it's a relief, because both he and the viewers were uncomfortable. It paralleled some pillar of society being sentenced to community service.

And I'm still chuckling over Flooz, whatever that is, mounting a campaign touting "valuable business advice from Whoopi Gold-

berg." I discussed this with my own financial advisor, Rodney Dangerfield, and we agreed to buy 100 shares of Day Old Bread, Ltd.

Flooz has other, bigger problems. Get this key slogan: "Flooz®.
Just what you wished for.™" And the Web links don't link. And . . .
But why should we give them free advice? It's too late anyway.
Flooz sank into bankruptcy, perfectly consistent with their market-
ing wisdom.

I'll tell you who needs advice: Pier 1. Their television commercial has zaftig actress Kirstie Alley careening around in what appears to be a savage attack of St. Vitus' Dance. And Minute Maid
orange juice has Popeye and his nemesis Bluto, in a strange anima-
tion that defies any relationship with the product.

One of the more puzzling ads is headed, "The artists, the
thinkers, the personalities and achievers, the great beauties and
fascinating women of our time . . . THE GOLD FASHIONED
GIRLS." Below a strange photograph of a woman wearing tights
and ballet slippers, doing the split, is this: "Darcey Russell, Principal Dancer, The Royal Ballet, London, one of those who always
go out in the Gold." That's it except for a logo which says
"anglogold."

Huh? This full-page, full-color semi-ad wasn't in a UK publication; it was in a U.S. magazine. What was supposed to happen as
the result of the strange overproduced puzzle? And how many readers of the magazine identify either with Darcey Russell or her con-
tortions?

I'm convinced that a huge percentage of celebrity endorsements
are the result of advertising people just wanting to get their photographs taken, standing next to or playing golf with "Who." If that's
your own hidden agenda, I know a celebrity who's available right
now and will be glad to pose with you, pending an assignment. Get
out your five iron and meet O.J. on the third tee.

Nike and Mike . . . John Paul, The Frito Bandito, Pierce . . . and Almost Everybody Else

Nike is the archetype of the shiny-new-century marketer: Big, gutsy, proud, fearless, and moderately unscrupulous.

Some degree of mourning has to drop Nike's flag to half-mast because Michael Jordan no longer hangs from the hoop. To hundreds of thousands . . . make that *millions* . . . of underprivileged kids, Michael Jordan *was* Nike. That made him into a greater-than-life icon, the being they could be. And they all wore Nikes.

(I'm in partial mourning, too, because Michael Jordan exemplified *class*, and except maybe for Tiger Woods we don't have that in sports these days. The class acts—Lou Gehrig, Ted Williams, Don Budge, Sid Luckman—they're all either playing golf or gone to that great playground in the sky. They've been replaced by "Look at me!" poseurs such as Latrell Sprewell, Dennis Rodman, and the nasty disciples of John McEnroe. We see lots of gold chains . . . and hear egomaniacal ravings of pure brass.)

Living in South Florida, where we have "Pro Player Stadium" and a hockey arena mysteriously named "The National Car Rental Center," I shouldn't be surprised by the peculiar and sometimes bizarre commercial sponsorships of what's supposed to be public domain. So why does it bother me that the Children's Museum of Manhattan had Merck Pharmaceuticals sponsoring its "Body Odyssey"? I can see future exhibits: parts of the body labeled with prescriptions. Why not be logical and have Lever 2000 soap as sponsor of "Body Odyssey"?

A STRANGE ODYSSEY

But stranger yet was the visit a couple of years ago of the Pope to Mexico City and St. Louis (a peculiar combination of venues, don't you think?). The papal tour was sponsored by Frito-Lay and

Hewlett-Packard and Mercedes-Benz and Pepsi and I don't know who else. I had always regarded the Frito Bandito as the antiChrist, but obviously an epiphanous conversion has occurred.

(Apostolic Nuncio Justo Mullor told the Mexico City newspaper *Reforma*: "We live in an era of advertising and we are men of that era.")

Product placement takes a quantum leap forward! The Pope can't wear a Brioni suit, as Pierce Brosnan does in his James Bond appearances; and I assume he doesn't carry a Glock. But his product placement parallels James Bond–Mercedes-Benz instead of BMW: "The name is Paul. John Paul."

We're early in the game, so the Pope didn't show up with emblems plastered all over his robes like a race car driver. But the trend is clear: Commercial sponsorships now extend their tentacles to every target that can smear some image on them.

So a generation from now we can look forward to sponsorships bringing religion into full focus . . . as in TV camera focus. The Shoes of the Fisherman will be Nikes, of course. The Lord's Prayer will be, "Give us each day our Rosen's Rye." The imperative will be, "Cast your Wonder Bread upon the waters and your Rexall vitamins will be returned a thousandfold." And Northwest Airlines can advertise: "Whither thou goest I shall go, although your luggage goeth elsewhere."

We've opened a huge Pandora's Box of opportunities. Remember the ancient "Suzy Chapstick" commercials? Well, in the words of Al Jolson, you ain't seen nothin' yet. The last syllable of the Palestinian leader's name lends itself to a memorable endorsement for Procter & Gamble: "My name used to be Ara-fat. Now it's Ara-Olean." Sometime Senate majority leader Trent Lott can make his spouse available to Morton's Salt, "the choice of Lott's wife." Monica Lewinsky can certainly speak for Nestle. (She's already been the mouthpiece for Cohibas.) William Shatner can have his pick of any number of sanitary supplies. (Sarah Jessica Parker can't.)

The biggest benefit will be to those who have trouble singing "The Star Spangled Banner." We'll bring those lyrics down to earth. "The rocket's red glare" certainly makes less sense than its successor, "The Alero's crimson exhaust."

PARENTHETICAL BLEND

The way to blend these cultures so the contagious cynicism behind them is less obvious is through a simple device: a pair of parentheses. Among those who prefer communication over pomposity and obfuscation, parentheses already are replacing asterisks.

We can save Social Security and start whittling away at the national debt by offering sponsorships, camouflaged inside parentheses:

"Oh, say does that star-spangled Banner (amazon.com) still wave ("L'Oreal), o'er the land (quarter-acre lots, $495) of the free (except for shipping, handling, insurance, and markup) and the home (in this desirable subdivision with a view of running water) of the (Atlanta) brave(s)."

You can see the happy future: We're architects (courtesy of the Frank Lloyd Wright Foundation) of destiny, leaving our footprints (Dr. Scholl's) on the sands of Time (Professional rate $39.97, you save 74% off the cover Price . . . and, oh, Waterhouse).

Lee Iococca, Look What You Did.

Until Lee Iococca came along, corporate chief executives were content with their overpaid salaries, their overstuffed perks, their overgreedy stock options, and the oversize golden parachutes they left—sometimes tiptoeing through the corporate wreckage they had caused. They were shadowy figures, despite little exposés such as the whimsical movie *Roger and Me*, about one guy's argument with the chairman of General Motors.

The only CEOs whose mugs we saw on television were the owners of car dealerships, stumbling over words on the TelePrompTer. They were just local entrepreneurs looking for recognition at their country clubs, so we could excuse the realization that today's celebrity is a guy who can afford television time. We also had and have retailers such as Sy and Marcy Syms, whose stores are in just 16 states, so they're sort of local. And they seem to be relatively harmless.

Iococca's massive ego changed all that. His face appeared everywhere. He *was* Chrysler. His ghastly cliché, "If you can find a better car, buy it," became as much a part of Americana as "What the hell" . . . although "What the hell" has considerably more impact. He also made an embarrassing guest appearance on the TV show "Miami Vice" for reasons best known to God and Don Johnson. Aw, what the hell. When he left, to the smaller-wheeled universe of bicycles or whatever, no one dared replace him.

But the notoriety attending ego has saturated corporate America, and now a strange variety of would-be's are telling their advertising agencies: "Forget Arnold Palmer and Ed McMahon. [Good idea.] Bill Cosby is maxed out. I can't deal with the women's soccer team's agent. I'll do my own commercials."

HERE COME DAVE, CHARLES, AND ALL THOSE OTHERS.

So here is tired Dave Thomas, hawking for Wendy's. Is he really a potent follow-up to Clara Peller's classic "Where's the beef?"?

I have no quarrel with Dave Thomas. He's a sort-of neighbor, and his wife and mine are on the same save-the-arts committees. But, really, aren't the commercials tailored to glorify him instead of the restaurants? Hasn't the rapport of the early days given way to a "Let's get on with it" indifference?

The key question: Does his appearance in the television commercials increase market share? Ray Kroc built McDonald's into a behemoth without even once appearing on-camera. (I wonder what he would have thought of "Did somebody say McDonald's?" Too many jesters scream, "No!" when that strange slogan appears. What the hell.)

Over the years, I've quietly watched Charles Schwab quietly age in his quiet television commercials. This guy knows how to deliver a sincere pitch without becoming strident or cute. I like him more than I ever liked Lee Iococca, but his success has spawned a batch of would-be brokers.

For example, here comes one now. I have a sizable chunk of Fidelity Mutual Funds. The broker sold me the idea based on stock market volatility (true) and Fidelity's solid, no-nonsense management (now in question). I think Peter Lynch is the name of the white-haired chap who keeps his hands in his pockets and mumbles platitudes such as "You've got to make a plan and stick with it for the long-term. 10, 20, 30 years out."

Whoever directed these spots should have provided a clip-board so this fellow could have something to do with his hands. Whoever approved the message–could it have been this same guy?—has a gnat's-eye view of what the typical investor wants. 30 years out? Tell it to my embalmer. What the hell.

Then we have Ruth Fertel, of Ruth's Chris Steak House. Isn't there one word too many in that corporate name? Okay, her first name is on the door, but so is Chris's, whoever he might be. I ask her and her legions of restaurateur followers: Aren't testimonials by diners more compelling than owner crowings?

I'll qualify this next one as an opinion, but I have to add the hope that you share it: One of the most annoying self-subsidizing spokespeople was a man named Victor Kiam (now defunct), who originally touted Remington razors with the line, "I liked it so much I bought the company." The concept was sound; the delivery was in a "Nyaah, nyaah, look at me!" tone that would have made Dale Carnegie cringe. What the hell.

These self-puffers aren't parallel to the spate of political candidates whose mugs we're beginning to see all over the tube and the Net. Political candidates owe it to us to let us see what their makeup experts, hairdressers, and clothes designers have wrought. After all, the winning candidates are going to control our destiny. Like it or not, they're our super-partners. An ugly thought. What the hell.

Hah! Isn't that exactly what the Iococca-pretenders also want? In their warped psyches, *they* become paramount over *what they're selling*. How Caesarian! (The emperor, not the delivery.)

So all right. Let these people strut and preen and sell themselves instead of their products and services. Let them think they have the polish of a professional spokesperson such as Arnold Palmer or what used to be Bill Cosby. Let their toadying advertising agencies feed their egos so the agency executives can feed their families. But we should have a say, because we, their targets, are unwitting targets, penalized by being forced to commit these faces to memory.

Yeah, we're marketers. But we're also consumers. You know what to do when they pop onto the screen: Shrug and say, "What the hell."

Hara-kiri, 21st-Century Style: Broadcast Is Knifing Itself.

If you're old enough, you remember a nasty World War II Japanese procedure—hara-kiri.

We saw the technique in "The Bridge Over the River Kwai," in which the actor Sessue Hayakawa, playing the role of a prison camp commander, found himself outwitted by British prisoner-in-charge Alec Guinness. So Hayakawa dressed himself in his finest silk robe and prepared to rip out his own guts.

Do you see a parallel with network, cable, and local television . . . and radio, for that matter? Both are/were committing suicide. But do you see the difference: The Hyakawa character understood what he was doing. Media managers appear to be oblivious to the implications of their actions.

Broadcast's darling-target, the 24–49 age group, is migrating to the Web. Fresh cable channels are eating up the new capacity of fiber-optic lines. And yet . . .

The established maximum allotment of commercial time within a television hour used to be eight minutes. Then it was ten . . . twelve . . . sixteen. Now some hours carry eighteen minutes of commercials. And in the same pod we'll see a Mercury automobile commercial back-to-back with an Acura commercial. Here's Volvo, followed immediately by BMW.

What's this? A spot for Honda, "completely redesigned." Without a beat or a blank frame, it's Chrysler, "completely redesigned." So sure, Burger King and Wendy's can be podmates.

Okay, if broadcast stations want to blur the competitive lines, that's their right. So it follows that if they want to commit hara-kiri, I guess it makes sense. It's the only honorable thing to do.

But I just flat-out don't understand why the advertising agencies don't kick up a hue and cry about one of the most obnoxious procedures television has ever implemented: butting up two commercials against each other without a fade-out/fade in, so the viewer can't even tell that one has ended and another one begun. It's bleep-bloop-bleep . . . where am I? What this "just-splice-'em-together" approach shows is contempt for the hand that feeds the medium.

NEVER IN DIRECT MAIL

Would we ever send out a direct mail package that included a pitch for a local Mercury dealer and a pitch for a different Acura dealer and the next day have Volvo and BMW wedded in an uneasy combination as uncomfortable as the principals of that "How to marry a millionaire" fiasco? No, I'm not referring to "marriage mail" . . . although if television sells its spots, especially network spots, as marriage-spots, both seller and buyer have a cranial defect. It's a marriage made in hell.

Those of us who make our livings by professional exhortation we carefully structure to generate *singular* buying decisions are totally out of sync with television's hara-kiri. Eighteen minutes of commercials? That's 36 commercials, minimum. If a third of those are split-30s, it's 48 commercials. At what point does the Law of Diminishing Returns turn that shot in the foot into a gangrenous mess?

The ludicrous invasion of television as an advertising medium by dot-com companies, accompanied by ludicrous commercials for dot-com companies, has been a bonanza for the stations. Sane commentators long since have agreed that aside from the confusion they add, these spots have dried up barter time and infomercial availabilities—the manna DRTV marketers have to feed on, or perish. But the benefit to the broadcast stations is that they don't have to deliver a specific audience. (Purists please note: I'm aware that the true meaning of "audience" is a group that *hears* something.) They air the "Whee! We're here for whoever out there might be interested in what we do, which we aren't about to tell you" commercials, the 21st century version of "I shot an arrow into the air; it fell to earth I know not where." Make that "I care not where."

I guess direct marketers can quit apologizing for their own brand of clutter—the multiplicity of "You've been pre-approved" financial mailings with dollar and percentage numbers that defy any eyeblink test. At least theirs are coherent mailings . . . with coherent messages.

Imagine two dot-com commercials back to back. If they're typical of what's been churning out of the "Let's prove we're in the big leagues" spots that play up names without giving us a clue of what the company does, TV viewers are like the line in "Fiddler on the Roof": "When a poor man eats a chicken, one of them is sick." (I prefer the old Pennsylvania Dutch saying, "You can't hatch chickens from fried eggs.")

EVERYBODY DOES IT.

Incidentally, the commercial overload isn't just independent or ethnic stations. NBC and ABC have been well beyond the 15-minute mark for many months, in prime time where the cost-per-spot is highest. NBC's West Coast President is quoted: "Compared to most cable networks we are rather conservative." Oh? The director of media research at J. Walter Thompson USA commented, "This is now out of control."

Now here comes radio. Broadcast stations have a new gimmick that cuts the pauses out of talk shows and newscasts. No dead air! They're adding two to three minutes of commercials.

The Numbness Factor has to set in. If broadcast marketers adopted the same disciplines direct marketers observe, they'd recognize that bulk can be self-defeating. Oh, the Food Section of a newspaper has a batch of competitors advertising side-by-side; but the assumption that newspaper advertising, with its clip-and-save and "let's take another look" capabilities, parallels having a Progresso Soup commercial and a Lean Cuisine commercial with parallel videos and parallel "Lunchtime" claims butted together without even a fade-out/fade-in . . . well, that's suggesting all media can transmit the same message.

But okay, let's be realistic and relegate idealism to classrooms, where analysis is an end, not a means.

We can draw these conclusions:

First, any medium is entitled to maximize monetary return. If greed results in a self-shot in the foot, that shouldn't bother anybody else.

Second, it's stupid and noncommunicative to tie two spots together without any transition at all, even a six-frame cross-fade. No, make that stupid *because* it's noncommunicative. These people are in the communications business.

Oh, well, how about this as a deal: We'll agree to quit criticizing the way TV stations put their commercials together if they'll agree to quit inserting promotions for their sitcoms, weakly designed as news, into their newscasts.

Oh, no you don't, commercial managers. You first.

"Please Stay on the Line for a Self-serving Message."

Telemarketing has fallen on evil times.

I'm so old I remember when a phone call was actually a phone call, not a recitation. In those golden times, telemarketers didn't have to worry about the disgusting "Here's another one of those unsolicited calls" factor. The industry was new, response was high, and the goose was laying foil-wrapped golden eggs.

Hey, guys, the Disgust Factor is your own fault. You run on tracks. Your scripts—well, to use a euphemism, they stink.

The phone rings. A recorded voice says, in ragged English, "Please stay on the line for a public service message."

You *know* the message is canned; and you *know* it's no more a public service message than "No dogs allowed" is a public service message. So those most able to respond to whatever they're pitching (in this case, attic insulation) are those who—if they stay on the line at all—greet the message with the highest percentage of skepticism.

Put yourself in my position: The phone rings, and you happen to pick it up. (In my office, we operate as a democracy.) A woman's voice, pancake-flat, says, "May I please speak with the owner?"

In happier times, I'd have played along: "What do you want to speak to the owner about?" But that was before the Disgust Factor roasted my tolerance.

So I donned my Minor Bureaucrat garb: "This is a division of a corporation. We have a number of stockholders."

Long pause. Duuhhh. "Well, uh, who's in charge of purchasing?"

"Purchasing what?"

Because I wasn't following the script, she couldn't follow the script. So she leaped ahead, past the damage: "This is a good news call. Due to a recent FCC ruling, you're going to get a 25 percent reduction in your long distance phone bill. If you'll tell me what you're spending on long-distance calls, I have a message that can save you a considerable amount of money." ("Considerable" was mispronounced . . . and what amateur communicator decided to start a verbal sentence with "Due to a recent FCC ruling"?)

A more sadistic individual, or one ready for a break in the business day, would have continued the banter for a while—"You mean you don't have a message if I don't tell you?" . . . or, "I'm a hairdresser. We don't make long distance calls" . . . or "Didn't they tell you we're already signed up with whatever long distance company you're with?" . . . or "Where did you get our secret CIA number?"

I was in the middle of a copywriting job, mildly irritated because I'd waited for three rings and nobody else had picked up the phone, so I couldn't continue the game. "Sorry, but we're content with the service we have. Thanks for calling." And I hung up.

But I wondered: Is *cold* telemarketing to a company office really effective *on a comparative level?*

And after a call that same evening, at home, I wondered: Is duplicity the next act for those who finally have begun to realize that "Hi, how are you today?" is a dead giveaway for a telephone pitch? A development I trace back only a couple of years has become so popular it's predictable: "Hello, this is a survey. Can you take five minutes to answer some questions?"

Hell, no, lady.

SURVEYS IN SHEEP'S CLOTHING

If I were in the survey business—the *real* survey business—I'd be beside myself. Among other problems, three of four calls claiming to be a survey *aren't;* they're a pitch-opener. The last one asked me to name three people who might buy a new luxury car, in exchange for which they and I would be entered in a sweepstakes. Huh?

Look, fellow communicators. I know you're out there, because telemarketing is a member of the direct response family, and some of you have to be reading this comment. Pretend you're a head-to-head salesperson instead of a tired boiler-room lackey. What might you say to grab attention, hold attention, and not generate the Disgust Factor that afflicts so many of your best targets because they recognize the same tired ploys?

My suggestion is to move up to the next generation of telemarketing.

And how, you ask, does the next generation differ?

I have a two-piece answer.

The first piece: It differs in recognizing that the Glory Days are behind us. Tens of thousands of homeowners are saying, sometimes with legal threats, "No more unsolicited phone calls. I've had it with interruptions at dinner to sell me a subscription to the newspaper I already get every day, or a long distance service, or solar panels." Ordinarily polite businesspeople are hanging up on recently-recruited stockbrokers who call them by their first name, in the middle of the day, with "hot tips." The danger-needle is way into the red zone. Golden eggs now are brass.

So the next generation of telemarketing calls might be straightforward. The caller might explain, in the first sentence, what the purpose of the call is. The company employing the caller and the person charged with creating the pitch wouldn't take the semi-paranoid view that the call is so unwelcome they have to hide its purpose.

The second piece: Whatever happened to the "Tip of the Pyramid" logic—telemarketing is productive only for calls to the very best targets? If you're aiming calls out into the open market, scattershot can be an expensive exercise in money-wasting. Ever hear of an ancient form of communication called direct mail, or its newborn giant offspring-incarnation, e-mail? Ever try using direct mail to set up a climate of acceptance, so the phone pitch isn't an ice-cold call?

Using direct mail as a pre-call device also helps defang the implicit antagonism stemming from the usually-thought but usually-unspoken objection, "Why are they calling me and where did they get my name?" (Telling someone how you got the name, if such a source exists, often extinguishes skepticism before it ignites.)

As an advocate, sometime practitioner, and long-time defender of telemarketing, I'm growing weary of watching this once-powerful medium shoot itself in the foot. I'm inventing new obnoxious answers to the obnoxious question, "How are you today?" I'm tuning out, where I once tuned in. And I'm in the business; imagine how exponentially we can multiply that reaction for those who *aren't* in the business.

A MODEST PROPOSAL

For one solid month, *test* a straightforward, businesslike approach—delivered by persons who speak the language as though they grew up with it—against masked, thoughtless, slow to the point, or deceptive techniques. Then tote up comparative results . . . being sure to factor in the "stick" rate (the percentage of responses that stick) for each approach. Depending on your preconceived attitude, you'll have a happy or unhappy surprise.

Probably this commentary will generate some nasty response from career telemarketers. That's okay: They're validating the Disgust Factor, generated by having stayed on the line for this public service message.

Reader's In-Digest-ion

Let's get this straight.

The Reader's Digest is in trouble. How can that be?

Those of us old enough to qualify as geezers remember two anomalies in the world of advertising: *The Reader's Digest*, which accepted no advertising; and Hershey's Chocolate, which didn't advertise.

Both those delightful aberrations are long gone, but certainly you remember when the *Digest* was actually a digest whose content was articles reprinted from other publications. How have the mighty fallen!

The Wall Street Journal says the *Digest* is implementing initiatives "aimed at trimming costs and raising capital." They've gone so far as to sell some of their art collection, which the guy at Christie's said may generate dollars reaching into nine figures.

An analysis of the publishing empire's recent travails isn't all that surprising. For the basic magazine, advertising revenues are down, and promotional spending is up.

In a recent demi-year the magazine didn't reach its rate base and missed the Audit Bureau of Circulations deadline. Subscriptions and newsstand sales both are down.

Does the nasty combination of revenues down and promotional spending up give you a clue? Okay, here's another indicator:

The sweepstakes response rate is down, and *Digest* management (again I'm quoting *The Wall Street Journal*) "now blames the falloff on changes in the marketing pitches on the sweepstakes mailings and on staffing cutbacks that led to the departure of skilled direct marketing staff."

Surprised? Then you haven't seen what *The Reader's Digest* was mailing.

NATURAL BORN LOSERS

Anyone who penetrated the blizzard of semi-impenetrable *Digest* sweepstakes mailings could have told that mailer its grotesquely overproduced sweepstakes mailings had to waste more money than they brought in. At the rate of about one per week, clogged by desperation and burdened with obfuscation, these mailings were a negative triumph—form over substance, substitution of production and mechanical flash for salesmanship.

So instead of selling off Monets and Renoirs and Chagalls, I have a better suggestion.

Dump the semi-pros who semi-created your falling-down weekly sweepstakes. Move back into the major leagues where savvy mailers such as *National Geographic* and *Vanity Fair* dwell.

What's puzzling is that this venerable and reasonably sophisticated publisher/marketer has continued trying to attract the attention of their targets by beating on the window with a sponge.

Insular, old-fashioned thinking built *The Reader's Digest* . . . but that was three generations ago.

What's your opinion of what seems to be this marketing direction: "We'll send another sweepstakes mailing this week, in a different envelope. How about a polybag? How about 'Postmaster: Please handle in conformance with mail security regulations as outlined in the USPS Domestic Mail Manual'? How about a rubber stamp, 'Reply Required Immediately'? How about 'Do we have your money in our prize vault?'? How about 'Contents to be hand-inserted in postbox'? How about a fake check visible through the envelope window, with 'Accounts Payable—Disbursing' as the return address?" How about 'NOTICE—POSTMASTER: The security of this package is guaranteed from tampering, inspection or delay under Section G011.5.1 of the United States Postal Service Domestic Mail Manual'? Yes, how about using these? Nobody ever used those wildly innovative ideas before, did they?"

Yes, ma'am, yes, sir, how about those? Nobody has used them . . . for weeks.

Can it be this giant organization is so insulated from contemporary direct marketing techniques it continues to lean on creative executions as old-fashioned and obsolete as Behaviorism—we'll repeat and repeat and repeat until the people getting our mail finally do respond?

Hey, that may work for the Chinese Water Torture but it doesn't work for those who have wastebaskets.

WHY CAMPAIGNS FAIL

Okay, rather than destroy, let's build. *Why* doesn't any particular direct mail campaign work? Yeah, yeah, I know the entire list of answers would eat up every page of this book and the next two on your shelf . . . but we have some strong hints here.

First, a campaign fails because whoever makes the marketing decisions excludes *testing* from the mix. Testing might have avoided the multi-sweepstakes fiascos . . . and might even have resulted in greater response at lower cost-per-contact. The word is that *The Reader's Digest* reduced mail promotions testing by more than a third.

Second, the company might be mailing (a) the right message to the wrong targets, (b) the wrong message to the right targets, or (c) the wrong message to the wrong targets. No question the *Digest* skews its magazines and its offers toward an older group. Isn't that the group that distrusts sweepstakes most? Isn't that the group that looks with bewilderment at music and video division offerings such as "Folk Rock Classics" and "Magic School Bus Video Collection"?

And third, much as I hate to suggest it, the magazine might take a look at its editorial content. I'm not privy to the renewal rate, but I suspect placidity has glued itself to the editorial helm.

To have this monument tottering after about eighty years of solidity isn't any more tolerable to us outsiders than it is to whoever is inside the company's headquarters. "Jurassic Park" told us that dinosaurs can be resuscitated.

Any volunteers? Go to Pleasantville, New York, and knock twice. If nobody comes to the door, go home and look for another "Postmaster: Deliver only to addressee" sweepstakes offer in your mailbox.

Where Does an Alien Go to Register?

In a single section of a single issue of *The Wall Street Journal* were a gaggle of ads that were both naive and assumptive. What a dangerous combination!

Here, in the "Marketplace" section, were ads typifying the contagion that has infected e.com advertising: "Whee whoopee, we're here and we're bright and we want your business." What's missing? The simple statement: "This is what we can do for you."

Oh, we've seen these ads wandering over the television screen. A batch flashed past at $2 million per, on the Super Bowl. And print media are loaded with them, to the delight of advertising agencies who share their clients' disdain for straightforward communication.

Media placement doesn't seem to mean much to companies whose on-paper worth is in the billions while their annual losses are in puny millions. So we aren't surprised by space ads whose entire text, except for a 7-point line across the bottom, is reversed on a grayed photograph of a desert island, another indicator, and is set just this way:

E-COMMERCE
GETS
YOUR BUSINESS
EVERYWHERE.
WE GET IT
THERE
WITH THE
TECHNOLOGY
YOU
ALREADY HAVE.

The line in 7-point across the bottom says, "For information on how our people and software tools can make e-commerce work for you, visit www.compuware.com/ecommerce."

See the aberration?

AND THE PURPOSE OF THE AD IS . . . ?

What, after all, is the purpose of *any* ad? To transmit information. This one, in sync with the attitude of the latter-day pseudosaints who have invaded our turf, is an ad whose purpose is to get us to ask for information the ad itself should have transmitted.

And for those of us who venerate our craft as a mighty force: How have the mighty fallen!

That ad wasn't an anomaly. In the same section of the same issue was an ad whose illustration was an "Important Memo" slip— a message from "Your mother" asking why it was so easy for her to hack into the company's intranet. Okay, this company sells hack-proofing software, right?

Uh . . . well . . . maybe and maybe not. The text of the ad is black-hole-murky, beginning, "The concept of 'e' has changed business virtually overnight." Wow, what a revelation! It goes on to say, "You know what your company needs to thrive." Another revelation. And the call to action, ending the copy block, is, "To find out more about our company and what we do, call 800-566-9337 or check our website."

Do you grasp this strange conclusion—"To find out more about our company and what we do, call . . ."? It's an admission that the ad, whose purpose should have been to *at least* tell the reader what the company does, is simply a "We're here" announcement.

Now, look, friends and foes: I'm aware that some heads will shake in disgust, the brain inside reacting, "What is he talking about? I know these companies and know what they do." Oh? Then what's the point of *this* approach? Why run the ad in a general circulation newspaper? Running an ad for Viagra in Marvel Comics makes more sense. (Come to think of it, it might.)

And I'm not totally without knowledge of e-business. After all, I've written two of those instantly obsolete books on the Web . . . not that this makes me, or anyone, a genuine expert. My point is: Assuming some of your readers know your field of business and some don't, so what? Obfuscation and writing around the point are never a proper use of advertising money.

Here's another ad, same issue, same section. The heading:

An e-business strategy that drives you to the bank,
instead of into a wall.

Okay, what does this company do?

Want to keep guessing? This is the first sentence of a two-sentence copy block: "FirePond's software products weave e-business into the rest of your organization."

Thanks, FirePond, for explaining that.

A full-page ad, same day, same section, is by a company I actually do know. Until I saw the ad, I thought I knew what the company does. The heading uses 9/10 of the page:

HIGHLY
AVAILABLE. ALWAYS
RESPONSIVE.
HIGHLY SECURE.
ALWAYS PROACTIVE.
THAT'S WHY
One company.
38% OF THE
TOP INTERNET
SITES HAVE
CHOSEN TO WORK
WITH US.

Don't you get the feeling some of the copy was accidentally deleted?

The body copy isn't much help. It's *one* sentence: "We're the outsourcing solution for securing, maintaining, and maximizing your company's mission-critical Internet operations."

Look, guys: Every one of you show-off advertisers could benefit from the rule every direct marketer has—or certainly should have–pasted onto the keyboard:

> *The purpose of a direct response message is to cause the reader, viewer, or listener to perform a positive act as the direct result of exposure to that message.*

Direct has claimed the Web, seized the Web to its bosom. Who are these parvenus, dilettantes, amateurs, and ad agencies, invading the Direct turf?

Idiots' Delight

One of my worst kept secrets is that I haven't been a fan of Cadillac's advertising.

Certainly the introduction of the Catera—the car whose name sounds like a sneeze—was remarkable for its silliness: "The Caddie that zigs." Saner heads seem to have prevailed lately, but it may be too late. Automotive publications say Cadillac is undergoing massive marketing restructuring.

While they're at it, can somebody get them to rename the "Escalade"? That would be nice. An owner says to a neighbor, "I have an Escalade." The neighbor replies, "Better get it lanced."

But obviously, other companies are suffering from the Caddiezig infection. A Ford ad has this slogan: *"Breakout."* We expect to see Nicholas Cage in a bullet-riddled Focus. (Can somebody get them to rename that car, too?)

Toyota has a car whose name could be tied to Viagra: Prius. The advertising is parallel, too: ". . . powered by a battery that never needs to be recharged and an intelligence system that knows when to use which." On Toyota's behalf, they finally changed their claim of "Everyday" to "Every day." Good dog!

Here's Oldsmobile Again.

Lame-duck brand Oldsmobile announced proudly its dependence on a massively advertised slogan for the condemned car. Budget? A cool $236 million. Ads were based around "Start something." Alero: "Start connecting." Aurora: "Start obsessing." Now, come on. I know they're obsessive-compulsive, but does this campaign represent $236 million worth of connection with car buyers?

Mazda recently had a shakeup in its marketing department. Anyone (other than whoever charged a ton for special effects) who saw the flashing, dashing, impenetrable "Mazda World" commercials wasn't surprised. Mazda's vice president of marketing was quoted as saying the company would be "communicating what the brand is." Gee, what a breakthrough idea!

Those of us who are long enough in the tooth remember slogans that succeeded because they related to the product: "What'll you have? Pabst Blue Ribbon?" . . . "How are you fixed for blades?" . . . and for that matter, "There's a Ford in your future" . . . and in more recent times, "Butter. Parkay."

The marketing professionals who created those slogans seem to have been replaced by word-bandiers, who trademark or service mark slogans with a happy abandon one would expect from a bunch of kids playing in the advertising sandbox. The puzzling aspect isn't that somebody spends a few million promoting a dot-com company's "We'll go to bat for you" slogan; it's that management, assuming that company has any, says, "Okay. Good. Run it."

A plethora of companies in computer-related industries take no chances at all. Their slogans or mottos or whatever you might call a nondescript line of type are inarguable. For example, AMD, the processor company, has this one: *It's just you, us and the world.* Well, they got that right. Ricoh says, *We're in your corner.* That's also where the wastebasket is. Tyan technology says. *Let Tyan Be YOUR Answer.* Fine, Tyan, if you'll tell us what the question is.

Samsung has a curious one—with the ubiquitous™ symbol, naturally: *"Everyone's invited™."*

Sony wants us to ponder its words: *"Sony. Our media is your memory.™"* Oh. Sure. Who can argue with that (except *media* is a plural)?

General Mills' newly coiffed, racially neutral, and sensually neutered Betty Crocker has trademarked this one: *"What a great idea."*

Brummel and Brown Spread seems to be proud of *"Creamy Taste That Swings!"*

We're bombarded by goofy slogans that don't relate to a specific. What a glorious waste!

Is a disclaimer in order—that these are aberrations, not typical of 21st century aggressive and dynamic marketing? I dunno. There are simply too blasted many of them to relegate them to the aberration-pile. If the trademark office wouldn't be so generous in awarding that symbol, maybe we could stanch the flow. Advertisers with impenetrable slogans such as the one TWA used just before the airline went into Chapter 11 and American Airlines took it over—*"One mission. Yours.™"*—would go nuts. (Delta's new line is "How do you want to fly?" On time would be nice.)

Should American, having gobbled up TWA, follow the lead of Lufthansa, which has a no-nonsense catchline: *"The global airline from Germany"*? The statement is clear, and no one can object to it. That's what Lufthansa is.

Now, come on, I'm not militating for dumbed-down slogans. Lufthansa isn't going to gain any interest, let alone creative awards, for "The global airline from Germany." But consider: Would you rather have Delta's "We love to fly, and it shows" or the one before it, "Delta is ready when you are"? The genuine marketer rejects both Lufthansa and Delta and asks, "What will *enhance* image and cause the phone to ring or the Web site to come alive?" So you won't think every comment is a gripe, here are some slogans that in my opinion add some value to the name:

For the Broadmoor Hotel in Colorado Springs: *"European Grandeur In The Colorado Rockies."* (I like it even though there's no excuse for "In" caps/l.c. It's infinitely superior to Hilton's *"It happens at the Hilton,"* which makes me itchy.)

DuPont is within the acceptable target area with "The miracles of science." Buick is surprisingly sane with "A luxury car for everyone." Viagra is right in there, sans Toyota, with the double-entendre "Love life again." The cholesterol medication Lipitor has the clear, no-nonsense "The Lower Numbers You're Looking For" (damaged, as so many are, by the upper/lower case addiction). Charles Schwab has the serviceable "creating a world of smarter investors™," total lower case losing impact as it helps equalize the overuse of capital letters.

But because intellect has a habit of skipping generations, it may be another generation before a marketer equals the Maxwell House "Good to the last drop."

New Uses for Software Campaigns: A Limp 3½-inch Floppy

I've learned this on the tennis court, the golf course, and the analytical end of direct response results: No matter how lousy your game is, somebody out there is worse.

Witness trade advertising by newspapers, magazines, cable and broadcast stations, and Web search engines. Too much of it parallels the shoemaker's children who have no shoes. Here we have media whose purpose is to provide a selling environment for advertising . . . and a lot of their own advertising is . . . well, to be charitable, it's execrable.

But running far ahead in the race to produce lousy advertising are computer manufacturers and vendors, along with their camp-followers—software and peripherals. They might have two excuses: (1) lack of their product's visual appeal, and (2) digit-head nerdiness, so they can say both they, their advertising agencies, and their targets don't know any better.

THE SUN DOESN'T SHINE

It's probably secondary radiation, but what other reason could Sun Microsystems have for the ad in its "dot.com" campaign, in which the dot is a double-jointed man curled into a ball, with the legend— I'm not kidding—"Our application server will help you do things never thought possible." Obviously that doesn't include effective advertising.

Tivoli has a neat ethnic slur. A guy displays a photograph of a Japanese man holding a metal detector. The headline: "Mission: Find those system errors before they become nasty business errors." Yeah, we can see one nasty business error right there. The company's slogan is "Manage. Anything. Anywhere.™" How about including your advertising, fellows?

Computer Select Web shows a baby tossing a professional wrestler in the air: "Suddenly your challenges are easier to handle." Maybe, except for the challenge of creating an intelligible ad.

Seagate Software has a puzzling campaign. Here's the head of a cute dog, fur and ears pinned back by the wind. The headline:

"You know," mused Henry, "if we dogs could share our combined knowledge with each other, we could take over the world." Until that day, Henry would patiently wait.

So help me, that's the heading. I haven't changed a word.

What is it supposed to mean? (The body copy makes a droopy attempt to make sense of it, beginning, "Fortunately, dogs have yet to attain more powerful means of sharing information. With Seagate Info™7, however, you can."

To compound the felony, the next Seagate ad shows the rear end of a short-haired dog digging in the sand. The heading:

Although he knew his current position was, to say the least, compromising, Oscar's urge to dig deeper was too strong to resist.

So is our urge to reply: Yuck.

X-number of those who read this nasty comment will defend those ads. On what grounds? That they catch the eye, as pictures of dogs tend to do . . . or that they're provocative. Guys and gals, I reject both those rationales as totally specious and beg you to do so too. Otherwise, advertising and marketing admits defeat, settling for boiler-plate attention-getting instead of arrowing to the core of salesmanship—*a positive response from the most people who can and will buy what you have to sell.*

Going to the Dogs, in Full Color.

Cabletron Systems also uses dogs. Is a puzzlement. The message is clear, if primitive: "Still begging for more bandwidth." The full-color, full-page, full-bleed illustration: A group of dogs. (The body copy opens with a subhead, "The SmartSwitch 6000 from Cabletron," followed by "A high port density, low-cost wiring closet switch that will satisfy the hungriest appetites." Oh, I get it. The dogs are hungry. Gee, what an inventive concept for selling a way to eliminate network bottlenecks! One of the great lies of our time would be: I wish I'd thought of that.

I've been bewildered by Compaq Computer's peculiar advertising for quite a while. None of us should be surprised by a *Wall Street Journal* heading, "Compaq Posts $184 Million Loss on Weak Sales" . . . not after seeing their ad headed, "Everyone is Going Ape for Compaq Monitors." Guess what the illustration is. Yep. And an ugly one at that. Get out the Prilosec, folks.

Here's Cable & Wireless USA showing a matador who apparently has lost his bull, because he's sticking his sword into a cloud. The creative team hasn't lost its bull, though: "Backbone. You either have it or you don't." Uh huh.

These ads aren't cheap rate-holders. Most are full color, bleed. Stick it to 'em, agencies!

More full color, bleed, from NetScout—a photograph of an older woman in hair-curlers with the headline, "How much do you love your mother?" They're selling a cure for whatever may be causing applications to slow down. Uh . . . how about a jolt of that for your ad team?

Digital River's full page ad shows a man's athletic supporter— not a fan, a fabric. The headline: "Our customer support couldn't be more reliable." Aw, you don't need that gadget with a message as flaccid as this. And may your descendants be afflicted with jock itch.

In that same painful neighborhood is one of my favorites, Xircom's ad which shows a Greek statue. We all know the Mamelukes broke the noses off statues, including the Egyptian sphinx. Now visualize a midget Mameluke who couldn't reach the nose, so he settled for a look-alike organ nearer the ground. The heading on this ad, which shows the result: "Lost the dongle." Sure. The whole selling argument is emasculated.

TSANet shows a pair of ice skaters. The headline: "World class IT performers depend on solid multivendor support." Does that mean Olympic ice skaters are in it for money? What a surprise!

What isn't a surprise is the 50-years-out-of-date hucksterism behind all these ads.

Technology Evaluation Center has a strange ad: a barefoot girl sitting in limbo, her chin resting on her hand.. She's wearing shorts, emphasizing her legs (nice) and her feet (big). The headline: "THINKING . . . of a Technology Selection?" Well, I suppose that's as good an analysis as any.

Food, but Not for Thought

Macromedia doesn't want to be left behind in the race for obfuscation. So here's an ad that has a chocolate bar, labeled "Sweet Code," dipping into a jar of peanut butter, labeled "Creamy GIFS." Headline: "Create tastier websites with Dreamweaver and Fireworks." I guess Dreamweaver and Fireworks are applications, but what causes them to think peanut butter makes chocolate sweeter? Do you see the relationship between illustration and copy? Neither do I.

What's with the food paralleling? Mitsumi's headline is "More beneficial than a well-balanced breakfast." Is this a "Huh?" or a "Duh"?

A company named DLT makes tape for backup drives. Its ad in a reseller magazine shows a soccer team. The player in the foreground is protecting his crotch from a kicked ball. The headline: "Protection from the unbearable." They could have used that slogan to prevent this ad.

A trade ad by a company named Keynote has this powerful headline: "Are you losing customers or revenue because your web site is too slow?" This heading is strong, it's pointed, it's clear, and it grabs by asking a question. So what's the problem? The photograph over which this message is set—two feet sticking out of a morgue sheet, with a tag on one toe, "Office of the Medical Examiner." The tag identifies the body as "Unknown customer, age 35, male," and so on. Yup, power seeps out because they got cute with the illustration. If your question is, "What illustration would reinforce this point?" an easy answer is, "If you can't think of one that isn't childish, who says you have to have an illustration?" Ponder that.

THE POINT: RELEVANCE

Hey, I'm not militating for dullness. I'm not even issuing a blanket indictment of parallels, despite the Unisys "Nice break" ad that shows two people at a pool table and Cabletron's "How to take on those monster apps." ad that shows, sigh, a monster. The point isn't to stifle creativity; it's to channel it with *relevance* so the reader senses benefit. We can go all the way back to the "Unique Selling Proposition" Rosser Reeves espoused more than two generations ago. What is your unique benefit? Is your parallel relevant? Does your advertising degenerate into chest-thumping "Me Tarzan!" cliché-shouting?

Or, far more simply: Do you have a clearer, more dynamic way to make your point? Then why did you choose the fatuous route? (Yeah, yeah, I know we're dealing in opinions.)

Yes, and here's mine (backed up by experience, both mine and others): Any communication is damaged when it deliberately avoids The Illustration Agreement Rule:

> *Illustration should agree with what we're selling, not with headline copy.*

What would be surprising if we weren't numbed to all these is that these ads are in trade publications, where attention-getting *has to* be backed up quickly by *a reason to do business* and where the offer should be paramount over the glitz. That's why The Illustration Agreement Rule makes sense.

Nobody told these guys that getting attention is a means, not an end. But–gulp!–the end is not yet.

Can you imagine any piece of direct mail to these same target-individuals, using these same sophomoric themes? What an easy litmus test!

To those who think cleverness for the sake of cleverness is a better sales technique than cleverness for the sake of selling something,

I have a suggestion: Instead of pinning that ad on the wall of your cubicle, pin up your resumé. Before long you're going to need it.

Hit-and-Run Appeals to Fragments

Our targets are suffering from sensory overload.

Correction: *We're* suffering . . . because our targets are suffering from sensory overload.

Old-timers think back fondly to a kinder, gentler era when a winning ad or direct mail package could last and last and last . . . when first class stamps cost three cents and first class mail arrived within two days . . . when folks could count the choices of evening entertainment (at least on a mass level) on their two hands.

More to the point: People coped with 15 to 20 percent of the number of advertising messages we pour onto them today.

So it really wasn't a phenomenon that the space ad for the Sherwin Cody School ("Do You Make These Mistakes in English?") ran unchanged for 45 years. Today it would be a phenomenon if such a message survived 45 *insertions*. No, cut that in half.

No wonder those who toil in the furnaces of creative communications have become shrill. No wonder we've beaten old dependables such as "Free" and "New" and "Personal" into phantom images of what they were even a decade ago.

THE DISAPPEARANCE OF OLD-FASHIONED VIRTUES . . . AND MOTIVATORS

I'm not veering off the point when I ask you to look back in time to the 1960s and even 1970s . . . hardly a primordial period; but even that recently the public at large didn't have a Woodward/Bernstein mentality. When the president came to town it was a big deal, and if a placard existed it said "We love you." Merchants could generate guilt by calling dormant accounts and saying sincerely, "We want you back," or asking, "Have we let you down?"

Today we salivate at muckraking. We're Tom Cruise watchers who love to catch Nicole Kidman showing some bitchiness, so we can say, "Seeee?"

What does that have to do with "now, today" copywriting? You see the connection, of course. Attitudes of the X-Generation are filtering upward and downward, and we'd better adjust. Advertising copywriters can't "con" readers or viewers or listeners the way we used to, *which reduces exponentially our ability to generate guilt.*

This pulls the canine teeth of a lot of offers that might have succeeded with gusto a generation ago. Some old timers sit in time-capsules, warming their creative hands in front of the pot-bellied stoves of their own delayed reaction-time, and wondering what happened: "This always used to work."

LIGHTNING-FAST COMMUNICATION . . .
AND LIGHTNING-FAST BURNOUT

A disclaimer, quoting Alexandre Dumas: "All generalizations are false, including this one." My justification is that the noble profession of trend-following *demands* generalizing. So . . .

A dozen years ago the double postcard was king of subscription mailings. I, for one, had a double postcard that outpulled a lavish jumbo mailing, not just dollar for dollar but piece for piece.

Ah, but that was a dozen years ago. Today a few publishers cling to the shreds of double postcards, but they do it primarily to grab names for list sales or swaps. Ask them what percentage of double postcard respondents who figure, "Why not? I'll spring for a free issue if all I have to do is drop this card in the mail," *convert.*

And that horrible conversion rate ties directly into the previous point: Only a Svengali can generate guilt today. The key to any "soft" offer, whether for a magazine or for a "30-day free trial," isn't sending a sample enabling the recipient to confer dispassionate judgment on the publication or collectible or weight-reduction plan or electronic device or appliance or or or.

Heck, no.

The purpose is to generate a little guilt: "We gave you that, and it's only right for you to give us this" ("this" being a paid invoice). Oh, how tough it is to generate guilt today!

For the last two generations (and maybe back to Moses) the principal motivator has been and is *greed*. Argue with me if you like, but if you mount an appeal to sensibility and I mount an appeal to naked greed, I'll beat you every time. We've trained ourselves and the X-Generation and the children yet to come to revere three elements: (1) Me. (2) Myself. (3) I.

That's why we're inundated with sweepstakes. People subscribe to a magazine not because they want to read the magazine but because they think it will increase the possibility of Ed McMahon delivering a house to their back yard. (It's also why people sue sweepstakes companies, claiming unsolicited mail promised them all kinds of goodies for doing nothing other than opening the mail.)

The cream of the jest: Worthy non-profit institutions raise funds by having sweepstakes. People give because they hope to get back more than they gave. What a spirit of altruism!

Don't look for a contradiction here, assuming the sweepstakes is one of the last bastions of our ability to con our readers. Sweepstakes *do* award the prizes they claim they'll award. Donations and orders are the frosting on the cake, proof that we copywriters still can aim an occasional weapon penetrating the barriers of indifference and burying itself in the always-present layers of greed.

But sweepstakes have begun to flag, as the double postcard has begun to flag. Why? Because they work. Anything—*anything* that works runs afoul of a little mini-rule sooner or later. And the difference between today and yesterday is that sooner is one or two years, not ten or twenty years. The mini-rule:

Sameness = boredom.
Overuse = abuse.

We don't have a chicken-or-egg quandary here. The speedup in ad burnout is a result, not a cause. It's the result of the information flood.

That's why some of the devices that worked so well in the United States a generation ago are working well in other countries today. Their *best buyers* get two to ten pieces of mail a week; our best buyers get a hundred or more. Their best buyers choose from two or three television channels; ours choose from 40 to 60, with a third-generation explosion coming up. Their best buyers have a computer and maybe a modem; ours have ISDN lines and e-mail offers up the gazoo. We're drowning in exhortation, and the *Sameness = boredom* equation is becoming more profound every hour, not just every day.

Cynicism Moves Upward, not Downward

Worse: Our kids are as cynical as we are. In fact, they're the fountainhead of cynicism, infecting *us*. They've rediscovered how to "boo" our once-heroes and heroines; they talk loudly and unabashed in theatres, laughing when adults go "Shhh." They note the number of post-transaction changes of mind, the number of frivolous lawsuits that pay off, the outrageous monies paid to semi-literate athletes and semi-talented actors and actresses . . . so they have to absorb these potential benefits and relate them to themselves. They're cynical by the time they're twelve years old.

Ah! We know this. We can cater to the evolution (or devolution) and continue our mastery over our targets by adapting our appeals to what they want to see and hear.

What Do They Want to See and Hear?

Okay, the core of this argument: *What do they want to see and hear?*

- Immediate gratification.
- Exclusive benefit.
- A competitive edge.
- Maintenance of their status as Master of the Universe.
- Reinforcement of their status as Fairest of Them All.
- Pleasure without guilt.

Not bad. We have half a dozen chinks in their armor without getting into any subtleties. Sensory overload or not, built-up layers of cynicism or not, devotion to greed or not, who says our targets are unreachable? Not the marketer who has the ability—mandatory in this brutal age—to think like the targets at whom he or she is aiming.

The Shape of Things to Come

Think for a minute: *Why* does karaoke (or "AllyMcBeal") exist at all? *Why* do we have such laughable television program titles as "Hair Loss in America . . . A Growing Crisis"? *Why* do we feel superior when an Olympic ice skater falls on her rear? *Why* do we applaud bad-mannered egomaniacs who break up meetings and then start meetings of their own? *Why* are television shows such as "Survivor" and those "Millionaire" quiz shows the most popular among the Twentysomethings? *Why* does a movie or cable-TV drama seem incomplete unless it's larded with four-letter words? *Why* do "loser" high school students not only show up in class with guns, but use those guns on their classmates? *Why* do movie studios let Kevin Costner continue to produce unwatchable losers and call Keanu Reeves an "actor"?

The minute is up. If your answer is, "Narcissism and instant gratification and a truculent 'in-your-face' smugness demanded by truculent in-your-face peers are the hot new keys," you've answered all eight "why" questions and their proliferation of newly-arrived cousins. If our offer turns those keys, we're winners with Generation X in the first decade of the new century.

So how does one write for this group? Lots of choices:

- One writes copy appealing openly to narcissism and gratification. No subtlety, please.
- One writes copy larded with truculent in-your-face smugness.
- One writes copy which teeters on the edge of sophomoric bad taste.
- One writes copy which promises no-effort benefits—"Draw a pentagram on the floor and you'll be able to speak Swedish."
- One writes copy which tells the reader he/she will be a hero, environmentally or scholastically or (danger!) socially.

Learn the techniques because high school students ape college students and the "Home Alone" next-in-line kids ape high school students. You'll need these proficiencies increasingly for some years to come.

You say the thought nauseates you? Great! That means you understand the fragmentation and polarization between and even within target groups. One person's gratification is another person's turnoff. We wouldn't advertise rock groups such as Skulker and The DeadSexTunes to the over-45s. They're a different target. (The fading baby boomer market is already folded into AARP.)

Awareness of market fragmentation can save us—and those who pay us—tons of otherwise wasted money. Target groups overlap in some areas and are light-years apart in others. Each item we sell needs its own theme in order to reach the biggest group of potential buyers.

"POST-LITERATE SOCIETY"? HUMBUG

Are you able to accept the concept of a "post-literate society"? We haven't ever seen a dissective definition of that term, but as explained by its advocates, it seems to mean a society in which literacy is obsolete.

The concept of post-literate society is the wrong prophecy of doom because it assumes people who have lost or never had the ability to read or write or spell or rationalize are good marketing targets. They aren't. They're marketing detritus, discards, rejects, because of the First Great Law of force-communication:

Reach and influence, at the lowest possible cost, the most people who can and will buy what you have to sell.

Not "the most people." That's the old, worn-out cost-per-thousand concept that has misled so many advertisers into running television spots which score high as "noted" and don't help sell a damned thing.

Don't confuse inattention with illiteracy. Long sales letters do work (on the consumer level), and they wouldn't if our targets felt we're talking down to them. Oh, sure, people don't know how to differentiate between *who* and *whom* or *its* and *it's*, but that's nothing new.

Computers have given us spelling checkers and grammatical hints, so defects in spelling and grammar are masked. Oh, surprise: Semi-literates abound on astoundingly high levels. I'm lucky enough to deal with editors who can spell and parse, but, my God, I see editors—and, worse, creative directors at advertising agencies—whose command of the English language seems to be limited to "I'm like" and "Y'know."

The Pandora's Box of 21st century communication isn't empty. Hope is very much in there. We can shrug, "So what?" We go *our* way, aiming at <u>our</u> targets and leaving the detritus behind.

No, I'm not claiming spelling checkers will supplant literacy, any more than calculators have supplanted the ability to add and subtract. I do claim we're devolving into a two-tier society.

Ah! That's the "So what?". Our best targets are in the upper tier. They're reading books, magazines . . . and our mailings and e-mail. They cruise around our Web sites. Let the lower tier go hang.

TYING IT ALL TOGETHER . . .

All right. We have a fragmentation of society. We have rampant skepticism among our best targets. We have a barricade of self-awareness separating the next two generations from us.

Our "So what?" response is based on the recognition that a fragmented society is—get this—to our benefit as direct marketers. We have logical ways of penetrating each fragment, and no other medium can compete with us effectively . . . or economically.

Skepticism? Barricade of self-awareness? We've lived with them for our entire professional lives. We've lived with and overcome the derogatory (and often wistful) term *junk mail*. (Parenthetical comment: Junk mail is nothing other than an offer sent to the wrong person.) We overcome accusations of e-mail "spam." And, with on-going mastery of word-use, we can and do overpower skepticism every day, even as the clouds of quick, jangling cuts in heavily-produced television commercials confound viewers. (Parenthetical comment: Confusion feeds skepticism and justifies the barricade.)

So where are we as the sales and marketing juggernaut roars down the communications highway? Postal increases notwithstanding . . . outrageous prices for mailing and e-mail lists notwithstanding . . . image-loss from semi-literate communicators notwithstanding . . . the greater fragmenting caused by the electronic superhighway notwithstanding . . . hosts of detractors notwithstanding . . . we're in our traditional position.

The competition is disorganized, reeling from inability to understand its own research and technology. Those of us who know how to communicate on our prospective buyers' level, feeding them what they want to see and hear, will blast through the chinks in their armor. The bags of mail with orders enclosed will continue to roll in and the phones will continue to ring.

If that isn't any marketer's Kingdom of Heaven, what is?

The Peanut Gallery:
A Digestive Directive

Think you've seen all there is to see about government intervention into commerce . . . greasy sand, sticking in the gears of progress? Well, you ain't seen nothin' yet. And as an indication that we communicators aren't the only ones snowed under by useless rules . . .

Just when you thought government regulation of the airline industry couldn't be more stupid, up they come with a new height in absurdity.

If you fly Delta or US Airways or United or American, or any other airline that regards a glass of water in a paper cup and a handful of peanuts as a gourmet meal, you probably were the lucky recipient of a foil-wrapped bag of peanuts.

Quick! To the emergency room!

Get this: Apparently one person in several thousand has a mild allergy to peanuts. Uh-oh! The airlines pass out peanuts. In fact, on Delta peanuts are as gourmet a feast as you're likely to get.

So the Department of Transportation, in its infinite wisdom, has told the airlines that each plane should have a designated peanut-free zone.

I'm not kidding. A peanut-free zone. After all, next to cigarettes and glue-sniffing and self-mailers, peanuts are the deadliest poison known to humankind, right? The argument seems to be that peanut particles collect in airplane ventilation filters over a period of 5,000 hours of flight (again I'm not kidding, *5,000* hours), and a peculiar law passed about fifteen years ago guarantees airplane access to the disabled. So allergy to peanuts is a disability.

That's probably why you've so often read about passengers, who look like harmless Arab terrorists, sneaking peanut cluster bars through the peanut detector, past all those uniformed peanut guards who are busy reading magazines. Ha! Once aboard, one of these miscreants waits until the plane reaches 33,000 feet. Then, when security is relaxed, out comes the peanut cluster bar. A hairy arm seizes a passing attendant: "Take dis plane to Atlanta. And, yeah, Allah Akbar . . . I mean, Allah Peanut Bar. Or is that 54-40 or fight?"

The attendant explains that the plane is already headed for Atlanta, but logic has no effect on fanatics. Driven by a carefully-orchestrated self-immolation campaign, the hijacker warns, "Come any closer and I'll bite into it."

A Delta Force undercover agent pulls out a jar of mixed nuts, concealed in a shoulder-holster, and aims it at the hijacker. Unlike such shots in the movies, he misses and hits the attendant with a Brazil nut, squarely between the eyes.

Bedlam. The hijacker yells, "I warned you!" He raises the bar to his lips as passengers try to kneel to pray but can't because the seats are too close together.

Chomp!

Peanut panic erupts. The pilot radios a mayday call—"Peanuts at 33,000 feet!"—and is forced to make an emergency landing. The landing is, yes, at Atlanta, where almost every landing is an emergency anyway because you're stuck on the taxiway for 45 minutes and can't get up to go to the bathroom.

The FBI arrives and takes the criminal into custody, while passengers, choking and filing class-action suits, wait for their lawyers and their turn to be interviewed by television reporters with big hair. Stone Phillips is there from NBC, as usual looking as though he's posing for a statue-in-the-park sculpture. The defense lawyers (a team of eight paid by the federal government and headed by F. Lee Bailey, who also pose for sculptures now that Sherman's horse is no longer available) claim it's all a mistake, because the guy thought it was Turkish Taffy. They offer a broken tooth as evidence.

Johnnie Cochran shows up, shouting "If the bar ain't there, check his underwear! If they ain't walnuts, the jury is all nuts! If it's troglodyte rhyme, I'm here all the time!" Larry King interviews Ross Perot, because he hasn't interviewed Ross Perot for at least three weeks. Monica Lewinsky hints that she's swallowed a four-inch piece of peanut brittle without chewing, and does this qualify her for the "Mile-High" Club? She's admitted to the God's Little Acre Club. (Her mother has the stained paper napkin in her vault.) Linda Tripp claims to have recorded peanut farmer Jimmy Carter smearing peanut butter on whole wheat bread, a social gaffe, but the garbled recording also might be ordinary cream cheese smeared on rye.

Hey, kids, why doesn't the Department of Transportation dedicate some time to finding out why nothing bigger than a tennis racquet will fit into the overhead bins, or why the airlines keep shortening the distance between seats, or why peanuts are their gourmet meal of choice?

Southwest Airlines has solved its peanut problem by distributing raisins. But what's the matter with those guys? Don't they know one person in 57,000 is allergic to raisins? That means a raisin-free zone.

And certainly we're entitled to a baby-scream-free zone; I propose aisles 1 through 50.

The cream of the jest is that the Department of Transportation admits it couldn't find even one medical incident resulting from airplane peanuts . . . but it went ahead with the edict anyway because the Department has to follow the Rule of Automatic Bureaucracy: If a regulation doesn't exist, create one.

Congratulations, D.O.T., on another triumph of government idiocy. And oh, yes . . . nuts to you.

Our Version of the Boston Tea Party

My son Bob has devoted several of his weekly columns in the magazine *InfoWorld* to proposing a holiday that would benefit not just the United States but every nation in the world . . . even including Serbia:

National Boycott Stupidity Day.

Bob's field of expertise is information systems (he's my co-author of *Selling on the Net*), so he's able to point to America's "Duh!" glorification of Forrest Gump with less involvement than those of us who deal every day with the Forrest Gumps of advertising and marketing.

I agreed to add my voice to the concept—no, the *need*—for National Boycott Stupidity Day after absorbing some of the names and campaigns for—what else?—automobiles. It's only right.

For example, how can anybody in our business buy a Buick when that company has as its *selling message* "Isn't it time for a real car?™" Unbelievable. Forrest Gump is alive and well, along with Dilbert's boss.

What gets me is the imbecilic arrogance behind adding a trademark symbol to that line. Hey, Buick, why did you pass up other winners such as "If you're driving, be sure to use a car™" or "If you're driving a fake car, your arse may be dragging™" or "How's my driving? *What* driving?™"

My constant refrain: That "™" symbol seems to add dignity to stupidity the way death adds dignity to despots and criminals. Just add the symbol. It's like the magic feather or Shazam! Somehow your lunacy becomes sane. The trademark office has to be laughing at some of the dreck advertisers submit, in the hope that the "TM" symbol will add ca*chet* to their ca*ca*.

Bob points to movies in which a guy with a laptop computer (about four megabytes of RAM) solves a problem baffling the entire bank of government mainframes. I'd rather point to the far richer field of advertising and marketing, where Preparation H has a super in its TV commercial: "Use only as directed." Preparation H, I don't want to rain on your parade (as indelicate as that cliché may seem), but I'm not about to use your product on my toast.

EASY GRIST FOR BOYCOTT STUPIDITY DAY

Gee, automobile manufacturers are such easy grist for Boycott Stupidity Day. If I were more charitable, I'd feel guilty about spraying them with verbal Flit. As this text has verified, I brood endlessly (and less than fondly) over the sitting-duck target, Cadillac's Catera, and its strangely-named SUV, Escalade. Is that Es-kuh-LAID or Es-kuh-LAWD? They're going with LAID. Oh, well, Chrysler had the Cordova (KOR-do-va), which they called Cor-DOH-va. After the ill-fated Allante, which no one knew how to pronounce, we shouldn't be surprised.

Now here comes doomed Oldsmobile. What did it call its last-chance car? Cheetah? Golden Arrow? Starburst? Flash? You know better than that. It's "Alero." Whee. Hey, guys, we still have fond memories of Rocket-88, when your product-namers still were on this planet.

Now, how do we implement Boycott National Stupidity Day? I have a couple of logical suggestions:

First, on that day we won't set foot in a store whose advertising or window signs uses "it's" for a possessive. Shock treatment, that's what it is.

Second, we all phone Buick and tell them we've heard that

along with the Procter & Gamble "Man in the Moon" being a symbol of the devil, we understand on good authority that Buick isn't a real car.

Third, we all send faxes or e-mail to NBC demanding that Jane Pauley actually be forced to cover a live story on her own, with no teleprompter.

Fourth, we bury up to their necks in an anthill any list managers who, without telling us, combine inquiries and buyers.

Fifth, on that day we discard every piece of mail we get whose envelope says, "You've been pre-approved." Stern stuff! Wastebaskets throughout the nation will overflow their banks.

Sixth—now, this may require a little work, but the emotional reward is exceptional—we prepare a questionnaire for long distance telephone companies. We phone a key executive of each company and explain that we're preparing an article which will appear simultaneously in *The New York Times, The Washington Post,* and *The Wall Street Journal . . .* and will they kindly explain their deal to us. We then position a photographer across the street from each office so we can have award-winning photographs of phone company executives jumping off window-ledges.

Now, what day should it be? An obvious positioning of National Boycott Stupidity Day would be dead-center between Christmas and New Year's Day.

But if logic is to prevail, it should be on the day following the telecast of the Super Bowl game. We make a list of those sponsors who have shelled out millions for each of the unmemorable 30-second commercials on that telecast. Our list is valuable, because they will be the only memorials to the departed but unmourned spots. Each of us sends a card—postage-due is okay—to those witless money-wasters, asking what the content of their spots was supposed to mean; can they give us a reason why, except for their megalomania and their advertising agency's willingness based on greed, they chose that medium; and how much business they antic-ipate doing as the result of those airings. Might as well ruin their day. Nah. They won't read our cards because they'll be too busy looking for venture capital.

So why not sign up to join "A real holiday™"? We can get Cadil-lac to give it a catchy name, such as Blftx or Jalallall or Ingrulz. And you have every reason to join Bob and me in celebrating National Boycott Stupidity Day. After all, you've been pre-approved.

It Ain't Necessarily So:
Ten Creative "Myths"

A point of personal privilege: If you've stayed with the text this far, you're open-minded enough to accept the author's personal preju-dices. My excuse: They're backed with plenty of professional scar-tissue.

Ever since some Stone Age direct marketer proposed the notion that a successful mailing produces a two percent response, we've been subject to—and sometimes victims of—folklore.

As we rocket into the guts of the twenty-first century, we're more and more able to separate wheat from chaff, fact from fiction, truth from folklore. Long since, when the first publicly-reported con-tinuity programs delivered financial success with a response rate of three-tenths of a percent and single-item promotions flopped with a response rate of five percent, the old two percent saw went out the window.

But for some, the window is still locked shut. I had the typical call from a client after I'd delivered a direct mail package:

"Now, this is going to pull two percent response, right?"

Understand, this is a sophisticated guy at a sophisticated company. But sophistication is a weak adversary of folklore, and folklore says response is two percent.

I asked him about list selection. "Oh, we're still working on that."

No, I didn't tell him if we pull two percent on a mailing to untested cold lists, I'd head for the nearest window facing east so I could watch the star rise. After all, some mailings—especially sweepstakes and freebie-offers—pull considerably better than two percent. Some hit twenty percent . . . and no matter how huge the response, somebody in the executive suite gripes.

Nor did I tell him I've had mailings to *house* lists (for continuity programs) that were considerably more than moderately successful at far, far under two percent.

Why tell him anything? An attempt at education would have been misinterpreted as an excuse.

Seems to me the two percent myth has endured long enough. But how do we retire it? Somehow this blasted number has worked its way into the universal direct response subconscious. How many times have *you* heard a would-be guru generalize: "The typical mailing pulls a two percent response"?

Ordinarily sane marketers lose their rationality in the percentage fable. It's almost like a legend, handed down from generation to generation: "Direct mail pulls two percent."

What I'm driving at is mind-set based on anecdote instead of fact. It bleeds over into many facets of our business. When I was still in school, I heard that two percent story. It sounded reasonable; but then, when I was a child I thought like a child. If I'm offering twenty dollar bills for ten bucks, I'd damned well pull better than two percent. If I'm pitching Rolls-Royces to *Cricket* subscribers, I won't look for a basketful of mail.

We live with edicts, pronounced grandly without a thought-process behind them. We hear unscientific guesswork masquerading as gospel. One example is the quantity we have to mail to get a readable response. I used to work with a "list expert" who said it's impossible to read response if one mails fewer than 40,000 pieces. Why? An annoyed "That's the way it is!" . . . spoken with authoritative high-dudgeon.

That concept came a cropper when the entire universe for a business-to-business mailing was only 18,000. A sudden shifting of gears, probably out of fear of losing a list rental:

"Oh, well, then, that's enough. Eighteen thousand should do it for us."

Huh?

COMMUNICATIONS CLICHÉS

Let's be careful about making flat statements of quasi-fact. Every angle of the world of force-communications is shot through with decrees:

- If you can't say it in one page, you can't say it at all.
- Long letters outpull short letters.
- Short letters outpull long letters.
- Color outpulls black and white.
- Self-mailers don't work.
- Photographs bring higher response than illustrations.
- If people don't see themselves in a photograph, they won't buy.
- Envelopes with copy outpull envelopes without copy.
- People won't read letters longer than two pages.
- People won't read letters longer than four pages.
- People won't read letters longer than six pages.
- All unsolicited commercial e-mail is spam.

- To sell subscriptions to a financial newsletter, a 16-page letter
  is a standard length.

A lot of these guesses-masquerading-as-dogma are based on
one-time personal exposure, certainly no bellwether of success or
failure. Why not, "My grandfather tried using the mails in 1926 and
it didn't work. Why should I try it now?"

How easy and logical these statements become when they're accompanied by the simplest of disclaimers: "My experience has been.
. . ." Heck, I'd settle for the single word "Usually."

So here we are, well into the 21st century, and some of the myths
still persist. Why do they persist? Because some of the self-professed
latter-day saints of our business make declarations unbacked by
testing under actual battle conditions. Myths are proposed as dogma
. . . and *all* dogma, however ill-founded, finds some takers.

Let's explode some of those myths.

**MYTH NO. 1: INCREASED ATTENTION TO PRODUCTION RESULTS IN
INCREASED RESPONSE.** What a beautiful package! It's an award winner for sure. Look here—the company name is embossed into the
100-pound enamel. And those photographs! Must be a 200-line
screen.

How did it pull?

More than a generation ago came David Ogilvy's one immortal
pronouncement: *What you say is more important than how you say
it.* Ogilvy was referring only peripherally to direct response, but
today—when even some of his former disciples are producing television commercials whose very purpose seems baffling—the dic-
tum-turned-homily is one we shouldn't ignore.

Two developments make the "What you say is more important
than how you say it" concept one we should recognize as yet valid:
1) The average individual who demonstrates any level of buying

power is exposed to more than twice as many "gimme" messages as was true in Ogilvy's day; 2) the advertising agency consolidation—make that explosion—has brought improperly-trained recruits into our ranks.

The mad scramble for attention has resulted in message-warping. Conventional advertising agencies traditionally confuse form for substance, and the trickle of art direction supplanting message impact has become a stream. Uh-oh.

One aspect of what we do remains immutable: A properly targeted message, underproduced, will outpull an improperly targeted message, overproduced.

Understand, please: I certainly am *not* militating for underproduction. I'm using it only as a parallel, in militating against overproduction.

I've seen too many creative teams specifying a paper stock they know costs more . . . but their targets not only won't share that knowledge, they wouldn't give a damn if they did share it. I've seen die-cuts and embossing and six-color printing that added zero to comprehension and sales appeal.

So a mild plea for some statesmanship, please: Let salesmanship triumph, not a selfish desire to produce an ad or mailer whose main purpose is to add a sample to your portfolio.

MYTH NO. 2: THE PURPOSE OF THE ENVELOPE IS TO REINFORCE THE SELLING ARGUMENT. Logical enough, isn't it? The only problem with this axiom is that it's untrue at least as often as it's true. Ask major mailers such as *Business Week*, who have had as many successes with no-message envelopes as with custom-converted heavily-produced envelopes. Ask financial mailers, who regularly find two-color envelopes outpulling four-color envelopes. Inevitably—if your approach is analytical and not prejudiced—you'll reach the conclusion so many of us have: It depends.

Not a satisfactory solution, you say? Then try this: If you change your interpretation of what constitutes an effective envelope, you'll invariably come up with a new dogma, totally valid in today's marketing ambience which has little reverence for snail-mail:

Except for keeping its contents from spilling out onto the street, the carrier envelope has a single purpose: to get itself opened.

For cookbooks and picture magazine subscriptions and mailings to highly targeted lists of some types of collectibles, the highest probability of getting the recipient inside might well be custom-converted envelopes loaded with full color, or a polybag that lets the contents do the inviting. For the appearance of a cold-blooded business offer or investments or financial services or the total suggestion of a one-to-one mailing, odds probably are with Spartan envelope treatment.

For almost any kind of mailing, a rubber stamp or a color bar or a few handwritten words often outpull either heavy production or no production.

So what do we conclude? If we accept envelope logic—it's a shill, a tout, an official greeter—we revert to our dogma: The single purpose of the carrier envelope is to get itself opened. With this philosophy, every other aspect of envelope treatment falls into place.

MYTH NO. 3: "LAUNDRY LISTS" ARE A STRONG SELLING WEAPON. This next myth-exploder may seem controversial . . . until you understand what I'm attacking—not content, but intent.

A listing of features, benefits, or components has its place: in the guts of a sales argument. To use it as the principal sales argument is abandoning the creative challenge in favor of clerkdom.

I'm looking at a couple of envelopes—*envelopes,* whose sole purpose we just discussed.

On the face of one envelope is this legend:

14 Ways to Media Success!

On another:

5000 ways to get better results with less work from your advertising or public relations programs

Hey, fellows, I certainly don't want to have to explore 14 different ways to media success. And 5,000 ways to get better results with less work from my advertising or public relations programs? Some of those ways better come up fast or I'm doomed to a lifetime of study.

What's wrong with these approaches is the implicit suggestion of a nasty four-letter word: w-o-r-k. It's *work* to analyze and implement 14 different ways to media success. I want *the* way; if you can't show it to me you've validated my suspicion that I'm just as professional as you are and have no reason to accept you as an authority. And 5,000 ways to get better results with less work? How can you say that when your very words tell me I'm going to have to wade through (and weigh) a list of 5,000 items? That's *work.*

The current champion is a direct response space ad:

168,000 REASONS WHY YOUR NEXT MEETING IN ALBU-QUERQUE WILL BE A WORK OF ART

Now, let's see. Assuming I can absorb one reason per second, that's 168,000 seconds or 2700 hours. If I work a 40-hour week, that's 67½ weeks—about 1¼ years. Any other activity has to be relegated to spare time. Albuquerque, this isn't quite fair.

My points . . . and the reasons we probably agree this myth-explosion is controversial . . . are first, it's the writer's job to separate valid from invalid, important from unimportant, useful from ancillary; and second, statistics are always a second-best way of presenting a sales argument. Laundry lists say to the reader, "I'm unable to select a key selling argument and subordinate the rest, so I'm regurgitating every point, equally. Please do my selling job for me."

MYTH NO. 4: CELEBRITY ENDORSEMENTS ARE A GOOD IN-VESTMENT. Celebrity endorsements ain't what they used to be.

If you're old enough you remember when Arthur Godfrey and Dinah Shore could endorse almost anything, and the force of their apparent sincerity could drive sales over the top.

But those were kinder, gentler times. In the Age of Skepticism, a celebrity is as apt to suppress response as he or she (or, judging by the appearance of some of these creatures, it) is to enhance response . . . and when we include a celebrity's fee as part of the cost, we can, with two exceptions, form a conclusion:

In business-to-business direct marketing, user endorsements are usually more effective than celebrity endorsements; in consumer direct marketing, endorsement by a celebrity who has no reputation or use-recognition relative to what we're selling usually is a poor investment.

(Remember Zsa Zsa Gabor for automobile mufflers? Muhammad Ali for a roach killer? Cybill Shepherd for the beef industry? "Tip" O'Neill for a chain of motels? Rodney Dangerfield for an airline? O.J. Simpson for Avis? As already stated in these pages, Dennis Miller or Candace Bergen for anything? And—the cream of the jest—Joe Namath for a financial service?)

Yes, we have two exceptions . . . and in my opinion these are transitory.

Exception 1 is the infomercial, which has to grab the viewer *on an entertainment level* or the channel gets changed in a flash. Celebrity entertainers are—well, they're celebrity entertainers. We need them to prime the viewer pump, although few have the salesmanship to run a solo infomercial. Even as we accept this exception the clock is ticking, because viewer skepticism toward for-hire celebrities is becoming more profound every day.

Exception 2 is the rare celebrity outside the hired-hand, tired-hand mold of Bill Cosby and Arnold Palmer and lip-flapping John Madden who can say, exclusively for one product or service, "I use it" . . . and convince the target-group to believe him or her.

(A possible third exception: An offering so weak it needs propping up with an artificial prop. This isn't worthy of tabulation because the promotion is doomed even as it starts.)

But we know, even as we consider these exceptions, that the cost may outweigh the benefits. Outside the orbit of intra-industry awards, we're supposed to keep score by the number of times the phone rings, by the number of orders on the fax machine, by the screen full of e-mail responses, by the number of pieces of mail on Monday morning. So might we better off spending the same money to reach more people?

Test it, of course. Test it dispassionately, forgetting autographs and celebrity shoulder-rubbings.

MYTH NO. 5: PROVOCATIVE PHOTOS AND ILLUSTRATIONS ARE EFFECTIVE. This myth is a first cousin of the one before it and the one that follows. I call your attention once again to the Illustration Agreement Rule:

> *Illustration should agree with what we're selling, not with headline copy.*

The Illustration Agreement Rule is often ignored because we're cursed with another ghastly device—remembering one element of an advertisement, as a defective surrogate for the unbeatable "acted upon." The creative team is so intent on being "creative" they overlook the reason for the message: to generate response.

Are you surprised to discover that most people are deadly serious about the way they spend their money? Are you startled by the truism that most people prefer the reassurance of actuality to the stimulus of unconnected "creativity"? Are you disconcerted by the ultimate perception of what marketing salesmanship really is—generating a desire and satisfying the desire?

The ultimate purpose hasn't changed. Radio didn't change it. Television didn't change it. The Web didn't change it. No, nothing changed except a deadly misperception in the minds of many whose dedication should be to serve that purpose: to induce your target to perform a positive act as the direct result of having observed and absorbed the message.

The two principal offenders are marketers of computer hardware and software and, amazingly, media. You've seen their desperately irrelevant "Look at me!" illustrations—girls in bathing suits, the Three Stooges, a soulful picture of a unisex creature looking placidly over the horizon. Have you *bought* as the result of these unconnected illustrations?

More to the point: One marketer shows product-in-use or uses easy-to-read text as a way of proving superiority or next-generation advances; another shows a horse and wagon, the point being that competitors are old-fashioned. Which message generates your confidence? From whom do you buy?

MYTH NO. 6: HAVING A DATABASE DIRECT THE CREATIVE PROCESS HAS TO RESULT IN A GRAY SAMENESS OF SALES ARGUMENTS. This myth is reality only for the semi-pros and would-bes. They're the ones who use database as a scattershot blunderbuss instead of relying on selected pieces of it as bullets for their rhetorical rifles.

For the professional communicator, who recognizes database for what it is—a compendium of fact and analysis—*any* additional ammunition is grist for the marketing mill. But regurgitating information from the database, undigested, untreated by the creative salivary glands (located in the fingertips)? That's not creative selling; it's a "one size fits all" mentality.

Want proof that database is ammunition and not the firearm itself? Two highly-skilled creative teams, each armed with identical printouts of the data an organization has collected about who responds to what, and even why, will produce advertising, Web sites, or direct mail packages whose thrust and response differs widely . . . and no one, no matter how expert, can predict which will be the victor.

Database fear is as unprofessional as database worship. Seat of the pants "mad genius" copywriting is out. We need every round of ammunition the database can give us.

What makes the concept "Success from database dependence" a myth isn't the concept of database; the only new component of fact-gathering and fact-analysis is the term "database" itself. Oh, no, no, no. What makes the concept of success from database dependence a myth instead of a working postulate is the accompanying *data uber alles* attitude that shoves data into the writer's creative gun-chamber and fires without measuring the barrel. An undersized shotgun sales argument comes wobbling out of the wrong-size barrel, competing with high-powered rifle bullets.

Too far-out an image? Okay, try this: The best salespeople aren't slide-rule types. They're the cream of marketers, able to distill the useful nectars out of a database . . . able to select and isolate key selling arguments.

MYTH NO. 7: COST-PER-THOUSAND IS A LOGICAL WAY TO KEEP SCORE. What an antique notion! The very edge the smart marketer has over the tradition-bound marketer is the recognition that we don't want to reach the most people; we want to reach the most people who can and will respond to our offer.

When a marketer starts to refer to "CPM"—cost-per-thousand—we know it's the reflection of an accountant's mentality or dependence on pseudo-score with terms such as "recall" and "noted."

The astute marketer regards "recall" as a myth . . . unless it's the only way of hanging on to dignity while explaining away a campaign that didn't break even.

Everyone recalls the Coca-Cola polar bears. They didn't improve the soft drink's market share. Coupons in free-standing inserts, a standard but unglamorous marketing ploy not regarded as particularly inventive or innovative, regularly improve a product's market share (usually at considerably lower cost than a campaign of "morphed" or animated television spots).

And how about e-mail, which has decimated other media in specific but often low-profile campaigns? CPM doesn't even apply to this lowest-cost medium, except as an embarrassing indicator of relative costs.

MYTH NO. 8: A MAILING OR E-MAIL LIST COMBINING INQUIRERS AND BUYERS IS ALMOST AS VALUABLE AS A LIST OF BUYERS. Let's suppose—and this isn't just a supposition, it's a common occurrence—you're communicating to two lists. One is a list of buyers from a specific company; the other is a list of inquirers to that same company. The inquirers haven't responded to the offer, so they haven't been converted to buyers.

Would you structure one message to both groups?

That might be the imperative, if the instruction coming down from on high is to "create a message." But what if this were a more wonderful world in which *you* called the tune? Would you structure one message to both groups?

Or would you recognize immediately the psychographic differential separating unconverted inquiries from actual sales?

Some of the list companies have generated an insidious bit of folklore: Inquirers are just about as valid as buyers.

What nonsense! An unconverted inquiry might, in fact, be an antibuyer—one of those literature collectors whose great joy is to ask for information.

If your experience parallels mine, you've found that in "cold list" mailings, inquiries lag desperately behind actual sales in comparable conversion-rates. So a list described as "Customers and Inquirers" warrants the question, "What percentage of these are inquirers?" . . . with fiduciary arrangements adjusted accordingly.

You say I'm overstating the differential? Take a look at some of the "teaser" space ads designed to attract inquiries and then decide whether someone who hasn't bought is remotely equivalent to someone who has. Take a look at the "don't contact me again" response coming back after your own mailing and then decide whether some of these inquirers will be grist, for years to come, for *any* offer.

A suggestion: Isolate the inquirers on the list. Tailor your message to skepticism, to the reality that these people <u>haven't</u> converted. Tell them you not only recognize and appreciate their skepticism, you share it. Then you have a chance.

The point, and it's a cosmic one: Customizing your message to *any* target-group will increase response.

MYTH NO. 9: CONTRACTIONS, HANDWRITING, AND REPEATED CALLS TO ACTION IN A SALES LETTER ARE UNDIGNIFIED. Well, maybe this myth isn't a myth. But so what? We can accept lack of dignity as long as we add, "Who cares if it's undignified if these inclusions cause the cash register to ring a little more often?"

For that matter, the most undignified occurrence in all of advertisng and marketing response is producing an ad or a mailer that doesn't pull. And too often, lack of response is bundled with a phony sense of what's dignified and what isn't. We all have been exposed to salespeople (maybe in our own mirrors) who talk stiffly and who are afraid to ask for the order. Question: *Are they salespeople?*

I'm not militating for an overbearing, carny-type pitch. My point is just as straightforward as speaking clearly and asking for the order are straightforward: The salesperson who harrumphs and hems and haws and won't ask for a decision because of fear of a negative resolution will always come in—at best—in second place.

Good salespeople establish rapport. They have "test" closes throughout their sales pitches. That's what we should do too. Dignity? Let our competitors strangle on their own dignity while we outpull them.

MYTH NO. 10: IF YOU CAN'T SAY IT IN ONE PAGE, YOU CAN'T SAY IT AT ALL. I'm concluding my diatribe with this myth because over the past year or so I've been hearing it in speeches. But you know who says it? People who aren't out in the trenches. People who don't test long letters against short letters. People whose lecture notes are so old even the moths have abandoned them.

Are long letters outpulling short letters or are short letters outpulling long letters?

Yes.

That's the answer, all right . . . because results run both ways. And the only way to draw a determination is to test.

I'll offer an empirical observation: Right now, in the first half-decade of the 21st century, long letters tend to outpull short letters for (a) continuity programs, (b) newsletter promotions, (c) financial and health offers. Short letters tend to outpull long letters for (a) two-step conversions in which the purpose of the original contact isn't to force a sale, (b) business-to-business offers in which the target has prior familiarity with what you're selling, (c) "hotlist" offers in which a long letter would be suspect.

I hope you've noticed two aspects of these mini-listings: First, more subjects are excluded than included. Second, "tends to" means just what it says—exceptions exist.

If you're going to accuse me of laying down an edict for this tenth myth or any of the previous nine, let the accusation be: This guy wants us to test.

I can live with that. So can you. In fact, your professional life will be a lot healthier than it would be if you picked up one of the myths of our business and swallowed it without chewing.

Process/Technology Abuse

S ome years ago, when I still used slides to illustrate speeches, I had a favorite slide worded: "Lawyers and accountants can't sell anything."

Later, viciously, I added academicians to the nasty list. And that list grew until inclusions seemed to outnumber exclusions. Here came Webmasters (I detest that term) . . . television term-throwers who knew all the in-words but nothing about selling . . . printers masquerading as marketers . . . computer "experts" who could open the case and add RAM but couldn't for the life of them open a selling argument. And on they came, legions of poseurs, dilettantes, and ghastly examples of The Peter Principle.

Of the bunch, the ones I despised most of all were the labelers, first cousins of the term-throwers. These people were and are masters of the acronym. They can reduce almost any procedure, any intention, any proposition to three letters of the alphabet. Triumph! We've labeled it, ergo we're the experts in it.

Take, for example, one of the labelers' favorite acronyms—CRM.

We all know that CRM represents Customer Relationship Management. And what a bonanza CRM has been for software producers, for seminar speakers, and for trade publication columnists who strut and preen and toss about the term "CRM" the way the Easter Bunny distributes his tokens.

(Oh, yes, I'm guilty too, because my attacks on mindless CRM probably has to fall into the same bucket as does mindless CRM itself.)

You may—I least, I hope you may—as you read the next section of this book, see the difference between using CRM as a label and actually practicing it. To a huge percentage of CRM experts, the dividing line between CRM and database doesn't exist. The two are inextricably scrambled, like an egg.

That true CRM necessitates a knowledge of primitive psychology, resulting in the establishment of that wonderful and irreplaceable ingredient *rapport*, seems to escape the labelers. They're in their safe haven, content to mechanize and depersonalize what should be the most personal element of a seller/sellee relationship.

What the heck, the proprietor of the corner grocery store, who not only knew our grandparents by their first names but also knew how to "schmooze" them, had a far better grasp of CRM than many contemporary CRM experts. The Chevrolet dealer of the 1950s, who instilled enough confidence to have our grandparents coming back every three years to buy another car, had a far better grasp of CRM than contemporary multi-brand dealers who run shrill television spots, conduct frantic telemarketing campaigns, and mail slick but unconvincing letters and brochures that never overcome the reality of a dealer fifty miles away offering an extra hundred dollar trade-in, underscoring our loyalty-free business relationships.

Loyalty? Airlines, restaurants, hotels, who knows who else, create loyalty programs. And how do they implement those programs? With restrictions and conditions and descriptive folders loaded with asterisks (see the "Customer Abuse" section of this book).

Loyalty doesn't exist on either level, neither on the part of the seller nor on the part of the sellee. But the sellee isn't guilty of establishing the program nor, really, of trying to implement it. After all, *they* started it. *They* lured us into their fouled nest.

We call an airline's toll-free number to make a reservation using our frequent flyer miles. Lots of luck. The wait is interminable, and the possibility of actually using those miles—even though we call eleven months ahead—is profoundly iffy.

We call a software company because the manual, if one exists, is either incomplete or incomprehensible. Lots of luck. The days of free customer service are over. It's a toll call, and we wind up in a queue.

We call the telephone service provider to ask why our bill doesn't reflect the promise the company made when recruiting us. Lots of luck. We're hung in an electronic loop, and the cream of the jest is that it's a loop created by the very company that supposedly was to lead us to the Promised Land beyond that loop.

We call our cable company because the cable either doesn't work or suddenly denies us channels we're paying for. Lots of luck. The recorded voice tells us average waiting time is interminable.

And here comes the grandest, most magnificent lie of all, carefully recorded but casually ignored: "Your call is important to us."

With that imprecation, take a look at some case histories:

Marquis de Sade, Author of Owner's Manuals

It's my own fault for dumping my teeny phone with its teeny keys. I did it because it tended to disappear in my shirt pocket. The only logical replacement was one of those jazzy new Nokias with a bunch of "advanced" features.

I don't claim technical electronic expertise. I do claim basic literacy. So my first basically literate decision—making a phone call—didn't strike me as one that required an advanced engineering degree.

I'm used to "Gotcha!" instructions. These were insidious, because they didn't seem to fall into the "Gotcha!" category. To make a call, enter the numbers and press *Call*. Press what? Nothing on this phone is labeled "Call." Oh, just a second . . . here's a button with "C" on it. That must stand for "Call."

Nope. "C" stands for everything but "Call." It starts erasing the numbers. Terrific. Where's "Call"? Oh, it's that key with nothing but a horizontal bar on it. Why doesn't the Owners Manual get into sync with what's on the phone?

All right, I now know how to make a call. Now, how do I end the call? The Manual tells me in two words: "Press *End*." Oh, yeah? Hey, Manual, I'll answer your two words with my two words: "*@#$ you." There's no "End" in sight. And to compound your sadistic obfuscation, you show a diagram of every button on the face of this phone. None of them indicates any relationship with "End." The end is not yet. Of course, I can always slide the battery out. That'll end it. What a marvelous electronic advance!

Well, wait a minute. There's the word "End" in the little window, taunting me. I'll press that bar with the horizontal bar on it.

Archimedes in the bathtub—Eureka! It ends the call! Just one question: Why doesn't the Owners Manual say, "Press the bar when the word 'End' appears in the window"? I guess it's because the Marquis de Sade, who wrote this Manual, wouldn't think that's playing the game.

Speaking of games, the Manual says I can use my phone to play three games—"Memory," "Snake," and "Logic." Sure . . . except they aren't games. "Memory" is what I have to use instead of the Manual to remember what does what on this phone. "Snake" is the serpent who edited it. "Logic"? Well, I guess that *is* a "game" for this device.

Bemused by the Owner's Manual

On we go to my dependable old Hewlett-Packard Laserjet 4 printer. Suddenly it wasn't so dependable. It wouldn't print, and on the computer screen was an instruction to adjust the "Timeout." What the hell is a timeout? Do I stand the printer or, better yet, the writer of the owner's manual in the corner for an unspecified amount of time?

I scanned the index of the owner's manual, which through some miracle I still have after all these years. For about 30 seconds, my faith in humankind was restored. But that faith reverted back across the border behind agnosticism to standard cynicism when I read the cryptic instruction:

> *Timeout, measured in seconds, refers to the time the printer will wait before ending a print job. The default value is 15. The scroll increment is 10 (hold down + to scroll.) If, when using multiple ports, data from other ports appears in the middle of your print job, increase the timeout value.*

Huh?

Maybe I'm not taking enough Ginkgo Biloba, or maybe I should have waited for the full moon. I couldn't make the instruction compute. After much fiddling around with "Menu" on the printer,

"Timeout" appeared on the tiny printer screen. Whee! I pressed the " + " button and the number rose from 15 to 30. That should do it!

Yeah, sure. I tried printing something, and that same instruction to adjust the Timeout popped onto the monitor. Aaargh. I called my computer guru, who admitted he had never heard of Timeout. After messing with it for an hour and puzzling over the Manual and switching cables and trying to use the printer with another computer and cursing, he had a suggestion: Get another printer.

So I changed the printer default to my other printer, one designed for color, and limped along for a couple of days. Update: Trying to re-create the actual onscreen message for this report, I re-hooked the Laserjet 4 and asked it to print. It did, with no Timeout message. Somebody up there hates me.

Proof of that is my *bête noir*, the imported Gaggenau oven in the kitchen. Although the oven itself is a masterpiece of advanced German engineering, the manual obviously was designed as an elimination device for the Mensa Society. Re-setting the clock is a nasty adventure for this oven, which defiantly challenges a switch to and from Daylight Savings Time.

I'd guess, though, that the ultimate proof of manual inadequacy is the book of instructions accompanying word processing programs. For more than ten years I've switched back and forth between WordPerfect and MSWord. In both cases, I've gleaned more useful information from easy-to-read supplementary books I picked up at Barnes & Noble than from the manuals themselves. Heck, if the words about how to use words aren't clear, how can we expect anything better from a phone or a printer or an oven?

So I have a suggestion for manual writers:

Assuming you really do want users to understand (a dubious assumption) and assuming you have a mother (another dubious assumption)here's a reasonable litmus test of your creative output:

Use your mother as a guinea pig. Let her try to program the

phone or fix the Timeout feature or set the oven clock, based on your instruction.

If she can't follow your opaque instructions, just assume that neither can some of the rest of us. Shock treatment is in order: Have whoever writes the owner's manual for Nokia phones generate one for Hewlett-Packard manual writers, instructing them how to write their books. Have the Hewlett-Packard obfuscator write one for the MSWord manual writers. And for the ultimate indignity, have whoever writes MSWord's manual tell their WordPerfect chums how to write manuals.

They'll all either improve or go out of business. Either way, we're ahead.

Invasion of the Term-Throwers, Part 1

All right, kiddies, what's wrong with this statement from an article in a respected marketing journal?

Database-driven tie-ins appear to be growing in all sectors. Here is a sampling gleaned from trade reports:

- *House of Seagram*, which has been building a database since 1986, recently teamed up with *Flowers by Mail* to test a vertical market tie-in to the Seagram database.
- *The Children's Company*, which maintains a database of more than 20,000 children for each of its retail stores, uses it to mail various offers, including third party offers from local food chains, Little League organizations and video game tournaments. . . .

And how about this one?

Database is the future of direct marketing, and the ability to analyze "who is buying what" will be the future determinant of success.

If you shrug and say, "So what?" you're on my team. I'll tell you what's new about this latter-day worship of database:worship of the word itself. Term-throwers and slide-rule operators have invaded our domain, seizing a technique direct marketers have been using for half a century or more and "discovering" it.

Like the thirtysomething bunch who are convinced that nobody ever got married before or had a baby before or bought a house before or had professional successes and setbacks before, the database worshipers are convinced *they* discovered the idea of segmented contacts, of categorizing buyers according to what they bought, and of targeting individuals based on where and (with luck) how they live.

Malarkey.

These techniques existed before most term-throwers were born, let alone before they foisted "impact" and "access" and "input" and "network" on us as verbs—*verbs,* for God's sake. What's new isn't the procedure; it's just the word.

I've read about Upjohn using its database "to provide additional services to people who have expressed an interest in receiving information on hair loss" . . . about Rand Materials Handling Equipment Company using its database to target customers by purchase cycle . . . about tobacco companies amassing and hoarding databases as a hedge against the day when they won't be able to use any mass media.

So what?

Database is just a word. Get over it . . .
and go beyond it.

The marketer who regards these venerable procedures as "innovative" just hasn't been in our world long enough to accomplish anything other than memorization of a word.

If we decide to be database innovators, let's innovate. The concept of hyper-penetration of razor-thin target groups has two holes in it. The first hole is The Incredible Shrinking Universe Rule:

Testing expands the universe of buyers. Inflexible repeats shrink the universe of buyers.

The second hole is The Basic Law of Database Parallels:

The more you pinpoint a buyer's specific history, the more you increase the possibility of parallel appeals by competitors.

If you're saying "So what?" to those two logic-holes, I'm not outraged. I just hope your question fronts the realization that database is one of our prime marketing weapons—our 1950s howitzer updated to a 21st century heat-seeking missile—and not a genuflect-worthy religious icon.

Database is *fact*. No rational marketer attacks fact. Without fact, we're snake-oil carnie-hustlers, pitching puff instead of reality. We should feed on data the way a supercharged car feeds on premium gasoline.

Gasoline and fact are our fuels. A full tank of gas or a full tank of fact won't do anything but spill on the ground if the starter—salesmanship—doesn't turn over.

Enough metaphor. Let's put this word into proper perspective:

Database is to *information accretion and measurement* what *chronologically challenged* is to *old*. It parallels a house of haute couture declaring that smartly-fitted knee-length dresses are "in."

Sure, they are. They've never been out. Novelty lies in the word and the declaration, not in the concept.

Now, don't accuse me of sponsoring a reactionary movement back to seat-of-the-pants guesswork. I recognize that database-fear is as dangerous as database-worship.

I'm the archetype of everybody who depends on response for both income and reputation. I want as much ammunition as you can feed me. I'd be stupid as well as irresponsible if I ever discarded usable statistics because I think I can write a powerful a sales argument without knowing who the target is.

What I'm militating for is recognition of the huge gap between the Self-Appointed "Instant Database Expert" (aka SAIDE) and the savvy marketer who isn't in awe of nomenclature but who does recognize the value of data. That savviness goes back to David Ogilvy and John Caples and Claude Hopkins and beyond. These were marketers who realized the need for constant replenishment of the buyer-base with *non*-buyers who haven't responded to targeting that, according to all available data, should have nailed them.

Ah! That brings me to obfuscator-databasers, who also are communications-debasers.

Oh, I'm perfectly aware that I'll probably get hate mail from database experts who don't subscribe to the unholy concept of opaquing what they do. No, guys, send your hate mail to your confrères who feel that fogging up a point with in-talk impresses outsiders. *Impresses? Depresses* is closer to the reaction we outlanders have to bylined articles in publications aimed at us (or so I assume, since somebody decided to send me the magazine based on whatever demographic assumption the circulation department came up with), bulging with befoggers such as . . .

- *It is a good idea to know how much input resource you consume compared to your peers to produce the same unit of output.*

- *In an entity-relation (E/R) diagram, the "supplied" verb is only an annotation in the diagram. There are no semantics in support of this verb. If the part-supplier relationship is many-to-one, meaning that each part is supplied by one and only one supplier, then we explicitly define a hierarchy that key relationships between the tables can enforce.*

- *One practical approach for managing many-to-many transformation multiplicity is to reduce the problem down to a common denominator: transformations between any two XML schemas* [sic]*.*

- *Complex business logic will always remain a combination of static data relationships and adherence to procedural sequences.*

Get the idea? The words all exist. "Transformation" is a perfectly good word. So is "multiplicity." The writer crazy-glues them together: "transformation multiplicity." We're at sea in a boat that leaks rhetoric from every bulkhead.

A truism: Two proficient creative teams, armed with and dependent on identical database-input (ugh!), will generate advertising and promotional materials whose results can differ by 50 percent or more. Yes, database has value; but the be-all/end-all it ain't.

Your honor, the prosecution rests . . . but uneasily.

Invasion of the Term-Throwers, Part 2: FYI: The SOBs have left us SOL.

In the Paleolithic pre-computer era I never gave much thought to acronyms—the use of initials to symbolize words.

That's because we knew what they meant. We've used initials to replace a word-title since before World War II. If you're a geezer you remember the initials WPA, which represented "Works Project Administration" or something like that. We had OSS, "Office of Strategic Services," which eventuated into CIA, "Competence Isn't Available."

Most people knew, in general, what these initials meant, so communication still wasn't unwired. And we knew IBM was International Business Machines. Long before any of us were born, Radio Corporation of America was simply RCA. We'd hate to have to use the long form of AT&T. These were and are harmless identifiers, corporate slang, stock market symbols . . . years to establish, logical to identify, simplifiers rather than obfuscators. I use the long form of DMA, the Direct Marketing Association, only when dealing with outlanders.

Y2K, THE GREAT FIASCO; B2B, THE GREAT CLICHÉ

The digit-heads brought Initialitis into full flower with Y2K, that overblown Chicken Little prediction that the sky was falling. In the desperation that comes from Initialitis withdrawal, they quickly came up with another: B2B, which neatly saps dignity and purpose from "business-to-business" communications.

I'm 150 percent convinced that Initialitis is the unhappy result of a desire to be recognized as an authoritarian source . . . by "labelers" who have no right to make such a claim. Get this, from an article supposedly explaining "B2B e-marketplaces" in a magazine that can't claim esoteric readership because it was sent to me:

> *From an architectural viewpoint, B2B data integration is closely related to EAI, also known as application-to-application integration (or A2A, the term I'll use here) . . . B2B technologies increasingly leverage XML and extensible style language (XSL) for data integration, in addition to the process-integration support via message brokering and work-*

*flow automation typical of A2A solutions . . . Given the nu-
merous existing and possible standard and nonstandard data
interchange formats—EDI, X12, SWIFT, delimited, positional,
multiple XML document type definitions (DTDs) and
schemas, and so on. . . .*

Yeah, and so on. Okay, CIA, put your cryptography section onto
this one. I'll bet you come up with the same diagnosis I did: Chronic
Initialitis, CMC (Call the Menninger Clinic).

THERE ARE ACRONYMS . . . AND ACRONYMS.

We've always accepted the notion that U.S. VCRs (videocassette
recorders) use the NTSC standard rather than the European PAL system, except for France which has SECAM. We don't know what
these acronyms represent and we don't care, because we realize
they aren't subject to sudden on-a-whim change.

Those are history. We live in meaner times. And what has
caused this nasty shift?

Originally I blamed the low-forehead self-important military
world, with their SESAC and DEFCON2. Years after the word *radar*
entered our vocabulary, I discovered—accidentally, while struggling
in one of those trivia games—that radar is a composite, an acronym
for *radio detecting and ranging.*

Acronyms no longer are the bastard child of the military. They're
an insidious takeover plot hatched by computer nerds.

IBM and NTSC notwithstanding, many of us became determined
initials-rejectors even before financial institutions decided to defy reality: The typical recipient of a "You've been pre-approved" mailing
doesn't know what APR stands for. Most common guess: *Average
percent of response*—harmless enough, if incorrect; and more benevolent than *Asinine public relations.*

APR typifies "in-terms" a latter-day generation of public-be-damned communicators has foisted on us: "We understand what we mean, and if you don't, TS."

Who are the prime exponents of this attitude? Computer term-throwers.

I've about had it with those smirking keyboardians. I read their magazines and their direct mail and their e-mail, and it's becoming clear: They don't want outlanders on their turf.

They keep us out by using arcane initials instead of spelled out words. And when they do spell out the words, they make no more sense than "Nov schmoz ka-pop."

But seriously, folks . . .

The supposed point of acronyms is clarity. I'm looking at a magazine article with the innocuous title, "Time for a Change." I wish the writer had changed this self-defeater: "Consider how difficult it is to explain benchmark results to management in terms of your support costs per CPU MIPs and disk GBs." Okay, I'm considering. I *think* CPU means "Central Processing Unit." MIP? Uh . . . Disk GBs? Imported from Great Britain? No reference, no explanation, no lifting of the filmy mist from which oozes the "public be damned" attitude of the in-group coterie.

Next: ". . . a document access description (DAD) construct enabling document-to-database mapping, and an XMLVAR CHAR column datatype. . . ." Not even consistency here. Why do we need DAD for "document access description," whatever that means, and not need DTD for "document-to-database"? Is the intention to educate the reader or to say to that reader, "I know something you don't"?

My current computer-related Murky Initials Adventure (MIA, which, aptly, also means "missing in action") began when I was writing copy for a company that offers a leasing option to customers of computer and office equipment stores. Some of the action involved space ads, and I got a subscription to a controlled-circulation trade publication.

The dam broke. Suddenly I was getting a dozen such magazines. Then, one fateful day, a phone call filtered through: "Mr. Lewis, is your company a VAR?"

Now, how do you answer that? Of course by that time I knew what the initials covered—Value-Added Reseller . . . which, in non-nerd terms, is a retailer. My company name at the time was Communicomp, which could be anything. So I let them play their little game: "What else would we be?"

Okay, so I'm a VAR. Who's to say no? But as the months passed, so did my currency with computerese. I was still laughing over the Internet's "URL"—Uniform Resource Locator—because if these guys didn't have the pomposity inevitably born of insecurity, they'd just call it "address" like everybody else does.

We're certainly used to that with the Internet: "What's your URL?" Sounds like a nasty report from your urologist. URL is archetypical of the new technobabble. We get drawn into a lexical maze. So a uniform resource locator is simply an online address? Why couldn't they call it that? My guess is because it isn't as obfuscatory.

The game is out of hand. No, worse—out of control. Looking through just one issue of a computer reseller magazine, I see the next generation of obfuscation. VAR now is too common a term: Too many people know what it is, and that's the danger signal: If this keeps up, the whole world will understand our private lingo. Where would we be then? We'd have to quit wearing Nikes. We'd better replace VAR while there's still time.

So here's an ad aimed at the SOHO VAR—*Small Office/Home Office Value Added Reseller*. Here's another aimed at the BYO-VAR—*Build Your Own Value Added Reseller*. Build your own *what*? A POC (*pile of crap*)?

I'm anticipating the BOOBOO VAR—*Big Open Office/Bad Office*

Odor, Very Angry Rankness? Or TOTO VAR—*Terrible Operation/Too Obscure, Vacating All Reason?*

THERE'S UPS . . . AND UPS.

The acronym field has become so crowded some initials are being usurped from other fields. Most people call UPS "Oops!" and the name gained immense popularity during any of the delivery company's ridiculous strikes. But you need a double translator when you say UPS in a computer ambience. These guys ship a UPS by UPS. To them the initials mean *uninterruptible power supply*. How'd you like to schedule one of their deliveries?

Got a cellular phone? U.S. and Canadian phones use AMPS (Advanced Mobile Phone System) or GSM (Global System for Mobile Communication—what happened to that final "C"?) North American, which also is known as PCS (Personal Communications Systems) . . . but Europe uses GSM European, a different set of frequencies. Do you give a damn about any of this? If you do, you're probably in the cellular phone business. That's my point.

Look, folks, I'm not inalterably opposed to acronyms. If we dumped them all, we'd also dump USA and FBI and maybe IRS (I know, I know . . . a good idea!). My membership in the USLTA would be in the ponderous United States Lawn Tennis Association, and I don't play *lawn* tennis.

Naw, my objection is to term-throwing, to creating a private world where outsiders are supposed to feel like outsiders. It parallels a scientist spending a lifetime to discover a previously uncategorized plant just so he can put his name on it.

Don't the digit-heads know how temporal their triumphs are? Look what happened to their first monument, DOS—*disc operating system*. Today a better translation is *dead on site*. Even Microsoft, its originator, doesn't include DOS any more.

Okay, let them have their Andy Warhol fifteen minutes of glory.

Every one of these acronyms-to-go will flourish like a weed and die the same way. Their users will be SOL. And isn't that TFB (too bad)?

Invasion of the Term-Throwers, Part 3: I.S.P. or S.O.B.?

My wife didn't know how to answer this one.

She said, "There's a man on the phone who wants to know if you're an 'I.S.P.'"

"Pretty close," I told her. "I'm an S.O.B."

"I knew that."

Obviously she didn't understand either the caller or me, which was just as well. But it amplified a nagging annoyance that's been growing like some sort of science-fiction monster for the last 30 years or so, ever since "disk operating system" became "DOS": The computer technonerds are slowly drowning the rest of us in an alphabet soup of initials. Worse, they're—well, I'll get to what's worse in a couple of paragraphs.

For a reason I can't fathom or justify, imprinted on a loose dendrite dangling in my brain is the legitimate English language definition of I.S.P.—Internet Service Provider. What would be hilarious if this weren't an industry sickness is that many Internet Service Providers themselves know "I.S.P." and toss the term every hour . . . but don't know what the initials stand for. So *assumption* becomes *recognition*.

INDECIPHERABLE ADS

The result of all this initializing is a gaggle of indecipherable ads which are certainly worthy of satire. In a computer magazine (addressed to me, not to a techie) was a space ad with this formidable subhead and text:

New Messaging/Groupware Platform
(Already Claims 8 Million Seats!)
Supports LDAP (client and server),
IMAP4, POP3, SMIME, and NNTP specs.

Yeah, I'll bet it does. I'm certainly not going to argue with *that* kind of logic. Those guys might cover me with Smime.

The guy who trouble-shoots our computers is always mumbling, and I thought he was insulting us when he talked about what came out as "Scuzzy." It wasn't. It was the way he pronounces "SCSI," which stands for some stuff inside the guts of a computer. He also was talking about risk. That made sense to me, but not in the connotation he meant. "Risk" turned out to be "RISC," which is "reduced instruction something-or-other."

Is a puzzlement.

Now, here's what's worse. It's also funny: The infection has spread.

Sure enough, a radio commercial begins:

SOUND: DOT-DOT-DOT—DASH-DASH-DASH, UNDER . . .
ANNC.: Mayday! Mayday! Your IRA is in danger!

Here we have not just two but three separate choices. Can you envision a doting mother, who just sent her son Ira off to the first grade, hearing that? She'll go charging out the door, umbrella in hand.

But hold it! What if this is a message from the Irish Republican Army, whose latest bomb has just been found in a crowded railway station, with Gerry Adams' fingerprints all over it?

Or maybe it's just a plain vanilla Individual Retirement Account at your bank or broker. After all, the advertising departments of banks are principal succumbers to technobabble. They still don't realize that a huge percentage of their targets don't know what APR means.

(Come to think of it, the technonerds may have usurped this one too. It might be Internet Rationalization Avoidance. Naah . . . that's too clear to be useful.)

In case you didn't guess, I'm being wry. But the syndrome is as clearly identifiable as the Ebola virus, and for communicators it can be just as deadly.

Look what has happened on the corporate level. Federal Express shortened its name to FedEx, which many of us used anyway; the difference is that identification now has a little mud in it. Proof? Consider the difference between "Chevy" and "Chevrolet," "Caddy" and "Cadillac," "Vegas" and "Las Vegas," "L.A." and "Los Angeles." Truncation breeds image-loss.

OBSOLESCENCE AT WARP SPEED

On the "remainder" shelf of a bookstore was a book of computer terms. Other books on that shelf covered antediluvian subjects such as Lotus 1-2-3, WordPerfect 5.1, and CorelDraw 3. Those books dated from the late 1980s and early 1990s; this one had a 1998 copyright date. Obsolescence strikes fast when you're having fun.

Except . . .

The rest of us aren't having fun. May I superimpose on your own brain one more time my favorite marketing litany, The Clarity Commandment?

When you choose words and phrases for force-communication, clarity is paramount. Don't let any other facet of the communications mix interfere with it.

So if the technonerds want to lapse into the huggy-blanket of their private jargon when they're in their own enclave, fine. They can communicate any way they like. They can speak Hungarian. If it's clear to the message-recipient, no problem.

But when they wander into our universe, let's not surrender to the arrogance so often postured by the insecure.

The mistake so many tyros and dilettantes and beginners and marketing-unconscious advertisers make is selecting a sound marketing principle and then contorting it, deforming it, misusing it. In this instance it's misusing the concept of having the reader or viewer or listener feel he or she is part of a private or preferred in-group.

Okay. No problem . . . yet. In fact, having your target feel included reflects one of today's great motivators, exclusivity. It's a totally sound marketing philosophy, 100 percent in sync with the concept of generating response. But the medium isn't the message. Being ahead at the end of the first half doesn't mean you've won the game. You need the second piece:

Your targets are part of your in-group. Now you spout jargon they don't understand. The Band-Aid phrase "As you know . . ." doesn't cover you because you've violated the Clarity Commandment. So the ploy backfires because your targets feel either a) inadequate or b) annoyed.

We're communicators. Let's communicate. Otherwise we take the RISC of being SMIMED.

The technique of stringing words together in an impenetrable sequence undoubtedly requires a combination of TUC (totally uncontrolled chutzpah) and adherence to ORC (obstinate refusal to communicate).

Take that, fellow SOBs!

What a Surprise:
Nobody Is Responsible.

Of course you know the difference between America Online and a computer virus: A computer virus works.

I was musing over this minor truism as I tried vainly to connect with just about *any* Web site, encountering the unsurprising message that Internet Explorer couldn't open the site:

A connection with the server could not be established.

Now, my mood didn't darken because Internet Explorer couldn't open the Internet site at which I aimed it . . . or any site that day. I hadn't wanted Internet Explorer in the first place, but when it comes to AOL I am a stranger in a strange land. No, make that a sucker in Suckerville. I actually signed up as a beta tester, only to learn it's a trap: You can't get out. They wait a couple of weeks, then make that beta version "inoperative" so you have to click into the next electronic cesspool.

In this case, no, my reaction wasn't to AOL or Explorer or even everybody's favorite target, Microsoft. It was to the standard technique of responsibility-avoidance: "It ain't my fault."

Note the plaintive no-fault voice. Whoever wrote the line is either a member of Congress or a public relations hack: "A connection with the server could not be established." Not, "America Online doesn't have enough capacity to connect you" or even "We're sorry, but we can't connect you with the server" or "Internet Explorer explores with a blind eye and a club foot." It's the Bill Clinton syndrome—"Mistakes were made." By whom?

RESPONSIBILITY? WHOSE?

Nobody takes responsibility any more. People ignore the Surgeon General's warning and then sue the tobacco companies, whether they get lung cancer or not. "It isn't my fault that I started smoking. It was their fault."

Mistakes were made? By whom? Not me. I'm passive. It was the famous "They."

Sure, why not? Passive voice is the classic way to avoid responsibility. A financial planner sent me a mailing: "Your portfolio will be analyzed." By whom? Hey, Buddy, don't you see the difference in *power* between "I'll analyze your portfolio" and "Your portfolio will be analyzed"?

The worst I've heard was a fisherman who was caught in a sudden squall and drowned. His family sued the Weather Channel. (This is not a drill.)

And you remember the family who sued the Jenny Jones television show, not for terminal sleaze but because their son appeared on her show, together with another guest who showed up to meet "someone who had sexual fantasies about him." The admirer was their son, and the other guy shot his unrequited admirer to death.

Just a second: Both these guys agreed to be on the show. They weren't dragged there, kicking and screaming. They weren't promised anything except an Andy Warhol 15 minutes of fame. So why sue the show and not the shooter? Because that's where the bucks are. That's whose fault it was. It couldn't have been the fault of the fellow who pulled the trigger, because he's judgment-proof. And of course it isn't the show's fault, because they didn't force either man to appear. A murder whose perpetrator is once-removed? Sure, because it's nobody's fault, except whoever has the most money.

Every now and then my computer—a reasonably new 1.3gH box with 256mb of RAM and a 43gb hard disk, supposedly state of the art—tells me "A fatal error has occurred." *Whose* fatal error? Not mine, Bunky. I was just sitting here. And you give me only two options, "Close" and "Details." How about "Fix"? I know, I know, you didn't do it. It "has occurred." *They* did it.

Aside from the fisherman who wound up with the fishes, the most disgusting examples of the "They did it" syndrome are closely tied to advertising. Now, I don't smoke. Well, maybe a cigar now and then. And I don't like smokers. Well, maybe whoever gives me a good cigar.

But anyone who, well into the 21st century, says he or she (or in the case of these suicidal lowbrows, "it") doesn't know cigarettes are deadly just doesn't read the advertising.

Or do they? All cigarette advertising *has to* include the Surgeon General's warning. Yet, repeatedly, lung cancer victims blame cigarette advertising for getting them hooked. And bear in mind, we've had the Surgeon General's warning for nearly 40 years.

So here's a guy who smoked three packs a day, never even pausing when the warnings were posted everywhere, including directly on his cigarette packages. Three packs a day. He died of lung cancer in 1997. What a surprise! For thirty years he ignored the warnings. So, quite naturally, his family sued Philip Morris. Quite naturally, an Oregon jury awarded his family $81 million. After all, the folks in Portland weren't going to be outdone by the San Francisco jury that awarded more than $51 million to a Marlboro smoker who still was alive, but barely.

WHO'S RESPONSIBLE? ANYBODY AND EVERYBODY . . . EXCEPT ME

Now, the point isn't whether cigarettes cause cancer. Of course they do. The point is that nobody is responsible. They want the world—especially those "stick-it-to-the-big-boys" juries—to know it wasn't their fault. They weren't responsible. Many of these self-caused victims didn't even start smoking until after the warnings were all over the place. (I guess their disdain for all the "Don't smoke" messages shows us how effective advertising really is.)

But no, it isn't their fault. After all, if we don't agree with any advertising message, we certainly shouldn't pay attention to it . . . until we need it to file a lawsuit.

Here's a 23-year-old Miami woman who got a birthday card that read, "Happy birthday from your friends at Marlboro." Should we fire the list broker and the direct mail moron who dreamed this up? Hold it until the story unfolds.

The recipient's mother called the Miami Herald, which in a story with a four-column headline took a gratuitous slam at our noble profession:

Maria Weener usually tosses junk mail. But she couldn't ignore the birthday card a cigarette company sent her daughter. . . .

All right, all right, we have to ignore the ignominy of a mother opening her 23-year-old daughter's mail. All right, we have to ignore the logical gap of wondering how, if she usually tosses junk mail, she even opened the envelope. We're stuck because Marlboro's siren song was mis-aimed. Happy Database, guys.

And here's a 15-year-old who boasts he has no trouble lying about his age to get the Marlboro catalog of free gifts available to smokers who rack up points while wracking up their lungs. Now, get this: He lied, to get the catalog. And the cigarette company, that malefactor of great wealth, didn't even check his birth record or give him a polygraph test.

Now the coda to those last two examples: Marlboro says Kim Weener had sent in a card stating that she was over 21, smoked, and was interested in receiving material. Mom, better check your daughter for smoker's breath.

Here's the point of all this: Just about every kid who starts smoking says he or she (or it) saw ads that made smoking seem "cool." Bull. They see other kids their age smoking and decide— note that word "decide"—smoking is cool. Only when their cool lungs turn to toast do they say they didn't decide anything. They were seduced by advertising. Yeah, make that partial advertising, because they ignore what they don't want to see.

But hasn't that been the history of advertising and marketing since Year One?

Before We Had "CRM," We Actually Had Customer Relationships.

What a kinder, gentler time we had before we started labeling our obvious business procedures. Remember when, as though the concept hadn't ever occurred to anyone before, the big advertising agencies came up with a term—Integrated Marketing? Gee, what a novel idea—offering both conventional advertising and direct marketing, in the same shop! So these agencies either bought or started a direct division, which was supposed to work in concert with the established fifteen percenters. The only problem was, the shotgun marriage degenerated into two armed camps: Get off my turf.

Meanwhile, the agencies that already had an integrated approach, geared to the clients' marketing goals regardless of media billing, continued their merry and effective way without bothering to announce the "Integrated" notion. They didn't need the terminology. And that could be a historic key. (Note, please: It's *a* historic, not *an* historic, poseurs to the contrary as they consult an history book.)

Then in came the next appropriation by the labelers—Database. If ever an effective, active procedure gave way to a compendium of mechanical listings, this was (and is) it. Lacking a personal relationship with customers and clients, businesses began to substitute the collection of data. Data. Data. The database says this guy buys vitamin E. So let's pitch vitamin E. The database says this gal buys panty-hose. So let's pitch panty-hose. What? He also buys anything and everything related to the prostate, but not from us? What? She also buys sports attire? How is our database supposed to store information we haven't entered?

WIDENING THE GAP

See the trend? As the gap between seller and sellee widens, the relationship becomes mechanized, computerized, and standardized. Data doesn't lie, but it reflects the cold, impersonal *collection* procedure rather than a penetrating look into individuals' actual buying patterns. Technicians and marketing-unconscious executives start to replace intimacy with technology . . . and wonder why "market share" (another precious term) shrinks.

A savage opinion: The marketing philosophy of marketing companies should be driven by marketers. We're seeing an invasion of non-marketers. They're administrators. And what's the difference? It's the difference in ability to establish rapport . . . as often as not because they don't consider *rapport* a valuable component of customer relationships.

So now we have CRM. Okay, great, let's "manage" customer relationships. A potential customer phones an online vendor of high-priced furniture. On hold, she hears heavy metal rock music. Nice job of customer relationship management. Oh, that's a different department? Then how about EIM—Employee Idiocy Management?

An "arm's-length" approach to CRM has become epidemic, led by marketers who certainly have the staff and the capability of implementing CRM programs that at least begin to approximate a personal relationship.

Example: Neiman-Marcus, who used to be the bellwether of managed relationships, sent a Valentine e-mail to its InCircle members, the elite of their customer base. This is how it begins (no personalization):

This Valentine's Day, shop in the name of love at neiman-marcus.com. From romantic to whimsical, practical to just plain fun, we have gift ideas to dazzle anyone on your list, in a range of prices.

A Valassis free-standing insert has a greater sense of customer relationship management than this coolly efficient message, which follows the opening with a list of floral possibilities. No recognition of InCircle, no "because you're you," not a shred of rapport. The writer obviously is somebody in the advertising department who, undoubtedly under instruction, wrote an e-mail ad. CRM? What's that? Whatever it is, it isn't our department.

My wife stores her furs at Neiman Marcus. No, make that past tense—*stored.* An undated terse note from the local store: "We are relocating the Florida fur storage operation to our central fur storage facility in Dallas, Texas." Margo called the same day to say she'd pick up the coats because she didn't want to wait for Dallas to send them back when she wanted them. Blithe answer: "Oh, they've already been shipped there."

How big a deal would it have been to notify customers before sending their coats off to Niflheim?

Following suit, American Express Platinum Card increased the damage it already had given Platinum's image by a heavy card recruitment campaign that obliterated the concept that this card is one to be sought after. AmEx's e-mail to Platinum Card members destroys CRM even as it claims it, by dealing in plurals:

Dear Platinum Card(R) and Centurion(sm) Card members: As an Event Net enrollee, you will periodically receive email updates about important American Express services and special offers which we believe would be beneficial to you. If you would like more information on how to set your email preferences, please refer to the bottom of this text message. The fol-

lowing events will be on sale through By Invitation Only(R)
by calling 1_800_321_RSVP (8am _ 11pm ET). Attention
handheld device users, you can now download the latest By
Invitation Only events to your handheld device via
AvantGo(TM) free interactive service. Visit http://tm0.com/
americanexpress/sbct.cgi?s = 12071463&i = 294843&d =
932834 *and click on the handheld icon for more information.*

Who can resist such a warm and personal greeting, especially
when AmEx so graciously calls us an "enrollee"? A reasonably
bright high school student could craft a more inviting and certainly
more personal "invitation."

These are just two examples of the widening seller/sellee gap
even as vendors lay claim to the term "CRM." So the obvious charge
to marketers who sincerely want to pet and stroke their customers,
who want those customers to feel chosen and appreciated, and who
regard the initials CRM as more than a journal entry: Forget that
MBA approach to your painfully acquired customer list and turn the
communications job over to . . . well, to a communicator.

CRM by the Pound

CRM is hot.

Everybody is claiming expertise. Maybe that's why everybody is
selling a CRM method to everybody else.

Have you noticed how many software programs exist? How
many of the dozens and dozens of CRM seminars you can attend?
How many experts are telling us how to apply CRM methods?

Here's a "CRM Software Buyer's Guide." For $895 this Guide
gives us "immediate access to complete information on leading customer interaction software products"—sixty of 'em.

That's nothing. If you use Google to look up "CRM software" on the Web, you'll find 33,100 entries. There are a lot of experts out there. Shorten your search to just "CRM" and you'll have 921,000 entries. Spell it out—"Customer Relationship Management"—and you'll have 483,000 entries to plow through. That's a lot of management, Babe. (These numbers are as of the day this is written. Check it now and you'll probably see a substantially higher number.)

Is customer relationship management a science or an art? Our grandparents, who ran grocery or hardware or clothing stores or repair shops or pharmacies, didn't need software. They *knew* their customers. They knew which cereals and cuts of meat their customers preferred. They knew the little idiosyncrasies that cemented seller/sellee relationships.

The gap between seller and sellee is widening by the hour. And so is the gap between genuine CRM and a hybrid database-demography compilation. Here are online merchants, installing CRM software whose purpose is to overlay controlled communications with their customers, depending on what and when each customer has bought. Hey, guys, that isn't CRM. You might call it CCM—Customer Contact Management—but in no way can all this computerized notification mechanism compete with shipping an order on time, with sending a signed "Welcome" letter, or with creating a façade of rapport.

As Personal as an Invoice

Here's a gift somebody sent, shipped by Harry & David. Uhhh—*who* sent it? There's no card. Oh, wait a minute. Printed on the box, between the UPC and a whole bunch of code numbers and letters (in the same font as those numbers and letters) is "Message from sender"—"Merry Christmas Love Bob." Gee, how personal can an enclosure get? Now, assuming this company had promised to enclose a greeting, no amount of software can overcome what seems to be a casual replacement of *relationship* with *procedure*.

Replacement of relationship with procedure seems to satisfy the lip-service so many marketers are giving those three precious initials, C-R-M. Zabar's, an upscale vendor of gourmet chocolates and coffees, follows Harry & David down the low road. A gift box arrives, with delectable goodies such as Schwartenbroek Belgian chocolate, cinnamon rugelach, chocolate babka, and Zabar's private blend coffee. They're listed on an enclosure, with item numbers and quantity 1 each.

Who's it from? The last item on this coldly impersonal list of enclosures is "1 card," followed by the wording "Gift Card" and the sender's message in the same sans-serif all-caps type face as the rest of the inventory.

Does customer relationship enter the mind of whoever approved this format? Absolutely not. It's pure *management*.

That's why the whole concept needs retooling. We're offered innumerable CRM software packages. More CRM seminars exist than Web seminars, and I hadn't thought that was possible. But the programmers and the organizers consistently miss the point: Customers shouldn't know they're bring managed. Get that? *Customers shouldn't know they're being managed.* (If you ask why not, don't be the one who deals with your customers.)

I'll offer this savage and uncompromising opinion: One-size-fits-all and customer relationships are out of sync with each other. Introducing the word "management" into the mix adds even more distance between seller and sellee.

Maybe that's why some marketers, recognizing the artificiality of bulk CRM, now are emphasizing *knowledge* management. Replacing synthetic "need to know" with realistic "philosophy sharing" may be a good deal more sensible for those who sense getting slashed by an impending two-edged sword—the skepticism born of sophistication by customers and the mechanized, march-in-place trend of middle and upper managers.

Actually, the very term *management* is at variance with *relationship*. It suggests vendor superiority, and that's a dangerous attitude, especially in a 21st-century ambiance in which customer loyalty is itself a fantasy. What's puzzling is that so many expert and professional approaches to CRM don't even touch the fragile thread holding the sellee to the seller, let alone strengthen it. For example, people buy online, at once fearful of whether or not the item will be delivered as advertised and on time. A reassuring e-mail will do far more to transform that customer from skeptic to advocate than would a supersophisticated entry system.

Most CRM software touts automation as the principal benefit. Certainly, in this era of "bulk thinking," without automation any vendor who can count more than a few hundred customers can't even begin to mount a continuity program. But is automation the point of relationships . . . or is it the antithesis of relationships?

Darwin Was Right:
The Evolution of Motivators

The Scopes Trial was more than three quarters of a century ago. Charles Darwin published *The Origin of Species* 66 years before that.

Here we are, supposedly evolved from pre-Darwinian thinking, and two groups still reject the concept of "Survival of the fittest"— die-hard religionists and die-hard marketers.

Why? Arrogance is always present when refusing to admit obsolescence.

If you're not locked in the twentieth century, brain wide shut, you're aware of the savage shift affecting how we sell. Yes, the Internet is responsible. No, blaming the Internet and doing nothing about it can be a direct and increasingly lonely road to a receiver's auction.

As I see it (and I quickly admit that I'm X-raying a marketing monster barely out of embryo), survival of the fittest means the survivors have to discard prior notions of what the two words "customer loyalty" mean. We're in a meaner, tougher selling ambiance . . . and we're proving Darwin right: Only the fit survive.

Techniques for vending merchandise and services are evolving quickly. What will remain, in a *very* few years, are three major levels of response and one minor one:

1. Price. This is far and away the major factor, and the Internet Generation may well recognize no other.

2. Status. Status can overcome price, but the major "status" retailers are becoming so terrified they're either defaulting into the first level or misreading what today's customers regard as status.

3. Convenience. This is what will keep some stores open and enable some entrepreneurs who deal either locally or quickly with a cadre of customers/clients to be competitive enough to stay in business.

PRIVACY? FORGET IT.

The minor level of response: Privacy. I call this "minor" because privacy not only is a disappearing luxury; a huge chunk of buyers no longer regard it as a factor. Stemming from no-holds-barred investigative reports, we have the "f" word in common usage; we have people casually releasing their true names and addresses to porn sites; we have local cable shows whose content is a view of the naked rumps of willing-to-drop-pants passersby (some of whom are stunningly unattractive); we have publicity-seekers who gleefully air their personal problems and stupidities for one of those obnoxious on-the-air judges or a neanderthal-directed talk show. Privacy ain't dead, but it's gasping for air.

The Web is price-driven. That's as it should be, because the Web has butchered, drawn and quartered, and thrown into the sea our conventional interpretation of customer loyalty.

We look for the lowest price for vitamins, for computers and software, for anything regarded as "standard." It's a comparison-shoppers' wonderland. Intensifying the syndrome is the realization that implementing "Permission Marketing" (Seth Godin's astute and accurate term) means sweepstakes, premiums, and freebies to gather names for subsequent e-mail solicitations.

No one is immune. I've dealt with the same car dealer for eighteen years. He couldn't (or, being a staunch traditionalist, wouldn't) meet the online price. This led to a fascinating development: Another dealer, to whom I disclosed the online price, underbid the quote. That's where I bought the car.

I'm sure people still visit retail vitamin/supplement stores, because they're still open. But no one I know buys from them unless it's a day in which their coupons make them competitive with online sources. And if an electronics store wants to sell a computer, it means entering an Arabian bazaar with deals and prices sometimes so arcane they're impenetrable (example: those endless $400 discounts for agreeing to a three-year arrangement with the resuscitated Compuserve).

NEIMAN MARCUS AND THE DECLINE OF STATUS

Status seems to be misunderstood even by those who have been its cornerstones. I'm a long-time "InCircle" Neiman Marcus customer. In days of yore, InCircle members had perks. A toll-free call on a specific day brought magazines, perfumes, and events tickets. The copy of the InCircle Quarterly I'm looking at as I write this confers as much status as the telephone directory. I can vacation at Telluride for $200 a night. I can mail a form to be eligible for a drawing for a mother-of-pearl and sterling bracelet. For $2,225 per person (double) I can go to Santa Fe from August 10 to 13, including a performance of *Rigoletto* and a commercial showing of "Ford Ruthling's folk art." If I spend $200,000 at Neiman Marcus this year, they'll give me a Brioni suit. The only toll-free call is for information telling me where I can see a Bentley Arnage.

See what I mean? These guys don't know that Ubid and eBay and Carshopper.com are bleeding the significance out of their hauteur.

Status? Loyalty? What about this program either recognizes or promotes status or loyalty?

A company specializing in what it calls "e-commerce solutions" sent me a mailing promoting a seminar titled "Developing Digital Customer Loyalty." Good idea, if it works. But the subjects announced in the brochure are "Digital Selling Techniques" and descriptions larded with familiar pitches—"be proactive" . . . "one-to-one experience" . . . "how technology can be utilized to respond to your most critical customers and to achieve true long-term relationship value."

The same day I was looking over that seminar brochure, my local newspaper had a big headline on page one of the business section: "Dot-com deals." Hey, that's what it's all about, baby.

The article underscored what every Web-head has known for three or four years: Auto Internet companies are "battling to be the first to 'revolutionize the auto industry.'" The CEO of Autobytel is quoted: "Every day there's a new company."

WE HAVE MET THE FUTURE, AND WE'RE IT.

And that's the future. How does a new company . . . or for that matter, an existing company . . . attract customers? If you or I were to approach one of these competitors with the suggestion that they can achieve dominance, or even parity, by stressing loyalty, we'd get a fast "Don't call us, we'll call you" rejection. Speed and price, *ja*. Loyalty, *nein*.

The parallel CEO, of AutoNation (a conglomerate of dealerships), offered this rejoinder: "They have zero dealerships." Analyze the circumstance and the brick-and-mortar response and you can see the direction. That delineates both the circumstance and the future: We use the Net to set the pricing parameters. The conventional marketers can fill the orders if they conform and adapt.

Brave new world? Sure, if you drop the word "Brave."

Will the Real Sax Lewis Please Stand Up . . .?

Years back, when we installed our first fax machine, the phone company called: How did we want the number listed?

My wife told the caller we didn't want a listing because this was a fax machine.

"What?" the phone company representative asked. "What was that name again?"

"No, it's a fax. F-A-X."

In the regular course of Murphy's Law, a listing appeared in the next directory: Sax Lewis. "F" does sound like "S" and if one is eager to make an entry, what the hell.

So over the years Old Sax somehow moved up the demographic ladder from "recent installation" to various homeowner lists. The fax machine would ring, and if it was between 6 pm and 9 pm we knew it probably was one of Sax's new friends, trying to wheedle a contribution or an investment in time-sharing.

Those calls to our family phantom had to be the prelude to mail. And Sax is still popular—so much so that I may nominate him as a speaker (albeit a shrill one) for one of those Customer Relationship Management seminars.

The mail that comes to Sax Lewis is a microcosm of a failure in direct marketing psychology . . . one of the reasons those outside our uneasy empire point at us and brand us fakes.

Example: A letter to Sax begins:

Dear Colleague:

As your organization is widely regarded as one of the retail banking industry's leading vendors, I wanted you to be among the first in the field to share some very exciting news!

On November 11–12, in Phoenix, Faulkner & Gray will host the <u>*inaugural session*</u> *of our new* **CREDIT CARD MARKETING CONFERENCE: Keys to Co-Branding Success.**

My complaint isn't because the writer used the word "as" twice within the first seven words. Oh, no. It's the early 20th century sales psychology. Does this company think their first sentence is even remotely believable? I'm an exponent of target-stroking, but credibility is the key to persuasion.

Count one more strike against their sales argument: If they think a credit card conference is "very exciting news," they'd better add some Prozac to their kaopectate.

Phony stroking isn't just out of date; it's an intelligence-insulter.

Think about this for a moment: When somebody deliberately insults your intelligence, giving you *zero* credit for the ability to wade through the rhetorical treacle, doesn't the neutrality that may have attended your attitude as you open a piece of mail sour into antagonism?

In a one-on-one phone call, "I'm calling you because you're . . ." has a chance. In a letter, "As your organization is widely regarded as one of the retail banking industry's leading vendors, I wanted you to be among the first in the field to share . . ." doesn't have a chance.

How Small is a "Small, Select Group"?

How about this one? A letter addressed to me comes in a heavily-produced four-color custom-converted envelope. It begins:

> *Dear Colleague:*
>
> *I'm pleased to invite you to participate in our new Math-cad Preferred Engineer/Scientist Discount Program during the initial sign-up period.*
>
> *The purpose of the program is simple: to introduce our newest and most exciting technical calculation tools as they're completed to a small, select group of people who . . .*
>
> The program sells for $79.99.

Whoops. Hold it. I'm among a small, select group of people. You're going to the expense of custom-converting a color-separated envelope to sell $79.99 software to "a small, select group of people." One of two problems gets in the way: Either we disagree by tens of thousands on what a "small, select group" is, or you'll have gone bust by the time my order gets there.

Official Airline Guide joins the smarmy group with this peculiar offering:

> *Dear OAG Customer:*
>
> *Give us your opinion and a few minutes of your time, and we'll give you a free gift.*

Okay, what's their deal? They're developing "a new product" for travelers' hotel planning. They're conducting an in-depth study which, on an interactive disk, can take considerable amount of my time. And what's my "free gift"? A free copy of the prototype and "a certificate worth 50% off the price of a subscription to this product." Do they give me one word of evidence that this "product" will have any value to me? Are you kidding?

Again, phony stroking is based on the standard phony assumption: What's valuable to them is valuable to me.

Look, folks, we're in The Age of Skepticism. Fake effusiveness should be the dodo bird of our industry, and instead it's becoming epidemic.

Consider, before you send out that next mailing which says to your best prospects, "We think you'll respond because we say you're a big-shot who will think this is important, valuable, and exciting": Stroking with a molasses-coated sledgehammer isn't all that pleasant for the strokee, especially if he's as worldly and sophisticated as Sax Lewis.

Some Attitudes Just Don't Compute: Smart Uses of Smarter Tools

You know the old homily—"I said it to Orville, and I said it to Wilbur: The damned thing never will get off the ground."

Well, it does. I sometimes wonder how a 777 can lumber into the air, weighed down with all the luggage my wife stashed onto it; but I don't have any question about the "what." Planes do fly, and I fly on them.

I bring this up because a fellow writer took issue with something I had written in which I pointed out that because of the computer I'm (opinion) writing better than I ever have.

"How can you say that?" this writer objected. "The computer grinds out *im*personal copy."

The follow-up was jarring: "I don't even use a typewriter. It's artificial. I write on a yellow tablet and have my assistant transcribe it. This gives me the opportunity to think as I write."

Oh, yeah? Then, buddy, you have too much sand in your gears.

Why not write on stone tablets? That would *really* give you time to think.

The funniest part of the conversation was the comment that the job this writer was working on was for computer software. And this intended squelch gave me a chuckle: "You aren't writing any more. You're word processing."

SHAKESPEARE IN LOVE . . . WITH WORD PROCESSING

So what? If Shakespeare had had a word processor he might have written twice as many plays. Better yet, he might have hit the "delete" key for *Titus Andronicus.*

Hey, we don't have Word Processing Police whose job it is to prevent us from thinking while we word process.

And who says "thinking" eliminates professional tools such as the dictionary or thesaurus? Aren't they on the same assistance-plane as the computer? (And isn't the dictionary/thesaurus in the computer a lot faster than the dictionary and thesaurus on your bookshelf?)

Years ago, when I broke into this business with the old Morlock Advertising Agency in Chicago—one of the first genuine mail-order agencies—I had an Underwood typewriter with a faded ribbon. Because clients saw what we typed, the results had to be moderately clean. So if I hit the wrong key on the typewriter, I tried to think of a word starting with that letter.

That's one reason I can claim I'm writing better now.

When the first word processors appeared, I bought one. I could type 1096 characters and then had to turn a knob to give me a fresh position on the tape. It wasn't all that convenient, but I felt I could make changes without having to retype everything.

I'm writing this on a PC with a 43 gigabyte hard disk, a 1.3gH chip, and 256 megabytes of RAM. Before I reached this paragraph, I made two insertions and some word changes. If I still had the old Underwood, the words would have stayed as they were.

Yup. I'm writing better now.

I'll make the first half-point of this diatribe:

We, the communicators, *dare not* reject new tools any more than we'd reject new list information. We laugh at those whose decisions stem from the antique "We've always done it this way" dogma . . . so how can we follow that same specious doctrine?

When I was less affluent and less electronically equipped than I am now, I had a typist. A client would want a mailing aimed at the house list and another to the open market. I'd write one of them, make a photocopy, type some changes from one to the other, make other chicken-scratch handwritten changes, string the pieces together with tape, and hope the typist didn't add too many fresh typos.

If the letter was too long, I'd have to cut, because the concept of using 11.5-point American Typewriter font instead of 12-point Courier wasn't even a gleam in somebody's eye.

For a brochure, I'd give the artist a copy sheet, with my own copywriter's rough layout. The artist would prepare a "marker comp," and it would be up to unseen others to see to it that the type fit into its allotted space.

GONE FOREVER

Them days is gone forever . . . and I don't miss 'em. Nor should you.

Why? Aside from convenience and polish, compare the "cycle time." When I finish this chapter, it's *finished*. No retyping. No fresh typos. No waiting until tomorrow because it's 6 p.m. Try that with a yellow tablet.

Nostalgia has no place in our busy world, except as a marketing ploy. It makes no more sense to reject those tools the electronic wizards have bequeathed to us than it does to reject a new way of increasing response to an ad, a mailing, or an e-mail message.

The sermon for today: Refusing to adopt professional tools (and the computer isn't all that new; it's been here for more than a generation) is just about as *un*professional as a professional can be. Only in fiction can the tortoise beat the hare.

Oh, sure, sometimes we become the slave of technology instead of its master. I've seen mailings so thoroughly saturated with artificial personalizations (often in half a dozen or more fonts) they've come full circle: They fight themselves, with the device betraying the writer's intended me-to-you artifice.

But let's not ever confuse misuse and overuse with *non-use*. They aren't even distant cousins.

RUNNING ON TRACKS = RUNNING ON EMPTY

Here's the other half of my point:

When we begin to run on tracks, *then* we really have become word processors instead of writers. I know writers who are nonplused when they're asked to generate two differing approaches to a space ad or a mailing or to test two e-mail approaches. They don't *have* two different approaches in their creative ditty-bags because they run on tracks. Now, *that's* word processing!

Hey, guys, let's use every tool, every weapon, every cannon and bomb and sword and grenade and club we can get our fists (read: fingertips) on. Our targets out there aren't standing still, so how can we?

But if you think I'm off-target, why not switch back to a yellow tablet? In short order, I'll have the field to myself . . . and my word processor will type out a neat "Thank you."

"They'll Never Know the Difference"

Some years ago I wrote the mailings for a company selling collector's plates. The plates were handsome American-made china . . .

which, as plate aficionados know, is cream-colored as opposed to conventional white porcelain. Ours was a "continuity" program—that is, an ongoing series with plates issued at intervals.

The supplier of plate "blanks" raised the price. At that point, my client decided to switch to a Japanese porcelain blank made with a coloring agent that somewhat resembled American china. The blank was about forty cents cheaper than the existing price, let alone the proposed raised price. A confident prediction: "They'll never know the difference."

Some did. They not only dropped out, but I picked up an extra assignment—writing placating letters in reply to "white mail." (Later, this same guy decided to drop the size from 9½ inches to 8¼ inches with the same refrain: "They'll never know the difference.")

The first "They'll never know" assumption wounded the program. The second one killed it.

And so it should have, because of a venerable rule that should govern all of us in the most holy of professions, advertising/selling: *If you make a promise, keep it.* (Separating advertising from selling is an insidious cop-out.)

Airlines claim they can't abide by that rule because too many people expect them to keep their promises. Hey, that makes sense.

So "biggies" such as American and United, subscribers to the "Loyalty is for passengers, not for us" *cynicreed* (hybrid word), imposed previously unmentioned expiration dates and increased the number of frequent flyer miles we need to get a free seat or an upgrade. After all, if they lived up to their commitment, "those people" would come piling in with outrageous demands for what they've been promised. How dare they! Thank God we reneged. Just in time. Whew, that was a close call.

And other airlines fell into line. If American and United can do it, so can Continental and US Airways (one of the most peculiar name changes since Unisys). And had US Airways been folded into

United, that simply would have compounded the felony. Continental and U.S. Airways figured out a marvelously obfuscatory tactic. They established tiers of frequent flyers—a caste system. With Continental, to book an award to Europe or Hawaii, you had to have an elite level—gold, silver, or bronze—or you can't make a reservation until 30 days before the flight, when seats may be available on a first-come, first-served basis. Or they may not. Tough. And that elite level expires each year, so you can't rest on your laurels or pile up miles. Clever, huh? That'll show those creeps who want to cash in their miles. Do they think we're as naive as they are?

US Airways wasn't to be outdone. If you had an upgrade certificate, you can phone for an upgrade three days ahead . . . provided you're Chairman's Preferred—that's 100,000 "tier miles" during the previous year. If you're just a peon-level Preferred (25,000 miles), you can't call until the day before the flight. And if you're a member of the proletariat, you have to wait for the check-in counter to open or the next time a star rises in the East, whichever comes last.

I have nothing against elite status. After all, I claim it. My objection is to these guys changing the rules they themselves have set up.

Now here comes Delta, clomp clomp clomp. "Us, too!" You have to be not just a Medallion Frequent Flyer. Silver Medallion is just a hair better than peon. Gold Medallion gets some perks. You have to have Platinum Medallion status to get full benefit. Getting your Platinum Medallion card means flying to Mars and back twice a week.

That's why Delta has me particularly piqued. I'm a "Lifetime Medallion" member, but I also used to be a Flying Colonel. I didn't ever quite know what that meant. Apparently neither did Delta, because they suddenly discontinued it. But being a Flying Colonel once had ample prestige. During their heyday Flying Colonels were the *ne plus ultra* of Delta's elite, including, of course, access to the crowded Crown Rooms filled with noisy mewling, puking infants, at various airports where Delta flights invariably run late.

Here comes a communication from Delta. I open it. Uh-oh! ". . . in order to ensure that our Crown Room Clubs continue to efficiently serve our members, we are no longer able. . . ." And a single enclosure, with that nasty (and unnecessary) word, "Application." If I want to get into the Crown Room after whatever date, I have to apply. I get a break, they tell me: It's only $100 per year. No phone number on *anything* in this demotion.

Fie on you, Delta. I'm stripped of my Colonial rank . . . no surprise, because your coldly impersonal communication is rank.

IS THERE A FORD IN YOUR FUTURE?

Then along comes Ford. You remember Ford—those wonderful marketers who brought you the Edsel. Ford made a deal with Citicorp to offer a Citibank Visa and MasterCard. The card offered a rebate of five percent on every purchase, usable toward a new Ford car.

Success! Thousands and thousands of cardholders took Ford up on the rebate. If all six million Ford/Citibank cardholders cashed in their rebates, the total would be far up into the billions.

So what did Ford do? You guessed it. Ford discontinued the program.

A spokeswoman for Ford was quoted in *The Wall Street Journal* with this explanation: "I know it's hard to believe, but the decision really reflects a fundamental change in how we are marketing vehicles, such that we felt an across-the-board rebate program wasn't an effective way for us to market our products."

Hard to believe? Lady, you win the prize for that one.

But the infection reached another auto maker. Gee, said General Motors, can they do that? Me, too. Me, too. So GM was quite rightly outraged that cardholders took the GM gold MasterCard at its word— rebates up to $1,000 when buying a GM automobile. "Those people" have a lot of nerve, demanding what we promised. So GM lowered the cap on its card from $1,000 to $500. That'll show those mooches.

Michael Auriemma of Auriemma Consulting Group, Westbury, NY, explained the reverse "Gotcha!" effect this way: "The hard part is, after the deal is struck, getting the program to work and getting cardholders to behave the way you want them to behave."

Da noive of dem cardholders!

WORSE THAN THE ASTERISK!

The difference between the "asterisk exception" and a flat-out withdrawal of promised benefits is a profound one. Much as I hate that accursed asterisk (the indicator that a promise isn't really a promise), it's light-years more palatable than an unasterisked promise its proclaimer later withdraws.

Oh, before I forget . . . somewhat off this premise but a worthy example of sudden attitude-change: My mother used to chuckle over a death notice in the paper in which a comma was misplaced. Instead of "Died suddenly, beloved . . ." it was "Died, suddenly beloved. . . ."

That's the U.S. Postal Service. Direct mail is suddenly beloved. So the Postal Service sent a mailing to businesses, signed by Robert G. Krause, touting direct mail. (The money might be better-spent improving the percentage of bulk mail the post office delivers.)

I have three suggestions for this ponderous organization that suddenly loves us:

1. Suppress the names of companies in the direct marketing business. In a message pointing out that "Direct Mail is more versatile than you would expect," you mention organizations that have improved their response by "modeling, segmentation, and geodemographic analysis to define their audiences and send them tailored messages." (Who the hell writes your copy?) Hey, why don't *you* use those weapons so you won't mail your refrigerator offer to us Eskimos?

2. Back off with the inquisition. Where do you get the chutzpah to ask, in a bulk mailing, what a company's sales volume is, without explaining why you want that information and what you plan to do with it?

3. Design a response device that fits into your business reply envelope. Direct mail certainly is more versatile than you expect; but that doesn't mean you should test the recipient's versatility by challenging him/her to fold, fold, fold until the blasted thing fits into your offsize reply envelope.

On that happy note, let's all revel in our new role as the suddenly beloved target of our beloved Postal Service . . . at least until the next page of this beloved book.

Sweet Sue!

I'm old enough to remember an ancient vaudeville joke. One guy says to the other, "What's green, hangs on the wall, and whistles?"

The other fellow ponders. "Uh . . . I dunno."

"A red herring."

"But it isn't green."

"So you can paint it green."

"But it doesn't hang on the wall."

"So you can hang it on the wall."

"But it doesn't whistle."

"So sue me."

Our overstaffed and overstuffed legal troops are filing class action suits for reasons far thinner than a bad joke, and a lot of them qualify as red herrings. "Legal ethics" is becoming an oxymoron. Anyone who sees some of the ads these lawyers are placing in mass media, inviting any and all to join the parade to the courthouse, simultaneously has to admire the chutzpah and cringe at the chutzpah.

Consider the class action suits against America Online. I know, I know, nobody loves America Online, including me. But who deserves this? Lawyers in Virginia, Arizona, Colorado, Ohio, Oregon, and New Jersey filed separate class action suits and are advertising them heavily. What's the basis? They say AOL failed to inform users that an upgrade might interfere with their ability to connect to competing ISPs.

I'm not kidding. That's the rationale. The Virginia suit alone asked for $8 billion. And—what a surprise—the same law firm was handling four of the lawsuits.

There's a parallel with all the class action suits by cigarette smokers—uh, that is, by lawyers representing cigarette smokers. The AOL upgrade clearly asks whether the individual wants to do this; the invitation to smokers is accompanied by the Surgeon General's warning. Oh, I forgot: Nobody is responsible for his/her own actions. And although the Virginia law firm says it got "hundreds" of calls and e-mails from AOL users asking to join the suit (how did those people know the e-mail address of the law firm?), most people seem to have installed the upgrade and gone on about their business.

The Arizona law firm ran two display ads in the same issue of a number of Sunday newspapers. They're professionally-produced ads, with similar reverse headlines headed "Urgent news for . . ." One piece of urgent news is for people who took Propulsid. It catalogues a laundry list of symptoms that seem to include everything except ingrown toenail. The other urgent news is for people who took Rezulin for diabetes and . . . well, let's not get into that. The ads say "Open 7 Days a Week," like a supermarket, and have a photo of an angry-looking eagle. Vulture might be a better symbol.

Coca-Cola Hits the Spot . . .

Then we have once-mighty Coca-Cola, whose recent griefs have been compounded by a discrimination suit filed by a bunch of former employees who also militated for a Coke boycott. What's the comeback against a discrimination suit? One reason companies settle is the reason these legal vultures know so well: Defending casts heat and light on the claim. And of course, Johnnie Cochran tends to look for appearances.

Then we have the Franklin electronic organizer. Again in New Jersey, a law firm filed a class action suit claiming the Rex PC Companion was defective because it "reorders the items to the user's To-Do Call List in an apparent random fashion when an item is added, deleted or marked as completed (the 'Alleged Defect')." Aw, those poor puddy-tats. Anyway, Franklin denied this claim, but agreed to a settlement in which all the plaintiffs got an upgrade and the lawyers got a piddling $235,000. That they settled for such legal chicken feed may be an indication of the merit of this suit.

Even the AOL litigation isn't as high profile as the Publishers Clearing House class action suit. An Assistant Attorney General, Regina Cullen, made a telling comment: "It's important to look at the numbers and do the math. This is a $10 million settlement, but attorneys' fees and other costs take away almost $6 million of that amount."

A lawsuit filed against Loews and AMC theatres claimed the theatres violate the federal disabilities law by—get this—failing to provide captioning for deaf people. One plaintiff said in all seriousness, "I can't lip-read cartoons." The suit asks the theatres to implement captioning for all movies.

The open question hangs in the air: Whose responsibility is it, anyway? Should publishers be forced to print all books in large type? Should karate studios provide classes for paraplegics? Should restaurants have full-time first-aid attendants for those who choke on food they've swallowed improperly and infants who get their bowels in an uproar as they "sit" in their high chairs?

The kissin'-cousin of the class action suit is the technique of blaming the media for advertising they carry. Sanity prevailed when the sometimes erratic Supreme Court ruled that the medium isn't the message. Had the ruling gone any other way, every newspaper, magazine, broadcast station, and ISP would have been held responsible for claims of irresponsibility against their advertisers. The case in point was filed on behalf of a teen-ager who claimed that somebody else posted vulgar-language messages on Prodigy in his name, so Prodigy owed him a ton of money. The Supreme Court said no, the medium and the message aren't the same. Prodigy can't possibly police every message; and if it did, even more legal actions would result.

My Fault Shall be Thy Fault

We're quite used to lawsuits by individuals who spill hot coffee on themselves or smash their cars into abutments or trip and fall in the lobby of an office building. The defense, "But thousands of others *didn't* spill their coffee and *didn't* smash up their cars and *didn't* fall" may be logical but unappealing to the legal mind.

So we whose dedicated job is to communicate now walk on eggs . . . and the eggs no longer are golden eggs. Some who have walked before us have smashed eggs by blurring the fine line between puffery and impossible claim. Our job is to retain credibility while still being able to motivate the reader, viewer, or listener.

Should legislation exist to protect consumer and business targets from being "had" by scoundrels who populate the periphery of every type of business? Oh, yes. Should marketers, their agencies, and their consultants be held accountable for deliberate misrepresentation? Oh, yes.

And should the courts look askance at lawyers who run their own ads, rounding up the dogies for a class action cattle-call they know will result in riches for them and pennies, if anything, for their clients? Again, oh, yes.

We already have the strange and laughable situation in which tobacco companies legally advertise . . . while defending themselves with diminishing success against those who made the advertising successful. Joe Camel has gone to that great oasis in the sky. The memory lingers on: If you're injured, insulted, or sickened, go ahead and seek legal redress. But don't invite the entire neighborhood to join in.

A Really Simple Way to Connect with Your Customers: Shipping and Handling

Adding "shipping and handling" costs to a purchase is both venerable and logical. Well, let's add one qualifier: It's logical if the amount is logical.

What isn't logical is a latter-day movement to transform shipping costs into a separate profit center. When the reader penetrates this procedure, the negative reaction taints the entire world of direct marketing, not just the marketer whose greed has tossed aside its seventh veil.

Case in point: Beethoven's complete symphonies for $5.95. Pretty good, huh? Oops: It's $5.95 *plus shipping & handling*. And how much is the shipping and handling? Doesn't say. What it *does* say, in the response device, is that I'm to enclose $5.95 and they'll bill me later for shipping and handling. Opinion: This is a disservice to our industry because the shipping cost could be anywhere from

$3.00 to $15.00 . . . and they're not likely to enter the lowest actual cost as a charge on their books.

Assuming this marketer wants to hold the customer he or she seduced by the $5.95 Siren Song, we have to make either of two subsequent assumptions: (1) The purpose of separate s/h billing is to validate, artificially, the $5.95 as a total number; or (2) the purpose is obfuscation, hoping the buyer won't quite remember what was shipped and will pay a bogus amount.

FREE SUNGLASSES . . . THAT IS, PLUS PROCESSING

Here's another one, a remarkable offering in an inflight magazine. I can get "Brand Name Premium Sunglasses" free. Copy says, "No catch—now or ever—It's a market study."

While they're studying the market, they're also adding $7.95 each for "Postage, Processing & Handling" one style and $17.95 each for "Postage, Processing & Handling" another style. $17.95? Must be a whole lot of processing going on. Last time I looked, even the un-benevolent UPS wasn't charging even half that amount for shipping sunglasses.

Do you believe you can get seven "blockbuster" movie videos for just 1¢ each? I don't.

Understand, please: I not only comprehend the procedure of charging $1.60 each for shipping (total, with the 1¢ cost = $11.27); I've often used the shipping/handling gimmick to keep the mooches out. But when we're up over $11.00, the validity of a 1¢ offer starts to pale.

The response device for this offer is a commitment, tied to a credit card, for a minimum of five more videos "at regular Club prices." And how much are the regular Club prices? Unspoken. The brochure makes a cloudy reference: ". . . Director's Selection—plus scores of alternate movies, including many lower-priced cassettes, down to $14.95." The letter's price reference is "as low as $19.95."

Neither component gives us a clue as to what the post-promotional shipping/handling cost might be.

HANDLING THE HANDLING CHARGE

While I'm fulminating, a question: Haven't *you*, as sophisticated as you have to be to share the joys of freebies and one cent deals, on occasion taken a cynical view of that word "handling"? I'm especially uneasy when I see the word used for mail order candy and other comestibles. I don't want somebody *handling* my candy. The projected image is some greasy guy who just emerged from the washroom without washing his hands, picking up each piece of candy and rolling it between his fingers.

Whenever they'll let me, I use "shipping/insurance." This works for UPS and FedEx because insurance is semi-automatic on their shipments. For the U.S. Postal Service, depending on the statesmanship of the company, it still works; that is, if the company honors claims of damage or non-delivery, "insurance" is a better-selling word than "handling."

SMART MARKETING

A business catalog I admire pegs its shipping/handling charges to the size of the order, not to the avoirdupois of any individual item. Their rate schedule:

```
$00.00——$49.99 = $5.90
 50.00——99.99 = 7.90
100.00——149.99 = 9.90
150.00——499.99 = 11.90
$500.00 and up = free
```

Who could ever object to those rates? This smart marketer makes it worthwhile to increase the size of the order. We can visualize customers searching for additional items to make the next discount point.

Another catalog sells an "ecosphere." Little beasties inside the sphere feed on stuff which, as organic waste, regenerates more stuff. The thing sells for $499.95, a nickel short of the other catalog's free zone. This one says, "Due to the living nature of these products, they will be shipped by overnight delivery at no extra charge over our regular shipping rates." Yeah. Good way to hit while the buying impulse is hot.

My total admiration is reserved for companies like Starcrest and those vitamin marketers who occasionally or regularly offer free shipping. The bounty isn't universal, because the next catalog might eliminate this offer; still, I'll wager the sporadic free shipping brings these companies business they otherwise would have missed.

If you've seen these same catalogs, you've noticed that when shipping is free they don't use that melancholy word "handling." Good for them. No greasy guys messing with this stuff!

I'll give the ultimate accolade to a company called Geerlings & Wade. This company sells wine at a remarkably low price. (Any good? Beats me. I haven't ordered from them, although they offer a red Bordeaux.) In a totally dignified and almost casual way, they mention they'll ship the wine free.

Look, friends, we're neck-deep in the Age of Skepticism. We have enough trouble inducing even nominal buyer loyalty. If you're inclined to test—and testing is the nucleus of marketing success—occasionally test free shipping. You say you'll have to raise product price to make this possible? Of course you will. The notion of free shipping isn't to kill your bottom line; instead, it's to engender buyer happiness.

What if, instead of pitching free sunglasses and having the prospective buyer say, triumphantly, "Aha! I knew it!" when he or she encounters the $17.95 shipping charge, you charge a few bucks for the glasses and a less formidable shipping charge? What if you astutely point out that Beethoven's Ninth Symphony alone is a ridiculous bargain at $12.95, but you're shipping all nine for $8.95, less than a buck apiece, with no shipping charge?

I certainly am *not* predicting what the outcome of such a test might be. I certainly *am* predicting that if many sellers looked at shipping/handling from the buyer's point of view instead of the seller's, we'd transact more business.

Am I picking nits? Certainly. Meanwhile, get your greasy mitts off my candy.

Some Really Dumb Uses of Really Smart Tools

If you want to cause what otherwise is a rational human being to feel totally inferior, send him/her an unsolicited CD-ROM.

I didn't ask for this CD-ROM. Like all the others, it sings a Siren Song. On its colorful outer flap is a semi-professional piece of copy:

You need to keep track of something. You want to use your PC to do it. DON'T GIVE UP!

Copy inside is better. It calls this "an outrageous multimedia experience."

The only trouble is: "Outrageous" has two meanings. They use one; I use the other. Then comes one of the Great Lies of our time:

If you can build a spreadsheet or use a word processor, you can do this:

After that colon is a formidable description. In the middle of it, the Siren Song shifts into Rap:

It's fun, even a little addictive.

Now, here's where some infernal company mailing CD-ROMs wins the game of "Gotcha!": Computers have CD-ROM drives. Usually the CD-ROM in the drive sits quietly, ready to add a font or disclose a point of history or literature. Some of those programs cost sixty or seventy bucks. Bam! One that's *free*!

So what's the prey to do but stick the thing into the drive? It's as simple (according to instructions printed on the CD-ROM in mice-type) as starting Windows, selecting "Run," from "Program Manager," and then typing "d:\setup." Right?

Oh, yeah? Okay, Mister, follow your disk down here and *you* try it. You'll get what I get: First of all, "Run" is a stand-alone. It isn't under "Program Manager." I'm smart enough to decode that; and your image slips a little, because now I know something *you* don't. This calls further instructions into question, and that question blooms like a nightshade when I type "d:\setup." I read, in a box loaded with red circles and "X"-symbols: "Cannot find the file d:\setup or one of its components."

Now, suppose I got it to work (which I did: My CD-ROM is the "E" drive, and the backslash is an instructional peculiarity). It grabs and holds, and my options are, in a word, zilch. Immediately, I'm told I've successfully installed the program; but it needs a sister program. If I don't have that second program, lucky me—double-click on this icon and eat up some more memory. Gee, thanks.

Nowhere does this offer me an escape—and by escape, I mean cutting the cancer out of my computer's guts.

SOMEBODY IS STUPID.

Unsolicited CD-ROMS seem curiously infected by the lethal "We know what we mean so obviously you know what we mean" syndrome. One came to me from a computer reseller magazine. The instruction was "Run, then Enter" (reads like a partial description of a decathlon competition). I ran, entered, and was scolded: "You first must activate 'Catalog' from master." Hey, Bud, I don't have a catalog to activate.

I certainly don't want to suggest that the demons mailing CD-ROMs are the only deliberate confusion-sowers. A golf organization (at least, I *think* it's an organization; its purpose and function aren't clarified) offers me a free hat on the envelope but not on the order form, labeled "Application for Membership."

(We interrupt this message with one of the least-surprising bulletins in the history of direct marketing: *Never* use the word "Application" as the follow-up to an invitation. That goes for weddings, too.)

Over the Edge

A magazine called *Edge* sent me a big, beautiful sample issue, tabloid size, enamel paper, full bleed, handsome graphics. At least, I *think* it was a sample issue, because this legend is on the wrap:

> *WELCOME TO YOUR FIRST*
> *ISSUE OF EDGE MAGAZINE.*
> *Coincidentally, it will also be your last.*
> *But don't take it personally. It's the last issue we're sending everybody, even our charter subscribers.*
> *Why?*
> *We're replacing EDGE Magazine with something* that will take IT professionals into the next century.*

Two questions: (1) Huh? (2) Who says I'm an IT professional? The asterisk typifies asterisk-infection: "That's all the specifics we can give you now. Any more details and we could not vouch for your safety." Or sanity.

(Proof: I opened the thing to an article. The title: "Anno Domini

2000: An Algorithmic Solution?" Sure. What other solution could it be?)

I guess I should be flattered that so many mailers give me credit for in-group intelligence. Here's a message from a company offering me a deal on an omni-directional CCD camera. I can't imagine how I survived this long without one. (CCD? Let's see—oh, sure, Cannabis Chewing Dolts. It's from a dummy company run by the Bureau of Alcohol, Tobacco, and Firearms, right?)

Wryness has its place in ridicule. At some point, we have to assume if our CD-ROMs generate intramural wryness, they have to generate a more overt ridicule among our targets out there in Prospect-Land. That means the wastebasket.

So here's my suggestion for peace in our time:

Don't assume people outside your office share your inbred knowledge of what your alphabet-soup of arcane initials means.

Don't assume they share your vertical "We know what we mean, so obviously you know what we mean" technical knowledge of what you're selling or how it works.

Don't assume they're salivating over the opportunity to buy a product or service they don't understand.

And oh, yeah—don't send out any CD-ROMs until somebody outside your office and outside the sphere of your core group has tested it and not complained.

Language Abuse

T oday's marketers throw terms the way they'd throw confetti
. . . and with just about as much impact.

Yes, yes, of course we have "Free" and "New" and "Important" used so often and so unrelated to a specific offer we have the feeling some child has hit a macro button on a computer keyboard . . . or, worse, the computer is operating without human intervention.

Here's an ad in a free-standing insert in the Sunday paper: "Great news! Metab-o-lite now has a full line of products for extra energy and increased metabolism!" By golly, they're right on the money. We haven't had such great news since Gutenberg. Here's a mailing from a company selling hams by mail. It's labeled "Urgent!" By golly, *they're* right on the money too. We'd better act now or they'll run out of hams. Then where would we be?

(Parenthetically, "Act now!" is another phrase that ought to be sent to that great Lexicographical Purgatory.)

We have offers from credit cards—dozens of credit cards, all leaning on the same everlasting arms of credit reporting bureaus— all telling us we've been pre-approved . . . and then asking us for so much financial information or warning us that we may *not* be pre-approved that we wonder whether one person wrote the envelope copy, went on vacation, and was replaced by another person who wrote the deadly-warning text while unaware of the commitment the envelope made.

One of the most puzzling aspects of marketing mayhem is the plethora of indecipherable automobile names. Who, oh, who, decided to call the cheap Cadillac "Catera"? The initial campaign for that status-busting car has (thankfully) been discontinued, but we should remember "The Caddy that zigs" as a no-brain totem. Denali, Escalade, Allante—who came up with these? What image is the car supposed to project?

And our tired old standby "Free" is reduced to limping, in The Age of Skepticism. Certainly more than half the offers that begin with a huge "Free!" are followed by an "if . . ." or "when . . ." condition. What we've done to that poor word is criminal, and what makes the criminality worse is that so many uses of free are the result of desperation. We don't have anything else to say, so we drag in "Free!" and because it doesn't fit, we have to saddle it with conditions and exclusions and exceptions.

No discussion of language abuse is complete without mention of actual raw abuse stemming from language *misuse*. We see "its" as a possessive, spelled "it's," and this is in an ad or mailer that must have gone through many sets of hands. We see plurals formed with an apostrophe-"s." We see singular subjects matched up—no, make that unmatched up—with plural verbs. We see present tense and future tense and past tense jumbled together in a crazy rhetorical Mulligan stew. We see unmistakable evidence of creeping illiteracy among those whose very function should be to combat illiteracy.

The language abusers don't care. They throw terms, they invent unpronounceable product names, they assault us with cliché after cliché. Response slides. And can you believe it, they're actually surprised to see their own murder victim die.

What we really need is an uprising, a revolution, a mutiny in which we organize and fight the deadly marketing-murdering forces of term-throwing. We need to impose a gigantic penalty on the use of "Important" and "Free" and "0% APR" . . . until and unless those terms once again run pure.

With that imprecation, take a look at some case histories:

Basically, I'd Like to Define This as a Paradigm Shift

Please say you agree with me.

When a speaker at a conference or workshop uses the word "paradigm" more than twice, I tune out.

When a speaker uses the phrase "paradigm shift" once, I tune out.

Unless you're that speaker, you have to agree with me.

We're infested with "labelers" who use cutesy-pie phrases such as "cocooning" and impenetrable terms such as "paradigm shift." That last 'one would make a pretty good title for a science-fiction movie: "The Paradigm Shift," starring Keanu Reeves, with a backup cast who actually know how to read lines.

Let's find a few members for admission to the Legion of Lousy Lexicon.

ON TO MORE (OR LESS) PROFOUND MATTERS

How many times a month do you make a long distance call that lasts more than 20 minutes?

In my opinion the most loathsome television commercial of the decade (well, it's at least among the top five) is the one for a peculiar long-distance service called 10-321. You may not have known this is MCI; if you had, your mind would have been colored beforehand. But watching John Lithgow, delightfully and rightfully ill-at-ease, pitch this deal, saying, "You save fifty percent on calls over twenty minutes" . . . it makes one ache for "Gilligan's Island."

Some competitor ought to come in with, "You'll save 32.6 per cent on calls between 10 p.m. and 3:21 a.m., not only to Lesotho but to Andorra!" (The exclamation point is mandatory.)

Incidentally, the FCC seems to have ordered MCI to switch to 10-10-321, bringing this even closer to a winless lottery.

MCI, you've got company. Sadly, it's my sorrowful duty to take a curmudgeonly look at a duplicitous mailing from AmEx.

They mailed me a "Connections" Card. Wow! I haven't been the beneficiary of such largesse since my Batman Card expired. The Connections Card copy begins, "As a valued Platinum Card® member, we are pleased to offer you . . ."—a grammatical reversal that isn't surprising, because I'd certainly think whoever sent the mailing is a Platinum Cardholder (with a Caesar-complex, referring to himself/herself/itself as "we").

Copy all over the place touts 15¢ per minute. But uh-oh! I taut I taw an asterisk. I did, I did! I taw an asterisk! And this ain't no puddy-tat, because the asterisk reinforces my long-standing objection to this insidious device: "There is a connect charge of 85¢ on each call." So let's see: It won't make a lot of difference on all those 20-minute-plus calls I otherwise might have made by dialing 10-321. But in a two-minute call to a client . . . and that's all the time most clients will put up with me . . . we're taking a jump from 30¢ to $1.15.

So what are we supposed to conclude? That all suppliers want us to keep the phone in our ear long enough to satisfy their obviously insatiable greed? And with all the complication and obfuscation we won't notice? I'm still brooding over paying 35¢ for a local pay-phone call because my cell-phone is out of juice.

THE REAL SAP

Paying a little too much for a phone call isnt't the worst or most expensive trick that someone has played on me. In the bigger picture, I guess it isn't *that* big a deal. But mailings for conferences can be a big deal, because we can be talking serious money and serious time wasted.

Don't you sense that most mailings for conferences are designed for an in-group and you aren't part of that in-group . . . and that someone purposely wants you to feel that way? I got a mailing for "SAP R/3 Information Day." What a hoot! I know what SAP stands for—sap. But "Information Day"? They could use the day to explain what the conference is. Key copy says:

> At SAP, assuring your success is our highest priority. We would like to invite you to attend an upcoming SAP™ R/3™ Information Day to learn more about TeamSAP™—our 100% commitment to provide your company with the *people*, *processes and products* required to deliver faster business results.

Huh?

I drew two conclusions: First anybody fatuous enough to throw all those "™" marks at ridiculous acronyms has so little ability to establish reader-rapport that we ought to offer *him* some ways to deliver business results.

Second, why hasn't our entire tribe retired "We would like to"? If you'd like to, and nobody is stopping you, then go ahead and do it.

Oh, all right, I know it's software. After searching intensively, aha! Here's a reference to "Features and benefits of SAP R/3, including Release 4.0." Wow, even including Release 4.0! What a bonanza! Just one question, Bunky: What the hell is SAP R/3? You addressed this to me, and a polygraph will verify that I haven't the vaguest notion what this software does. Come to think of it, maybe the writer doesn't have the vaguest idea either. Yes, that explains it. All right, we've cleared that one up.

In the midst of chaos, a ray of hope: someone—at least one someone—is trying to communicate the actual benefits of doing business with them.

My wife has been a loyal Starbucks Coffee customer. She called to re-order a blend we'd been enjoying for months. Oops! The telemarketer said they've dropped that grind. Okay, said Margo, in that case I'm back to Gevalia.

But hold it! Here comes a letter from Jan Brown, whose title is "Direct Response." And direct it is! Ms. Brown, may her tribe increase, not only explained the circumstances clearly and logically but added: "Although we cannot offer you each of our coffees in espresso grind, because of your extensive customer history we have created a special gift for you based on the coffees you have ordered." Two pounds of incomparable coffee were enclosed.

So a salute—first, to the bright telemarketer who reported the conversation; and second, to whoever in the Starbucks hierarchy pays attention to the company's database. Starbucks, we're b-a-a-a-ck! You deserve no less.

So basically, what we got here is Paradigm Shift, to worthwhile communication for all us SAPs out here. 10-321, and all that.

Cell-phone Phonies:
Abbott & Costello . . . and
P.T. Barnum . . . Are Alive and Well.

I'll categorize the comparative advertising by AT&T, MCI, and Sprint with a one-word definition: peculiar.

I'm being nice. Their advertising is "peculiar" not only because the claims themselves are as murky as duplicitous copywriters can concoct; it's also peculiar because their comparative benefits are both contradictory and beyond the ken of many who see those puzzling television commercials flashing by.

How many mailings have *you* had, supposedly from airlines but actually a pitch for frequent flyer miles if you switch to the long distance carrier who's really sending the mailing? And not since Ponzi have so many fake checks gone out in the mail. Not since Muhammad Ali have so many "I am the greatest" claims filled the airwaves and our mailboxes.

A plague on all their houses.

COMPARATIVE + RELEVANCE: YES

I'm 100 percent in favor of comparative advertising . . . provided it observes a basic rule of salesmanship:

> To be effective, a sales argument has to be relevant to the person at whom it's aimed.

"Numbers people" have a low batting average when they're Peter Principled into positions of authority over the communications process. The reason, I figure reasonably, is that they're lacking the benefit-projection gene.

So let's assume these major long distance carriers pick up (or swipe) customers by accident, by semi-duplicity or by that old standby, customer indolence. When the typical customer gets a call asking which long distance service he or she prefers, as often as not the answer will be "I don't care" or "it doesn't matter."

Voila! The acme of duplicity! A Texas long distance company has registered more than 50 trade names, including "I Don't Care," "It Doesn't Matter," "Any One Is OK," "Whoever," "Anybody," and "I Don't Know."

So get this: You're asked which long distance carrier you prefer. You answer, "I don't know." Thank you very much, says the telemarketer, who then registers you with the company named "I Don't Know." Shades of Abbott and Costello!

CONFUSION IN THE CELLS

It's epidemic in the phone business. How about those cellular phone companies? They're establishing a new standard of confusion. I still haven't forgiven them for grabbing so many numbers my town was kicked out of comfortable old area code 305. I still have a batch of dead stationery I use for second sheets.

And I'm not about to forgive my cellular service provider for its big, blaring ads offering a far better deal than I have . . . "for new activation only." Hey, guys, loyalty programs are supposed to work both ways.

Now the cellular phone Barnums are out to destroy what's left of my sanity. They're creating competitive offers so confounding I turned a couple of them over to the CIA's Cryptography Section. They couldn't decode them either.

I've had a cellular phone for quite a while. I don't use it to show off by waiting until I'm in the car to make a call. So when I bought the thing, I got the phone for one cent in exchange for signing a one-year contract with the provider. Fair enough.

That year is long since up, but under the rule of the game of "Gotcha!" I'm not about to switch. That would mean breaking in a new number. But here's my own company—the one I've been loyal to, paying a monthly minimum even though at most I reach that minimum one month out of six. An ad screams: "Wow! $5 per month" with a big reverse, "GET 352 HOURS OF AIRTIME EACH MONTH." My eye goes to it. That's what they had in mind.

Uh-huh. Gotcha! Here's mice-type, between "Wow!" and "$5 per month"—"for an additional." The Bell giveth and the Bell taketh away. And what's this next to the free 352 hours of airtime? An asterisk.

You know what asterisks mean: Exceptions. Much to say about those in this book. This one—and if the other is in mice-type this is in mouselet-type—says the 352 hours are nights and weekends. That's fairly common, and it's a pretty good deal, *except* for the obvious ploy of obfuscating the point. So I look at a competing ad.

That one has a giant headline: "FREE UNLIMITED AIRTIME."

How can that be? Easy: It ain't. At least, I don't think it is, because the ad says nights and weekends are $4.95 per month ("Digital only $4.95 per month"—does that mean "only $4.95" or does it mean the deal doesn't apply to non-digital phones, which gives them extra impetus for a pay-more-for-digital pitch?) but doesn't tell me how much regular daytime activation costs. I'm gun-shy.

Uh-oh. Here comes the flood of contradictory, hit-and-run television commercials. First up is Sprint with a 15-second quickie: Fridays are free until next year. One question, Sprint: Do you have a grab-bag of "hooks," taking out one at a time to try to catch more fish? I hadn't seen or heard the "Fridays free" pitch before . . . and I'm not attacking shotgunning, because I've used it myself. But, as structured here, aren't you risking the ire of other new Sprint recruits who responded to a different siren song and aren't getting Fridays free?

Now here comes Radio Shack: "Get Digital Service for Less Than $1 a Day! . . . Plus 25 Minutes of Airtime Included Each Month!*"

That pesky asterisk has found a warm, snuggly home in cellular phone advertising. Here it has *two* separate correspondents. One says "Offer for new BellSouth Mobility customers signing up for blah blah blah." The other is more deadly and, by this time, more expected: "Advertised price requires a new activation and minimum service commitment (usually 1, 2, or 3 years), upon credit approval. An activation fee may be required." And it drones on with exceptions.

In the same paper is an ad for "CELLULAR WEEKEND!" (120-point red type) telling me this same provider has "waived digital activation fee*—a $50 value! (Asterisk = "Offer available to new digital activations only. Requires 24 month service agreement . . . Certain restrictions apply . . . See store for details." Other specials in the ad are tied to other asterisks. I especially like "$100 CASH BACK ON ALL ANALOG CELLULAR PHONES!**" in which the double as-

terisk says, among other rejections, "May exclude select rate plans
. . . See store for details." I have a couple of analog phones I'd give
them for five bucks.

Cellular phones parallel car leasing companies in their deliberate
attempt to mask the actual deal. I can lease a car for $699 a month
. . . provided (mice type) I plunk a $7500 own payment. Down pay-
ment against *what*? That money is *gone*, and if I lease the car for a
couple of years and add 1/24 of the down payment to each month,
it costs . . . oh, what the hell.

It burns me that everybody in advertising and marketing gets
tarred with the accusation of embroidering the truth with qualifiers.
At least the word "truth" is in there somewhere. Go thou and do
likewise, you giant phone-phonies.

And personal to Sprint: Tell you what. You did your part, so I'll
do mine. You got rid of those revolting Candace Bergen commercials. So I'm willing to talk.

But Wait, There's More!

I'm sitting here admiring my new cellular phone, marveling at the
advertising minefield I've crossed to get here.

The Wall Street Journal says AT&T dominates the cellular business. Okay, AT&T, I've switched to you.

But it wasn't easy. Oh, when I dumped my toy "StarTac" phone
a few years ago, it was easy enough. That phone is made for Win-
kler's Midgets, and being able to hide it in a shirt-pocket is a mixed
blessing, especially since most of my shirts don't have pockets. I
was always misplacing the thing, and the "provider" didn't provide
much long distance nor roaming service, beyond the next block.

Still, now wired up with digital and whatever, penetrating new offers from various competitors . . . well, it's like having half a dozen Toyota dealers side by side.

For example, in *one day's* newspaper were ads by four wireless providers. One offered 100 "Anytime MinutesK" for $39.99 a month, with "Free long distance to anywhere in Florida," free voice mail and Caller ID, and free first minute of airtime on every call received. But wait, there's more! They throw in an "Instant $25 service credit on most rate plans" and a car power charger.

So why didn't I consider this deal? First of all, the pomposity of that "K" symbol turned me off. Second, as I recall, the United States has several other states besides Florida. And third, what I'm not in-cluding in this description is enough mice-type disclaimers to feed a colony of rodents well past the third millennium. And, oh . . . I find that company's television spots sophomoric.

In that same newspaper was an ad by the carrier I currently had. The heading: "A cellular offer to get pumped about." Okay, the headline transmits a vaguely erotic overtone, and I guess that's good. And it offered the peculiar premium of "$60 in free gas when you buy and activate a cellular phone.†" But I was annoyed that the basic offer—$22.50 a month which included 450 Anytime Minutes (hey, wait a minute, didn't the other company service mark that cliché?)—was a better deal than they'd given me, a loyal sucker. But wait, there's more! That 450 minute deal had a double dagger after it. Oops! I shouldn't have dug out the mice-type on this one. After three months it's $45, not $22.50, and time over 450 minutes is 35¢ a minute and there's a $1.24 monthly charge for any month "in which a call originated from a cell phone is terminated through the landline network," whatever the hell that means. Auf weidersehn.

Believe it or not, the third newspaper ad was from the same company. This one had at the top a huge black rectangle into which four clover-like ovals were carved, each with the word "Send" reversed in green. The main heading: "Register to win a trip for two to Ireland, courtesy of Motorola**."

What was peculiar here was that the offer—$22.50 a month for 450 anytime minutes, with that accursed asterisk pointing out that after three months it's $45, plus all the extra add-on charges—was identical. But wait, there's more! Well, not much more. The double asterisk says "No purchase necessary." It doesn't give any details at all, so I'd have to visit one of the stores listed in the ad to register, to find out how long the trip is, and to have a chuckling clerk answer my question, "Is this first class or economy class?" with a knowing, "What makes you think you're going to win, Buster?" Here's an ad that originates more questions than it answers.

The fourth ad shows two interlocking hands, one of which is holding a phone. The heading:

> *it's for you*
> *digital. wireless. samsung.*

This lower case fetish represents an art director who doesn't care who's out there. And why no period after "it's for you"? So I was turned off by the artifice. And I can't generate a partial recovery with "But wait, there's more!" because there wasn't any more. No offer. Just the arrogant "for the location nearest you, please call 1 800 480 4PCS." Whee! Upper case for "PCS." What havoc that must have wreaked in the art department!

The Flood Continues

I said those four appeared on the same day. But the flood continued. Other days brought other offers. Here's one touting $29.99 per month for 120 minutes, plus "No long distance & no roaming charges on calls made from anywhere within our nationwide network." But wait, there's more! I get a $30 rebate on the phone and "300 Bonus Anytime, Anywhere Minutes." Interesting!

Oh, one question: How extensive is your network, Buster? If coverage is national, I'd suggest you say so, because your competitors consistently debunk your ability to make that claim. Still, I felt this deal was the most valid I'd seen, until I saw the last line of asterisked copy, 6-point lightface type reversed: "Some restrictions apply." Darn!

Then there was the ad whose headline had me nodding in agreement: "It's a Circus Out There! Let us make sense of the wireless circus for you." The ad was a catchall. "Digital phones starting at 1¢*" . . . "You pay only $22.50* per month for first 3 mo." . . . "no activation fee." And of course, but wait, there's more! A clever offer: Convert your own phone to that company "and we'll pay you $50**." And "Plus . . . no activation fee!**" A symphony of asterisks. (That second one was a real bear: "**Waived activation fee requires 24 mo. agreement. Certain restrictions apply. Subject to credit approval, cancellation and activation fees. A connection charge of $1.24 blah blah blah." And in this land-mine field of asterisks was a dagger whose antecedent I couldn't find. Just as well: "†Price does not include taxes, long distance, roaming or universal service fee." Gee, I feel like Lady Macbeth: "Is that a dagger I see before me?" Forget it, Charlie.

So AT&T, I'm yours for the foreseeable future. Yeah, I have a new cellular number, which is a pain. Yeah, my new phone came without a car charger, which is a pain. Yeah, you didn't even give me one of those imitation leatherette cases some of the pretenders were offering. And yeah, it really wasn't the phone I'd have preferred, a Mitsubishi.

But wait, there's more. I actually understood the deal. And I'm living in an asterisk-free environment, phoning and roaming all over the place.

L.O.L.: Take Out the Periods and It's Short for Lollygagging.

One of my pet annoyances is the punctuational shorthand the Internet has thrust upon our consciousness. "(:" is supposed to mean something—smile or frown or whatever. Virtual limbo! We don't even have to move a facial muscle to transmit a fake reaction to another virtual nonentity.

My least favorite is "L.O.L."—which means "Laughing out loud." Okay, friend, if you're able to laugh out loud and put that stupid reaction on e-mail at the same time, you do have an animal-like talent.

Let's analyze this: I tell you a joke; you laugh, or you don't. I e-mail you a joke; you e-mail me back, "L.O.L." Thanks a lot. Should I believe you? Can that bit of nonsense remotely compete with a typed out "Hey, that was really funny!"?

250 HOURS OF FUN TIME

All right, you Webheads, I'll use your semi-language. Here's the L.O.L. of the newest century, from our inept friends at America Online. This one is a real dilly.

In a pocket of the plastic sleeve holding the Sunday newspaper is one of those CD-ROMs America Online tosses around indiscriminately, like the Easter Bunny throwing his tokens in all directions. On the face is "As seen on TV," a tribute to a competing medium.

What's the heading? "250 HOURS FREE!"

Wow! Assuming you're on the Web two hours a day, that's 125 days, well over four months. *Quel largesse!*

Oh, yeah? Come on, you know better than that. On the back, in mice-type, is this ridiculous but unsurprising legend:

FREE TRIAL DETAILS: 250 HOUR FREE TRIAL MUST BE USED WITHIN ONE MONTH OF INITIAL SIGN-ON.

AOL, in your own lingo: L.O.L.

Let's see: The average month has 30 days. That means to take full advantage of this wonderful offer I have to be online well over eight hours a day, seven days a week. No fair taking a day off. So how do we make it work?

Well, here's one way: Up at six, a quick coffee-and-bagel mini-breakfast, and an hour at AOL. It's a quarter of eight. Off to work, from nine to five. Home by six. A quick decaf-and-tofu minidinner so we can be back at the modem by seven. No, scratch that. Decaf might let us sleep. Make that a double espresso. Putting in our additional seven hours brings us to two a.m. Quick! To bed! We have to be up by six. No time to change clothes or bedding.

So at the end of our trial month, rumpled and filthy and probably having been fired for sleeping on the job, triumph! We got in our 250 hours.

And here's where the ploy backfires, like having liter bottles of Coca-Cola come out of a vending machine: We're glutted. It's like those tough-love treatments for smoking that have people lighting up and inhaling until they never want to see another cigarette in their entire lives.

We laugh, whether out loud or online or in the fitful sleep we get after having spent most of our waking hours reading spam. Laughing is a reaction based on ridicule, not on analysis. Analysis becomes us better, because after all we're professionals who should have exhausted our laughter after America Online's tortured acquisition of CompuServe resulted in all those impenetrable deals with computer manufacturers—apparent discounts in exchange for a three-year CompuServe durance vile.

But wait! There's more!

COMPUSERVE FOLLOWS THE LEADER.

What the . . . ? Here's the same CD-ROM offering 250 hours free . . . from CompuServe. In fact, they saved money by having the exact legend in the exact typeface with the exact same wording.

Our analysis ordinarily would tell us to buy MindSpring stock, because MindSpring is a genuine competitor. Ah! Here's the Mind-Spring CD-ROM. Uh . . . what's that on the cover?

150 HOURS FREE!

SPECIAL OFFER 250 HOURS FREE!

Huh? They're infected too? Where's their explanation of two side-by-side unexplained mismatched headlines? Nope, not here. And not here. Not anywhere. What *is* on the sleeve? Installation instructions for PCs and Macs . . . some totally nondescript promotional copy such as "Click and you're there" and "Fast, reliable connections with 56K access in most areas" and "Award-winning service and technical support," plus an early candidate for the Most Uninspired Key Advertising Line of the Year Award: "With Mind-Spring choosing an ISP is a decision you make only once." That brilliant slogan suggests they got their award from the guy who draws Dilbert.

But nothing about 150 hours. Nothing about 250 hours. (Going once. Going twice. Can I hear "350 hours"?) It's hit-and-run. They hit. We run.

They haven't learned that the incentive to stick a CD-ROM into the guts of your computer should be on the package, not on the CD-ROM. The universe is full of semi-pros, and the Internet is their prophet.

Shakespeare had it right: "When sorrows come, they come not as single spies, but in battalions." And the word to describe these promotions is *sorry*. Instead of L.O.L. it's S.O.L. (an old army contraction for "Out of luck").

So what would *we* do, if we were in command? Oh, we'd probably list a couple of sites to visit, as our guest. We'd probably arrange with some portals or search engines or sites to offer special deals to visitors to an extension set up for us. We'd probably pitch the dickens out of the benefit of visiting a hot spot on the CD-ROM, and make it worthwhile once our hard-won guest hit that spot. *And we'd say so on the sleeve.*

Or would we? After all, who says the Internet and the World Wide Web really exist? Probably a couple of lunatics like those two guys who claim they can get a machine full of passengers to fly through the air.

A Blockbuster of a Marketing Mistake

The Blockbuster chain of video stores may be, in their current incarnation, parallel to a charging bull elephant with a bullet in its brain: It's dead but doesn't know it yet.

Video rental is a perilous business to be in these days. So Blockbuster is testing new marketing ploys to keep its franchise in moderate health.

Here's a program called Blockbuster® Rewards™. Oh, sure, the combination of the registration symbol and a trademark for the common word "Rewards" is in itself an admission of desperation. That isn't of any significance in an era in which we're likely to see a trademark symbol for the word "The."

What called this program to my attention is the sales literature Blockbuster created to sell this program. The sequence: You walk into a Blockbuster store to see what movies are for rent. At the checkout counter, the clerk suggests signing up for Blockbuster Rewards. For $9.95 you can get 12 "Blockbuster Favorites™" (yep, another trademark symbol for this one).

BLOCKBUSTER FAVORITES = BLOCKBUSTER OLD MOVIES

Talk about confusion! Blockbuster Favorites becomes a euphemism for Old Movies. (They also call them "non-New Releases," and at least "non-New Releases" seems to be exempt from the registration and trademark symbols they usually assign to awkward phraseology.) New releases aren't part of the deal. So okay, that's acceptable.

But additional conditions come in a swarm: You can get additional free rentals of non-New Releases but only Monday through Wednesday and only in combination with a paid rental. You "earn" (a ghastly word in any selling situation) a free movie or game rental for five paid movie or game rentals, each month. It isn't clear whether you get nothing if you rent fewer than five a month.

On the back of the descriptive folder the clerk has handed to you is a heading: "Terms and Conditions." Uh-oh. It's reversed in six-point type, which means something nasty is hidden there.

By golly, there it is. Check this wording—and, believe it or not, this appears on a piece that's supposed to describe *Rewards*:

> *BLOCKBUSTER Favorites are movie titles labeled as such in stores, and are determined by BLOCKBUSTER® at its sole discretion. . . . Our way of providing you with such offers is through the mail. Therefore, when you join BLOCKBUSTER Rewards, you overrule any election you may have previously made to opt out of receiving regular communications from BLOCKBUSTER. BLOCKBUSTER is not responsible for coupons lost in the mail. Coupons are not transferable and have no cash value. Other restrictions apply.*

Other restrictions apply? Hey, Buddy, *you're* supposed to be selling *me*. Blockbuster isn't yet through torturing us. Get this one:

> *BLOCKBUSTER may change the BLOCKBUSTER Rewards program rules, regulations, rewards and special offers at any time without prior notice. BLOCKBUSTER reserves the right to end the BLOCKBUSTER Rewards program with three (3) months' prior notice.*

Golly, fellas, how can anybody resist such an attractive offer?

Are you wondering why any sane person would sign up for a program whose multiple "look out!" signals are described with all the warmth and friendliness of a Miranda warning? So am I. I'm not bothered by the listing of conditions. We all are used to those. What bothers me is that this folder typifies what we're beginning to see: "Buyer beware." "The customer is our enemy." "Do unto others before they do unto you." Result: Negative wording, combined with the repeated negative word "earn." We become their indentured servants, their lackeys, their Cinderellas to push around.

That just ain't smart marketing. Any one of us in our superior universe of marketing critiques could transmit the same information without annoying the reader. How difficult is it to *optimize* the information instead of generating what seems to be a "Welcome to Leavenworth" folder? In thirty minutes, anyone reading this could write terms and conditions that still satisfy any legal requirements but don't outrage the customer.

I'd recommend this as a project in any Communications 101 class. To carry it beyond that level would be an insult to sophomores.

Oh, well. Blockbuster didn't ask us. And with the arrogance implicit in this little customer-harassment folder, we aren't about to volunteer.

But on behalf of those old enough to remember when stores actually posted little signs saying, "The customer is always right," I'll volunteer this: Guys, the Web is out there. It's everyone's competitor and it's the worst nightmare of retailers who forget that the last bastion of brick-and-mortar ongoing existence is that most fragile of all assets, customer loyalty.

Oh, Blockbuster isn't alone. Airlines show increasing frenzy in offering incentives to get us to sign up for their frequent flyer programs . . . then leave us in a frenzy when we try to book a flight using those miles. Restaurants establish loyalty programs, then carefully and cannily insert enough exclusions to turn off all but the greediest takers. Don't they realize that the greediest takers, like the greediest givers, are the least desirable prospects?

How typical it is, how 21st century it is, to extend what appears to be a clean and clear offer and then weight it down with conditions and exclusions. That alone is a reason to treasure any offer that seems to be free of self-injected negative-condition viruses.

Blockbuster, heal thyself. I'd hate to have to go back to pay-per-view, but if I get infected with your virus, I might start writing copy like yours.

The Importance of Saying "Important"

I'm getting more and more steamed at hit-and-run copywriters.

Who or what are hit-and-runners? They're the ones who know a couple of action words but don't know what damage they're doing by using these words and not justifying them.

Some of the words:

- Important
- Urgent

- Personal
- Hurry
- Rush

I've left off the mandatory exclamation points . . . although adding one after "Personal" is an Open Sesame to anyone other than the target, to peek inside (and be the first one to be disappointed).

What's wrong with all these imperatives? you ask. Not a thing— IF what follows *is* important or urgent or personal or legitimizes the demand for fast action.

But here's an envelope—a 9"×12" jumbo—from a publication in the meetings and conventions field. In big stencil type on the envelope is the word "URGENT."

Urgent, huh? Then why does the postal indicia say "Bulk Rate"? How come it's urgent for me but not for you?

And what's inside? No letter. You're reading right, *no letter*. Bulk rate urgency without any semi-personal communication? Gee, that'll do a lot for the credibility of everybody else's direct response.

What *was* enclosed was a beautifully-printed brochure, on whose cover is the cryptic message:

*Can You Imagine Having the Power To
Increase The Value of Gold?*

Yeah, yeah, it's not only too prettily laid out to be "urgent"; it's also too lyrical. (The eventual reference: Gold awards for the best hotels and resorts and golf courses.)

Look: Stay in character. How easy all this is if you STAY IN CHARACTER.

Aw, but I know what happened. Some consultant told them to put "Urgent" on the envelope. He or she was hired only for the day, so there wasn't time to explain that if we cry, "Wolf!" we'd better show them a wolf.

"Urgent" isn't the abused word winner. By far the most abused word we have—even surpassing "Free" and "New"—is "Important."

Hey, guys, *Important* isn't a stand-alone. Every time you kick it in the head, you weaken it a little more for the rest of us.

Here's a double postcard—a *postcard*, for God's sake—with this legend on the face of the card:

**Important
message inside.**

Somehow it's suspect before we flip open the flap. Inside is a printed pitch in advertising language for a "High Yield Tax-Free Income Fund." To those looking for tax-free income this isn't really *un*important; but the problem here is the mismatch between "Important" and "message." To some, it can be "Important information"; a message it ain't.

A letter to me whose envelope has non-profit indicia in the upper right corner has this envelope copy:

An important National Survey is enclosed.
Do you
❑ hike?
❑ bike?
❑ ski?
❑ run or walk?
❑ ride horses?
❑ or just plain enjoy the outdoors?

See the self-canceling nature of this envelope copy? Somehow I can't attach *any* importance to the bland questions on this envelope.

Inside is a load of stuff. We have have a five-page letter (it's no misprint—*five* pages, with a blank back panel, a direct mail no-no).

We have a survey that would get a "D" in any class taught by Nielsen:

1. How do you (or would you) enjoy trails? (check all that apply)

___ bicycling

___ birding or other nature activity

___ commuting to work or school

(and 9 others including wheelchair)

2. Do you feel that your community needs more trails?

❑ Yes   ❑ No   ❑ Undecided

You get the idea. It's about as scientific a survey as asking a passerby, "Does your brother like cheese?"

"I don't have a brother."

"If you had a brother, would he like cheese?"

At the end of the "survey" is a *Membership Acceptance Form.* Also in the package is a "buckslip" offering a free booklet if you join this organization; a lift note; a small bumper sticker; and a business reply envelope.

Not a bad mailing; but what made these people think "Important" is the right adjective? Why not envelope copy that doesn't generate a grimace when unmasked, such as "We need your opinion" or a rubber stamp with "Survey Documents Enclosed"?

LEANING ON THE TIRED OLD CRUTCH

What slugs we are. Rather than take the time, trouble, and even talent to mount a legitimate selling argument in which we actually convince our targets to respond, we lean on the tired old crutch, "Important."

Wait a minute. Who's this "we"?

As Samuel Goldwyn once said, "Include me out."

I became moderately gun-shy of the word when a letter showed up, with an all-caps label and a bulk mailing indicia and the word "Important!" in a fake rubber stamp effect on the carrier envelope. The letter was addressed to "Resident."

I made a PowerPoint slide of that envelope and folks chuckle over it when I show it. But their chuckling doesn't seem to affect their dependence on the word as a hit-and-run attention-getter.

On into muddy waters: Suppose you open an envelope—a nondescript envelope which delivers a mixed message (first class stamp but address on a label).

Inside is a four-page document printed in red and blue, with a big heading:

. . . News Flash . . .

Has war been declared? Is Madonna or Michael Jackson at it again? Has the Dow-Jones dropped 500 points? Has a professional football team moved to Joplin?

None of the above. It's an announcement for a mailing list.

I'd never attack flat-out promotion. Wording such as "Brand new—grab this list before your competitor does!" not only wouldn't jar me but might move me to take a *positive* look at the list. "News Flash" doesn't do this because what follows is a letdown.

That's the key. Go ahead and yell "Urgent" . . . *if* your target regards the information as urgent. Scream "Important!" IF your target actually regards it as important. Send a "News Flash" if your target regards it as hot news.

But don't hit and run. In every interpretation, that's leaving the scene of an accident . . . or a crime.

Hey, you creative types, don't you understand the Law of Diminishing Returns? Every time a reader sees that word, unbacked by evidence, cynicism grows another inch. That cynicism adds another inch of rejection to the next "Important!" message some other un-witting and unthinking marketer throws in the mail, on the screen, or in a space ad.

IMPORTANT TO WHOM?

Here's an envelope. It says, all caps: *IMPORTANT FINANCIAL DOC-UMENT ENCLOSED*. Yes, it's a manila envelope with those fake "In-structions to postmaster" instructions we've all used. Yes, the window shows "Pay to the order of" next to my name. But I *know*, as I open the envelope, the importance is to the sender, not the recipient.

Yep. It's a standard fake check, with the words "This is not a check" printed on it. It offers me a home equity loan, if I qualify. A reply card lets me choose between bill consolidation, home im-provements, major purpose, refinancing an existing loan, or other. Okay, I choose other—a not-for-profit campaign to stamp out unau-thorized use of the word "Important." Where's the importance here? It's a flat, standard financial offer every homeowner gets two or three times a week. That key misused word on the envelope has no backup inside.

Another problem: The "Important" infection has spread so it's now an epidemic. Two competitive mailings, mailed within a week or two of this one, use the same fake check gimmick and the same claim of importance. One tells me: "IMPORTANT: Your Single Fam-ily Residence has been reviewed."

Gee, I guess that *is* important. It isn't every day that my Single Family Residence is not only given caps/l.c. treatment but is also re-viewed. I qualify for $35,000 more (than what?).

The American Express Platinum Card is never far behind. It shucks its mantle of dignity but manages to water down the promise:

IMPORTANT

INFORMATION

For Automatic Flight

Insurance Enrollees

I hadn't known I enrolled for this, but maybe it was a negative option. Anyway, the "Important" information is that I can upgrade my coverage "to the highest level of accident protection." Now, is that elite status, or what!

One "Important Information Enclosed" fibber adds a deadline date and "Final Notice" in a second window. Uh-oh! (And of course it has the boiler-plate "Postmaster . . ." imperative.) Final notice? What have I done? Or not done? Aha! It's my last chance "to upgrade your present vehicle to a brand-new Honda or KIA." Hey, fellas, I hate to rain on your parade, but I'm driving a Jaguar convertible. How about having a clue about who you're selling to?

What's the next one? A plain white jumbo window envelope with "IMPORTANT INFORMATION ENCLOSED" in red above the window. Of course, the Bulk Rate indicia, in the same red, rides serenely above this legend.

Inside is one of the most impenetrable documents I've ever tried to look at. It's a prospectus for Fidelity Advisor Funds Class A, Class T, and Class B. No letter. No indication of what makes this important. Every indication of why the word "Bulk" is more apt than the word "Important."

And on we go, into this pseudo-psychological jungle. The Discover Card takes a stern parental position:

Important:

Please open at once.

DO NOT DISCARD.

Yeah, guys, but you've joined the "Bulk rate" parade. Oh, what the heck—even though it parallels the dire warning on the tags attached to pillows and mattresses, I'll open it.

I wish I hadn't.

The message from Discover (I haven't used this card since 1992, when Costco wouldn't accept any others) tells me, "Enclosed are four Discover® Card Checks just for you. Use them to . . ." Naturally, that "®" symbol destroys any rapport, but this doesn't bother me because I've built up an immunity to ® and ™ symbols, legal necessities for immediate identification and pomposities when overused.

A SIMPLE LITTLE RULE

I have a theory: Somebody writes the envelope copy, goes on vacation, and is eaten by a shark. Somebody else rushes in to write the enclosures; in the heat of getting these out, whatever is written on the envelope is overlooked.

How simple it is!

I have a little rule I've both preached and employed ever since the Fake Importance Syndrome showed up and developed into a Nile virus-like plague:

If you claim importance, prove it.

See how uncomplicated those six words are? They *force* the creative team out of the hit-and-run bunker, onto the open battlefield.

So when Sprint sends me a letter (presorted first class . . . I'm moving up!) with the legend "Important news about your telephone service," I first take a deep breath, hoping it won't be a stupid message tied to Candace Bergen or Sela Ward, then open it to find what I expected to find: "Now your small business can get the same quality and value you enjoy on long distance, for all your *local toll* calls, too.)

Is a puzzlement. My business isn't that small (should I be insulted?), and Sprint isn't our long distance provider. I wouldn't expect a company with the creative depth they have to die in the heading with limp words such as *quality* and *value*. Those are peculiarities, but they aren't germane to the point here, which is: What's so important? Couldn't the creative team have adapted envelope copy to intrigue me rather than generate just another weak cliché?

Hey, Sprint and Discover and AmEx and all you Honda dealers out there: Want to add some octane to your messages? *If you claim importance, prove it.*

Remember that, will you? It's important.

"Free at Last"? Well, Sort of . . . Except . . .

One of the great wonders of our time is that the word "Free" survives.

We've kicked it in the head, stomped on it with golf shoes, strangled it with adjectival qualifiers, drowned it in a sea of asterisks, maimed it with "if" phrases, and suffocated it with cheap rhetorical varnish . . . and still it survives.

As any resident of the former Yugoslavia might point out: Survival isn't equivalent to thriving.

Today's target doesn't accept "Free!" as really free, the way his or her forebears did a generation ago. Today's "What's the angle?" hesitation is often precursor to a consultation with one of those lawyers slathering for the typical unreasonable percentage of a class action settlement. We can be next in line for that reaction.

> **"It isn't 'Free,' you dummy. It's 'Complimentary.'**
> **Or it's 'No extra charge.' But it isn't 'free.'"**
> **"Oh."**

Writing for credit card companies and financial institutions, I often encounter the warning: "We can't say it's free. We can only say it's complimentary or at no extra charge."

That a difference in perception between "free" and "complimentary" exists (and only the sedate marketers heed that difference in perception) is an indication of the litigious, looking-for-trouble early 21st century societal structure. That one of the mailings coming to me spelled the word *complementary*—a word that has a totally different meaning—is an indication of the borderline literacy of some of our confrères.

Anybody who has practiced advertising, marketing, or basic salesmanship for more than 20 minutes is aware of the idiosyncrasies surrounding the word "Free." For example, we all refer to "Free Gift." Now, come on, have we ever heard of a gift that isn't free? That isn't the point. The redundancy "Free Gift" pulls. That's what matters, because we deal in response, not logic.

So I suppose we'll expand to "Totally Free Gift" and then to "100% Totally Free Gift." Does that make us charlatans? Certainly not. It makes us salespeople, sensitive to what motivates our targets.

When I was about six years old, living near Pittsburgh, I visited relatives in Detroit. Detroit had a paper called *The Free Press*. Gee, I wondered, how could they make any money? (The last few years have proved me right. Apparently they can't.) My aunt didn't disabuse me of the notion, and I was lucky that I didn't just grab a paper off the newsstand: After all, it was free.

So was Radio Free Europe. The magic of the word has been inescapable. In David Ogilvy's *Confessions of an Advertising Man*, published two generations ago, he singled out *Free* as one of the powerful motivators. That power still drives the marketing engine, although it no longer purrs on all twelve cylinders.

Why has *free* begun to sputter, running so roughly it even backfires now and then? Because of a venerable monolith of a rule affecting all forms of force-communication:

Sameness = boredom.
Overuse = abuse.

We lean on "free" the way a cripple leans on a crutch. It may not save us, but it supports us. But it doesn't support us as profoundly as it supported our predecessors a generation ago.

A generation ago, a free offer wasn't a novelty but neither was it a daily occurrence. Today, we fish around for something in an offer, something we can isolate so we can say we're including it free.

The most miserable of these I've seen lately is in a Valassis-type free standing insert ad for Yoplait Yogurt. If I get a "You win!" message under the top label of a six-ounce cup, I can mail in that label for a free cup of the same type.

Thanks a heap, Yoplait. The local supermarket sells Yoplait at two for 89¢. So a cup is worth 44½¢. A stamp costs 34¢ and the envelope is a penny. That pays me 9½¢ for drying the lid, putting my name and address on a sheet, addressing the envelope, and mailing it . . . assuming I find a winner. (The winner is the supermarket, which sells its house brand at two for 79¢.)

The creeping cynicism among those who read, see, or hear our messages is based on two factors. They're responsible for the first one and we're the generators of the second. Theirs:

A universal "I want mine" attitude has replaced the kinder, gentler "Gee, thanks!" of earlier times.

Ours:

To work the magical word into the mix, we hedge—"Free with your third shipment," "Free when you've collected the complete set," "Free if yours is one of the first 50 replies we receive."

(I hate the "Fast 50" development. I know it works, so I use it, just as I use peel-off involvement devices. That doesn't keep me from hating it. Some of my clients tell me it induces "white" [negative] mail, such as, "How can I hope to compete when I live in Vancouver and you're in Atlanta? This whole promotion is rigged in favor of people who live near you." I've developed an answer to this objection, but I won't share it here.)

And we have the old dependable "Buy one, get one free," which usually outpulls "Two for the price of one" or "Buy two and get 50% off." So even though the clock is ticking, even though worn spots are showing, even though the FCC occasionally growls, the Old Dependable still churns out response for us.

Understand, please: I keep score the same way I hope you do: by response, not by critical accolades or art directors' awards. So I'm in there, milking our favorite word just as you are. I'm not going to let pride stand in the way of response.

But I'm glad I'm operating during this generation. By the next one, we may have damaged our durable crutch so deeply it may not support those who follow us in our most noble profession.

An Embarrassment of Riches

Checks. *Checks.* CHECKS.

I'm looking at $223,367 worth of checks sent to me over the past few weeks. The biggest one is for $80,000. The smallest (piker!) is $20. I didn't have to do a lick of work to get them. And I don't know what to do with them.

Correction: I *do* know what to do with them. Ready, round file? Every one of them is an unsolicited "check" with sticky strings hanging all over it.

For example, the biggie—the $80,000—isn't a check at all. Gee, what a surprise! It says "Pay to the order of" and spells my name correctly and has a bunch of code numbers and a printed signature. Uh—what bank is it drawn on?

And what does that four-point type say, there in a corner? Aw, shucks. It says, "Non-negotiable. No cash value. This is not a check." Yeah, and Richard Nixon said, "I am not a crook."

Hey, Buddy, this gimmick is old and gray. When I was in the first grade (back in ought-six) one of my classmates brought one of these faux-checks to school. Our myopic teacher wanted to throw a party, until a neighboring teacher, hearing the clamor, pointed out a hidden line—"Wouldn't you like to have a real check like this?"

Ah, here's the deal on this one: "YOU HAVE BEEN PRE-AP-PROVED FOR A LOAN UP TO $80,000.00."

What do you mean, "up to"? That non-negotiable no cash value checklet is for a flat eighty grand.

Okay, let's agree we all knew when we saw that check-like image in the window, with "bulk rate" in the upper right corner of the envelope: We knew it was a virtual reality check. I'm intrigued by the mice-type on the reverse side of the letter, not the check:

> *How you were selected for this pre-approved offer: Informa-*
> *tion contained in your consumer credit report was used to de-*
> *termine if you met our credit criteria. After we have taken*
> *your application, we will verify your creditworthiness. We will*
> *also verify your ability to meet other applicable criteria such*
> *as income, job status and debt ratio and will ask you to fur-*
> *nish any required collateral. If you do not meet all of our cri-*
> *teria, we may cancel this offer.*

So much for being pre-approved. Sob.

"THIS IS NOT A CHECK."

One of two $50,000 checks is a little more subtle. Oh, sure, I found the hidden but expected "This is not a check." The attached letter says, "We are pleased to inform you that your home may be eligible for a low interest 2ndmortgage in the amount shown above." Yeah, "may"—better psychology. And they invite me to "discuss a possible increase in the amount shown above," light-years better than that nasty word "apply."

I really admire whoever designed the other $50,000 package. On the envelope—the standard governmental manila, with the standard "Deliver to addressee only"—is the legend "Buy U.S. Bonds." Terrific! That's a clever touch.

This one says "This is not a check" as a light green line on a light green background, visible if you hunt for it. And the attached letter—except it isn't quite a letter, since it's set up as a display and has no signature—starts, "Dear Herschell." An anonymous admirer, probably.

My reciprocal admiration is tempered by the multitude of asterisks in the text. They're all over the place, following provocative semi-truths such as "No equity limitation!! means no appraisal" and "Some bad credit o.k.!!" (How can anybody have *some* bad credit? It's like being pregnant—a simple yes or no will do.)

Yeah, the asterisk at the bottom sucks out the romance: *Subject merely to verification of debt ratios, credit scoring and of owner occupancy of property. Some programs may require equity.*

That word "merely" is a professional touch, but anybody who uses two exclamation points in a pitch like this already has two demerits against the score.

One mailing tries for verisimilitude by offering $43,200. Its envelope is even more patriotic than its competitor: "Buy and hold U.S. savings bonds." And the checklet says flatly, "Check no. 2484739." Check no.? That "no." is just plain "no" because there it is—"Non-negotiable coupon." And they misspell my first name.

A REAL CHECK! BUT . . .

Here's a real check, but it's for just $100, and I can't deposit it in my regular account; I have to deposit it into my (yet to be established) VISA Platinum account. Some obfuscation here. See if you can decode it:

> *It's easy. Simply fill out and sign the back of the attached check and mail it to us—then we'll send you your VISA Platinum card. Make VISA Platinum your preferred account, and we'll credit your account with $100 to spend as you please!*

See it? How does one make this the "preferred account"? More mice-type on the bottom of the reverse side. Buried in the mound is "We will pay you a reward for trying all the benefits of this VISA Platinum account, which simply means you must charge and transfer minimum amounts to your account once it is opened. Transaction fee for cash advances is 3%. Minimum $5." Oh, well. Didn't your mother tell you never to say "You must" to strangers?

We've all had checks—real ones—from various long distance carriers, bribing us to switch. Checks are good, and even their non-sibling imitators are eye-catching, especially in an era of direct deposits.

But easy on the double-talk, huh? Our embarrassment of riches is turning into just a plain old embarrassment.

When It Comes to Award-winning Artists, We Mean Business. Let's Shake on It.

I just got a mailing from a company called ScanSource. The heading:

BackTrack—The Complete Database and Tracking System For Companies That Mean Business.

Clever, huh?

It matches the space ad in the current issue of a meeting-planning magazine:

Texas Means Business.

Wonderful. That makes an even 176 examples of this cliché in my collection. To keep Texas company, among destinations I also have "Florida Means Business," "Seattle Means Business," "San Diego Means Business," "Taipei Means Business," "Britain means Business," "France Means Business," and a batch of others. Lots of weak business offers out there.

What doesn't seem to be out there is a sense for imagination blended into creative selling. In speeches (as entertainment rather than instruction) I often rip through about a hundred examples of ads and mailers by various dullards who mean business. And I grant you, the first time this play on words appeared—in the year 1895, as I recall—it had some impact.

Them days is gone forever.

More insidious, because it isn't as quickly recognizable, is "When it comes to . . ."

Here's an ad for a software company called Symantec:

WHEN IT COMES TO <u>NT VIRUS SCANNING</u> WE RUN CIRCLES AROUND THE COMPETITION.

Okay. It's what we'd expect, since Hewlett-Packard has a full-page ad in *The Wall Street Journal*, headed:

WHEN IT COMES TO 8-WAY NT® SERVER AVAILABILITY, DON'T LOOK TO COMPAQ®. THEIRS WON'T BE AVAILABLE FOR ANOTHER 6 MONTHS.

What's fascinating isn't that these are all caps or that Hewlett-Packard uses the ® symbol for NT and Symantec doesn't. No, no. What's fascinating is that each of these ads cripples a strong selling proposition by using the impact-free "When it comes to" wheelchair.

These two bring my "When it comes to" collection to 134.

LET'S SHAKE HANDS ON THIS.

When I switched from slides to PowerPoint I threw out more than 300 slides I'd shot of ads featuring handshakes. It struck me that these represented "Generic Ad," available for use by every Peter Principle dimwit. So, rather than immortalize this zero-concept theme, I'm dismissing it with a single imperative: If your imagination is so sterile you can't think of any illustration stronger than a handshake, may your own hands shake so badly you won't be able to put the blasted picture in position.

WAIT, THERE'S MORE.

Did you ever pay attention to the ads for collector plates by the Franklin Mint in free-standing inserts? Typical are ones featuring art by "Award-winning wildlife artist Randy McGovern" and "Award-winning nature artist Hilary Scoffield."

Before Wyeth and da Vinci start entering their works in a fine art awards competition, they should be aware of some of their rivals—"award-winning artist Laurel Burch"; "award-winning artist Dave Troutman"; "award-winning artist Craig Nelson"; "award winning folk artist Lowell Herrero"; "award-winning wildlife artist Mike Wepplo"; "award-winning wildlife artist Michael Matherly"; and so on and so on and so on.

Some are bizarre: "Award-winning animal artist Nigel Hemming." Watch those fangs, Nigel! One is charming—an award-winning teddy-bear artist. I'd like to be there when that beast takes the award in its paws.

Now, I'm not suggesting that all these artists—have you ever heard of any of them?—haven't won awards. I'm just wondering who the hell dished out these awards. Well . . . on second thought, I'm not wondering.

Oh, I've lost count of these. I have about eighty or ninety, I guess.

Speaking of da Vinci, Leonardo makes quite a hit with our gang. I now have 87 ads and mailers featuring the Mona Lisa. Here she is with a wireless phone for NetExpert. There she is in the screen of a Smile/KFC monitor (can't be a Kentucky Fried monitor, can it?). She's even the spokesperson for Los Ranchos Restaurant.

I'll say on behalf of La Gioconda and her employers: Many of her images are tongue-in-cheek, unlike the deadly seriousness of the "Means Business," "When it comes to," and "Award-winning" candidates. Better yet: Mona Lisa doesn't have an agent. Free use. Take that, Michael Jordan and Tiger Woods!

Michelangelo doesn't have an agent either. So here's the ceiling of the Sistine Chapel. Who's using it? Disney, of course (and probably Disney will claim royalties from now on). Inc. Magazine. The Minneapolis Gift Mart. Ashburton Investments. "Miracle" chip. Black Starr & Frost. And so on and so on and so on.

SINCE THESE ADS ARE EXCRETIONS . . .

If we're dealing in such inanities, why not expand our vistas? How about that statue in Brussels or Amsterdam, or somewhere near there, in which a little boy's weak kidneys spout day and night (example: *When it rains, it pours*)? How about Attila the Hun (example: *Attire by Attila*)? How about art by those award-winners, Hieronymus van Bosch (example: *Even St. Anthony would be tempted by these chocolates*) and Georges Seurat (example: *If you're nude and descending a staircase, better wear Reeboks*)?

You get the idea.

What I'm hoping is that some others will get the idea. If my col-

lection of "Means business" stretches to 500, I won't feel particularly triumphant. Is it a triumph when one's confrères sit there
lazily, leaning on non-motivational clichés?

If my collection of "When it comes to" reaches 250, that won't
be a genuine milestone. No, it'll be a *millstone*, with another marketer wondering why response isn't at the level it should be. (Not
that it ever is.) And the 250 mark will disappear faster than a previous Olympic record as new contenders for mediocrity push their
way into the arena. Anyway, when it comes to that, nothing will
have come of it.

As long as we have printing presses, we'll have enough art
awards, so I'm not worried about running short of these. I do think
a potent promotional stunt would be to rent Yankee Stadium for an
assembly of all those unfamiliar award winners, to give them the ac-
claim they deserve. The star should be the teddy bear artist, who for
the evening can wear a big unisex bow.

Are you exulting because the juggernaut missed your favorite
cliché? Careful, now. "Your partner in . . . " and "Unleash the power
of . . . " are coming dangerously close.

If you're poised at the keyboard, ready to excrete today's banal-
ity, you'd do well to pay attention to these suggestions . . . because
when it comes to predictable bromides, I mean business.

If Your Caddy Zigs, Does Your Jaguar Jag? Does Your Saab Sob? And How about a Pap Test for Your Volvo?

A brutal question: When was the last time national advertising for
automobiles caused you to take any positive action other than sti-
fling a yawn? Or scratching your head?

I'll be kind and use a euphemism:

Most automobile "catchlines" are . . . execrable.

I blame the decline of salesworthy vehicular rhetoric on the current buzzword: *Brand*.

Every couple of years a new term for a venerable concept bubbles to the surface, bobs there for a while, then quietly sinks. I've brought that up before in this text—remember when that term was "Integrated Advertising" (for most advertising agencies, one of the great lies of our time)? Then we had The Database Era. Now it's Brand.

Everything is brand. Martha Stewart isn't a person, she's a brand. (Others think she may be an android.) Tiger Woods isn't a golfer, he's a brand. Some publications tell us they aren't magazines; they're brands. Fair enough. While reading this brand, ponder: Does brand recognition have any value if it doesn't produce enthusiastic *buyers*?

Selling be damned, the latter-day sinners of automotive autoeroticism declaim. We want to be known as a *brand*, and we'll spend millions establishing brand identity. If you build it, they will come.

Fellas, do you really want to do that? Remember the Edsel. Remember the Allante, which nobody knew how to pronounce, and the Cimarron. For that matter, look at Isuzu. On second thought, no, don't.

Mazda brings out its next year's model almost in time to celebrate New Year's Day of the year before. As I recall, one year Mazda had this slogan: "The all new Mazda Miata. It's waiting." So were we. When does the selling season begin? Oh, I forgot the tagline: "Get in. Be moved." They got that one direct from the New York subway.

Mazda is reintroducing its rotary engine, and they say this time it won't wear out before the car gets out of the showroom. But Mazda doesn't have to worry about ridicule as long as Cadillac defies the Angel of Death with its hopeless Catera. The car started off in zero-gear with "Catera—the Caddy that zigs." I look back at the days when I owned a Cadillac, before Cimarron and Allante. It was considered a luxury car then, and it zoomed comfortably without zigging aimlessly. What puzzles me isn't that some brand-fanatic of the "That which is different = that which is good" cult proposed this image-damaging campaign; it's that the automaker accepted it and the dealers didn't hire a hit-man.

Let's not forget Nissan, with its peculiar "Life is a journey. Enjoy the ride." Yeah, but what about the car? Dealers didn't enjoy the ride. They ultimately raised the roof about this campaign, but not until Nissan's sales fell nearly 30 percent. Like roller-coaster addicts, apparently the brand-aware and marketing-unaware creative team enjoys the ride downward.

Infiniti finally abandoned those insufferable, snotty Jonathan Pryce commercials. And what was the first substitute? Peggy Lee's old song, "You give me fever"—which, in an automotive ambience, suggests the air conditioning isn't working. The tag line is "Own one and you'll understand." Yeah, right on.

The Mysterious East: Mitsubishi (I wonder how many Mitsubishi owners can spell the company's name) came up with "spirited products for spirited people." Oh. And Honda has "An Accord like no other." Hey, Honda, nobody else is making Accords. You're welcome.

HUPMOBILE, PLEASE COME BACK

Toyota refuses to be left out of the Vague Cloud Club: "Toyota. Everyday." I guess Toyota doesn't have a dictionary, which defines "everyday" as "ordinary." Or are they proud of that? Don't wake them up by pointing out the difference between "Everyday" and "Every day." Hupmobile, where are you now that we need you?

Mercury's theme is "Imagine yourself in a Mercury." What a two-edged sword that one is! I'm old enough to remember the Mercury Comet, and imagining myself back in that thing . . . well, that would make both the ad-writer and me masochists.

Mercedes-Benz reached back, back, back into history with Marlene Dietrich, or a Dietrich foghorn sound-alike, burbling through an off-key "Falling in love again." The commercial ended with the all-too-revealing line, "I can't help it." Yeah, we figured that out.

Historically, automobile advertising has been a chimera ever since form overtook substance as the rationale behind advertising. We've seen that idiotic "Fahrfegneugen" campaign for Volkswagen. We've seen "This isn't your father's Oldsmobile," which suggests you're driving a stolen car. What we haven't seen is a serious attempt to show and tell us what the benefits of a car might be.

Let's relate these television campaigns, every one of which runs into eight or nine figures, to what professional marketers regard as the reason for a sponsored message. I'll repeat our catechism:

The purpose of a sales message is to convince the reader, viewer, or listener to perform a positive act as the direct result of exposure to that message.

If a prospective customer showed up at our premises and asked for a reason to buy, we might be in trouble if we recited, "Get in. Be moved," or "This isn't your father's Oldsmobile." Come to think of it, soon it won't be anybody's Oldsmobile.

Can you visualize a potential buyer asking a car salesman, "Why should I buy this car?" and having the salesman break out in an offkey rendition of "Falling in Love Again" or "You Give Me Fever"?

Well, I've figured it out, courtesy of Webster's. Two of the definitions of "brand": a mark burned into the flesh of criminals; and a mark of disgrace or notoriety, a stigma.

Okay, car makers. You show me yours and I'll show you mine.

Rocket and Roadmaster, Where Are You?

Oldsmobile is on a death watch, complaining that sales just ain't what they used to be.

Well, let's see. There's a sameness to most cars today. You're sitting next to one at a stoplight. What kind is it? A Mercedes? A Dodge? Oh, it's an Avalon? Who makes that?

Image seems to have disappeared. And Oldsmobile has become the bellwether, the pack leader, in disappearing image.

Remember when Olds had the Rocket 88? That word "Rocket" really drew a dynamic image. Owning a Rocket was a status symbol.

Then things changed. Rocket 88 gave way to Delta 88. We had Cutlass, which had a certain panache, and Calais and Cierra, which didn't. But now, here's Alero. Who in the name of Zilch chose that name? Alero? It isn't as bad as Catera or Denali, but then what could be? Another Oldsmobile sub-brand is Aurora. It's lyrical but feminine, and that has to cut into sales.

If Oldsmobile wants to recapture market share, marketing expertise has to back up engineering expertise. A venerable rule of salesmanship says that a product is what it is, plus what the prospect thinks it is. Perception of Alero isn't within light-years of the perception of Rocket.

ADD THIS TO THE MIX

Can the looking-for-a-job marketing executives at Oldsmobile really not have a clue what went wrong, after approving advertising which was about as distinctive as "Yes, we have no bananas"? The negative mix is complete. Okay, quick: What's Oldsmobile's selling proposition? If you guess it's a frog sliding down the window of an Alero or the "Intrigue Virtual Mystery Tour," you're as out of touch as the advertising is. What, from that multimillion dollar advertising budget, would persuade *you* to head for the showroom?

The combination of weak advertising, weak image, and weak car names is deadly. Imagine having a car called Ciera and the parent company having a truck called Sierra. What's next, See-Era?

I'm picking on Oldsmobile, but that marque isn't alone. The Chrysler brands are in free fall. Early in the model year, advertising for a whole batch of cars often centers on rebates, an indication of buyer indifference.

It's too late for Oldsmobile, but what might have been the answer? Back to Rocket, the way Chevrolet has resuscitated Impala? Oh, sure, names wear out, but sometimes the manufacturer *thinks* a name is worn out before it actually is. Ford has had Mustang since 1964 and the name still has guts. Cadillac dropped Fleetwood, a name that reflected the top of the line. Lincoln dropped the "Mark" series, which puzzles me. Buick dropped Roadmaster, which during its reign was king of the road. Chevrolet dropped Caprice, and people still ask the dealers why.

So Oldsmobile isn't alone. Kia has a car named Sephia, which sounds like a disease. Ford has Probe, which sounds like a step in diagnosing the disease. GM has Jimmy, which sounds like a toy. Toyota has Previa, which sounds like it's been released too soon.

The Japanese cars seem to be the victim of dropping a letter from the spelling. What if Acura were Accura and Galant were Gallant? Would that damage the image? If Sentra were Sentry, would prospects rebel? If Altima were Ultima, it wouldn't be as high in the alphabet but it might have a stronger image.

And a domestic manufacturer, Pontiac, has a new one called Aztek. Why the "k" instead of the "c"? For that matter, why the design of that one?

Here's one named Tiburon. That's okay, but Tiburon means "Shark"—which strikes me as a far more salesworthy name.

Some names defy analysis—Passat. Jetta. Bravada. Integra. Tercel. Cirrus. Leganza. Stratus. Breeze. Aspire. Protege. These are just a little out of focus. Yeah, that's one too—Focus.

The name "Grand" has not just survived; it prospers to the point of total confusion. Jeep has Grand Cherokee. Chrysler has Grand Voyager. Dodge has Grand Caravan. Mercury has Grand Marquis. Pontiac has Grand Am and Grand Prix. Suzuki has Grand Vitara, whatever that's supposed to mean. Isn't that mutuality of names just grand?

Do all those Grands cause confusion? Well, maybe not as much as New York street names. One manufacturer has the Park Avenue and another has Fifth Avenue. Hey, guys, Eighth Avenue is still available, and they have all those movie houses that show racy films. Let's suggest it to Madison Avenue, which may be the breeding spot for some of the outlandish car names.

Even the giants stumble. Rolls-Royce maintains its "Silver" series, which had glory days with Silver Cloud and Silver Spur, with Silver Seraph. Huh? Verbally, it seems to be not a celestial being but a typeface.

I'm puzzled by names such as Golf and Focus and Millenia, which seem to have been awarded to the wrong type of product.

Some names still have "bite"—Viper. Tracer. Mystique. Blazer. Silverado. Sunfire. Firebird and Thunderbird (is that one still alive?). Mountaineer. Ram.

Oh, well. No matter how obfuscatory or unmotivating car names have become, any one of them can look with disdain at Unisys and Diageo and say, "What low-voltage computer came up with those?"

THESE ACCIDENTS AREN'T ACCIDENTAL.

The most bewildering aspect of car-appellation is that these names aren't accidental. They're the result of not just hours but probably days, weeks, or even months of brainstorming. How many of them would have survived the first guffaw a generation ago, when car manufacturers were far more sensitive to their market and more in touch with it . . . and tailored model names to what turned on potential buyers, not what was a peculiar but yet unused combination of letters, originated by a computer?

You may argue that the name on the car isn't of such major consequence. Okay, let's argue. I opine that the name on an automobile should suggest one of three "buyer incentive virtues"—power (Thunderbird, Cobra, an "X" something), status (Imperial, Royale), or exclusivity (Mark XI). Being able to name your car with chest thrust out is simple child psychology. Next to a home, cars are the most expensive purchase an individual will make. Positioning, or lack of it, is welded to the name. That'll be $300 million, please.

Having cast those pearls, I'm off in my Stanley Steamer to get a price on the newest Nash Rambler.

Lawyers on Skateboards

If one word describes about half the output of conventional advertising agencies and their witless clients, that word would be: *Duh.*

An absolute indication of marketer moronity is a "Look how clever we are!" attitude implemented by obfuscation, sophomoric cleverness, or both. We certainly have known for generations the peril attending ignorance or avoidance of The Illustration Agreement Rule—*Illustration should agree with what we're selling, not with headline copy.* We also acknowledge and revere The Relevance Equation (*Irrelevance = lower response).*

But those guys out there—they love it when a bewildered televiewer asks, "What was that all about?" They revel in their full-color, full-bleed space ads that have readers puzzling over not just the message but the intent. Why? Duh.

In a single issue of a trade publication aimed at top corporate management are so many non-communicating ads one wonders if the advertising department has turned over its pages to a group of silly, not-quite-bright grammar school students whose intellectual achievements are dim enough for them to flunk a course in Clay.

Here's an ad whose big and only illustration is a barefoot youngster on a surfboard. The entire text, and yes, ellipsis and lower case are theirs: ". . . representing emerging growth companies, multinational enterprises, and everything in between . . . we help clients capitalize on opportunities around the world" (no period at the end, of course). Below this is a giant word: mofo. Yep, that's it—mofo. Who or what is mofo? No, the word isn't from "The Sopranos." It's a law firm. Go figure.

Same magazine: An investment firm says, with initial caps to make reading a little more difficult, "We Look Beyond The Surface To Ensure Your M&A Success." Illustration: x-rays of two skulls facing each other.

Same magazine: A software company offering "e-business solutions." Headline: "The sky's the limit when you leap into the Internet economy. Illustration: aerial view of skydivers. Opinion: A better line for this nonsense would be "Softbrains selling software."

You may think it's impossible to slide farther downhill, but a few pages beyond is a photograph of a great ape, its angry open mouth framed in a monitor. The headline: "Primal Stream." It's for a streaming provider, get it? If you don't, the first line of text helps initiate some dry heaves: "Going ape over trying to choose the right streaming provider?" So help me, that's actual copy.

A rather fuzzy photo of a convertible driving away from us (full bleed, naturally) occupies more than two-thirds of a page. The headline, below the photo: "B2B—It's not a luxury. It's a way of life." Whose ad is it? A company claiming, in Spartan text, to be the only one that "allows you to create a smooth, collaborative environment between you and your business partners." Better take out some key-man insurance on this one, guys.

At the top of a page is the legend, "powering e-market networks™." A huge butterfly, with a string of smaller butterflies trailing behind it, sits astride the heading, "The power behind the Fat Butterfly." Total explanation: "A software platform for value-based e-markets, connecting buyers and sellers of business-critical products and services." Oh. Thanks for the explanation.

Turn the page and uh-oh. Against a solid black background is a vicious-looking basketball player stuffing a ball into a net. The heading: "The Power Move That Puts You in e-Business—Fast" (again, no period at the end, but they do use initial caps to prove they aren't ready for prime time).

Inside the back cover is a wrench (photo) about to tighten a nut (loose art). At the bottom is a tiny block of text headed by, "E-BUSINESS SYSTEMS BUILT LIKE NOBODY'S E-BUSINESS."

Look, folks, I grant you I find these annoying. But am I being overly picky when I point out how nonsensical it would be if somebody asks you, "What does your company do?" and you answered, "We're the power behind the Fat Butterfly" or "We supply e-business systems built like nobody's e-business"?

It's Not the Time for Foolishness.

Attention-spans are short and comprehension is down. Everybody knows this . . . except for so, so many so-called professional communicators who don't seem to have a clue how to influence anyone except one another.

Should we blame the agencies? Really, the blame lies squarely on the sloping shoulders of marketers who let the agencies get away with such nonsense. What's most bothersome is that this unholy, unprofessional trend seems to be epidemic, a spillover from the fiascos a couple of years ago when dot-com companies, flush with investment money, rushed out like the naive gamblers they were and splattered away their marketing dollars on campaigns that temporarily boosted their egos and permanently damaged their bottom lines.

Enough, already. If these goofs can't learn the principles of communication, replace them with professionals who not only can but who already have.

Anybody out there? Well, on the back cover of that same magazine is an ad for Infiniti that actually shows the car. Great heavens! What's the world coming to?

Aw, Come On, You Know Better Than to Use These Words.

A mailing from a direct marketing service company had this heading:

Where You'll Find Quality, Service, and Value

Somebody got paid for writing that. Ugh.

Uh-oh. I can sense a reaction—"What's wrong with that?" I'll tell you what's wrong:

We're motivators whose connection is always long-distance. We're trying to generate a highly emotional reaction, culminating in an orgasmic "I want that!" We're <u>force</u>-communicators, hurling action-words, not sponge-words.

Quality, *service*, and *value* generate no image. They're clichés. Oh, sure, I know Ford had "At Ford, Quality Is Job 1" as the company's slogan. But at the moment of truth, in the showroom, a salesperson would score zero by using this as the kicker-line. And in this Age of Skepticism, with credibility and attention spans both near zero, we'd better *start* our sales arguments at the moment of truth.

Why "Quality" Has No Quality

Why doesn't "quality" hack it as a motivational term? Because of a basic rule of force-communication any effective advertising copywriter should know implicitly:

Specifics outsell generalizations.

(Actually, Ford's thin slogan wasn't true anyway: The J.D. Power survey of customer satisfaction at the time showed the top five cars to be Lexus, Infiniti, Saturn, Mercedes-Benz, and Acura.)

A negative-test tip: Take a look at some of the ads in the yellow pages. If your nouns, verbs, and adjectives match what you see there, chances are your copy stinks.

Who Needs "Needs"? Nobody.

Example: The word *needs* as a noun—"For all your insurance needs." Wherever you live, take a look at the yellow pages. Some local insurance agent, or more probably the yellow pages salesperson who lives with a batch of ridiculous restrictions on claims, thinks that's good copy. The message he or she—or, God help us, you—may be excreting is, "I don't know what you want, and I'm afraid to make a specific claim, so please write my ad for me." Next to "*[WHATEVER]* means business," seeing this word in your copy has to be the low point of your career.

Nondescript Words

Some words aren't terrible; they're just blah. Using them means you're writing in black-and-white instead of color.

An example: the word *special*. We all use it, the way we drink water when Diet Coke isn't available. "Your special discount"; "This is a special offer"; "Special to Collectors"; "A Special Announcement."

Nothing really wrong here. Nothing unprofessional here. But nothing suggesting a meistersinger talent, either. The way out of this corner is a simple self-asked question: "What about this makes it special?" If the question has an answer, and you use the specific instead of the generality, impact jumps exponentially.

One more, and this one is my pet peeve: "The finest (or *best*) in . . ." First of all, why do we need the word "in"? Is "the finest in furniture" more communicative than "the finest furniture"? But "in" is just the symptom; in this use, "finest" is the ailment.

Once again, ask yourself: "What enables me to claim this is the finest?" The answer, if you can think of it or if a supplier will provide it for you, will transform your copy from blah to wow. (Oddly, the complaint doesn't apply to *fine*.)

In the friendly spirit of meanness designed to ruin your day, here's a short list of words you should be inspecting for possible replacement. None of us can avoid these altogether; all of us should be on the alert for more vital substitutions.

(A suggestion: Look through each piece of copy for any three. After a month or so, you'll be hyper-aware of flatness. Consciousness is 72.8 percent of the battle against dull copy.

administration	constructed
affinity	contradictory
amendment	"Dear Friend"
approximately	define
attractive	dispatch
available	earn
configuration	facilitate

features	purchase
fond	quality
formulate	reliable
humorous	replacement
indeed	requested
merchant	respond
moderate	rethink
needs [as a noun]	selection
pamphlet	standards
peruse	value
prearranged	service
product	utilize
proven	various
provide	work

If you're wondering why words such as *beautiful* and *wonderful* aren't on this list, along with a few hundred more, consider: When you first learned to ride a bicycle, you didn't do wheelies. Take it slow and your copy will gradually shine with a patina that might have you—and, better yet, others—admiring your ability to sell with words.

I Admire You, You Rascal, You.

Ever hear the phrase "Information optimizing"?

It's a favorite of mine. I admire creative people who use creative thinking to project a creative halo around a creative idea. Information optimizing is behind one of my favorite rules, the Generic Determination Rule: *The generic determines reaction more than the number.*

The Generic Determination Rule points out that 60 seconds

seems to be less than one minute. One pint is less than half a quart. Attention is to the generic, seconds and minutes. If you don't believe the Rule, ask yourself, "What if McDonald's 'Quarter Pounder' had been named McDonald's 'Four Ouncer'?"

So, in keeping with that Rule, I sort of admire the ad headed "A Historic First" for the "World's First Year 2000 Golden Dollar," which claims to contain "124.41 grams (1,920 grains) of Pure Silver." Note, please: I said I *sort of* admire. I didn't say I admire. After all, a grain of silver is .002 ounces, so 1,920 grains is 3.84 ounces. And the statement would have been stronger without "grains," a word that emphasizes smallness. But consider: To the American-educated (or uneducated) experience, grams and grains are exotic. 3.84 ounces are mundane.

This "Golden Proof" of the strange and still novel Sacagawea dollar coin is 3½ inches in diameter and priced at $99. Is it, in fact, a superdollar, acceptable across the counter at banks and McDonald's? Copy says it's "an exquisite adaptation." Although I'd prefer 99 of the originals, I have to say: Nice job of information optimizing, guys.

IS OBFUSCATION SYNONYMOUS WITH OPTIMIZING?

I can't be as benevolent toward some of the other deliberate obfuscations we see in the mail, in space ads, and increasingly online. That applies to another "Mint" whose headline uses an ungrammatical pomposity—"Announcing an Historic Release . . ." *An* historic? I've seen that too often, and one of my recurring nightmares is that "An historic" will worm its way into common usage. As I said earlier in this text, I guess we'll see it in an history book.

Ahh, let's move on. The line "My idol has feet of clay" applies most appropriately to American Express Platinum Card.

I've had a Platinum Card seemingly forever, and even though it costs three hundred bucks a year (against the host of free cards),

I've treasured it, used it both for protection against deals that might not be as represented and for frequent flyer miles, and touted it to others. Now here comes a mailing from Platinum Card, headed "IMPORTANT NOTICE." Uh-oh.

The Important Notice is insidious enough to warrant my using the Platinum Card to protect myself against it—Catch-22:

> As a "Thank You" for being a valued Platinum Card® member, you are entitled to receive one or more American Express VIP Awards. The maximum redemption value of your Reward is shown on the Certificate below.
>
> Any portion of the maximum Reward value that remains unused after you have made up to 3 Reward selections will expire and cannot be redeemed for cash or credit. . . .
>
> After your Reward period, you'll continue to receive uninterrupted service at the low annual prices. . . .

The "Certificate" at the bottom of the letter has a "Reward Value" of $46. For what? Aha! Magazine subscriptions: 90 days free, then I "continue to receive uninterrupted service at the low annual prices." Note that word "service." It's optimization for "subscription," a less-motivational term, just as "Reward" is a euphemism for "first issues free." Nowhere—*nowhere*—in the text of the letter does either the word "magazine" or the word "subscription" appear. In fact, neither word appears on the face of the certificate.

Is this worthy of Platinum Card? In my opinion, it's a big step down, beyond information optimizing and leaning toward deliberate obfuscation to induce readership. Cleverness pays off when the recipient doesn't think you've tried to put one over on him/her.

SCRABBLING AROUND

With the decline of subscription/sweepstakes offers, magazines are scrabbling around for alternatives. *Business Week,* a most astute user of the mails to build subscriptions, generated its version of the classic *Wall Street Journal* "On a bright spring afternoon" letter. Their letter begins, "Two brothers went off to work . . ."

Well, all right, but a pitch like this is out of sync with the envelope copy which says, above the address panel, "Free subscription voucher for:" Actually, it's an eight-week subscription with the standard boiler-plate wording: "If you decide to continue, you'll receive 51 issues of *Business Week* (including your eight free trial issues) for the low rate of just $37.95 . . . that's 81% off the cover price. Otherwise, you will write 'cancel' on your bill. . . ."

Positive: *Business Week* astutely proposes eight issues, establishing a reading habit. Negative: We in DM have seen this pitch a thousand times. And so have about 50 million others who don't share our information optimizing background and cynicism. When credibility dulls, words lose their power.

What indignities we've heaped on the sloping shoulders of the word "free"! Here's a colorful envelope from Transparent Language, with "FREE UPGRADE!" in 60-point type. Yeah! Uh . . . what's that extra tidbit hidden to the right, not quite in mice-type, so make it rat-type: "With purchase."

YEAR OF THE YAHOO

Yahoo! Magazine boldly sends an invoice—an *invoice*—with the wording, "We have not yet received your check." Yeah, that's understandable, Yahoo!, since I haven't subscribed to your magazine.

Remember those fake newspaper pages with a stick-on note saying, "Mary, you ought to follow up on this. J."? The technique has invaded e-mail. Here's one addressed to my e-mail address, with the subject line, "hglewis1, a stitch in time." The message begins, "Hi! Just a quick note! Thought you might be interested in this site. It's got online descriptions of the coat of arms for families around the

world. Cool! Carol asked me to forward it in case you were interested. Here's the site from my bookmarks:"

Clever? Or insidious? I have two Carol-candidates, and neither
one ever heard of this deal (family heraldic crests, which may interest the Prince of Monaco but not me). Was it a lucky guess, or did
somebody break and enter inviolate non-list territory?

An Anti-virus Virus

One more, and this one really has me griped. For years I've used a
program called Norton Anti-Virus to keep outsiders from messing
up whatever is on my computer's hard drive. I like Norton Anti-
Virus because every now and then I can upgrade it just by a mouse-
click online.

In came a program called "Jammer," which claimed to be the
next generation of protection. Jammer was free for 30 days and then
$19.95, supposedly forever. Forever? Suddenly here's a dire e-mail
from something called Agnitum. After telling me, "Thank you for
using Jammer! You made a wise decision . . ." it makes that conclusion unsound by continuing, "The development of more sophisticated Trojans in recent months means your system has once again
become vulnerable to attack." It pitches "a superior, yet user-
friendly Trojan Horse scanner called Tauscan" . . . at $29.95.

The message winds up its infuriating spiel by saying Jammer
and Tauscan "work hand in hand like Batman and Robin." Oh, no,
they don't. They work hand in hand like Bonnie and Clyde.

Am I getting crotchety, annoyed by jackals picking at me before
I've even given the embalmer a chance? I hope so.

If John Caples Were Alive Today, He'd Be Turning over in His Grave.

A lot of young people in our business never heard of John Caples. It isn't surprising: The oldest person they recognize is Mick Jagger.

Caples wrote one of the two most historic mail order ads of all time—"They Laughed When I Sat Down at the Piano." (The other: "Do You Make These Mistakes in English?" for the Sherwin Cody School, the ad that ran unchanged for 45 years. Based on the grammar in a lot of advertising, we could use that one again.)

Caples isn't with us any more, except as a shadowy name on an annual group of direct marketing awards; but the melody lingers on. Every so often an advertiser picks up the golden threads: "They Laughed When I Sat Down at the Computer." (Must have been a copywriter.)

How far is this piracy supposed to go? In the same issue of a magazine aimed at would-be entrepreneurs were two ads. One was headed, "They All Laughed When I Said I Was Going to Start My Own Business." According to this guy, the business is mail order. Wow! In the body copy is this lead nugget:

> *The secret of getting rich in Mail Order lies in financial leverage. It's a little-known, almost secret method—using other people's capital to make money for you!*

Well, there goes the secret. Now everybody knows it.

I'll say for this advertiser: Unlike most ads in that magazine, his doesn't ask for immediate cash. It's a free details deal, and free details are rarer and rarer. Later, I imagine, he switches to using other people's money, just as we all do.

But the killer is the other Caples ad in the same magazine:

> *"They Laughed . . . When I Said I Wanted to Clean Carpets!"*

Laugh? Buddy, I'm not laughing. Come on over and indulge your aberration in my living room.

Hey, I didn't make this up. The ad shows a reasonably well-groomed couple sitting at what appears to be a patio—no carpets. Well, maybe it's just a fantasy. Some men want to dress up in women's clothing, some women want to be strippers for a night, some couples want to be lion tamers, and some people want to clean carpets . . . but they're back to normal by daylight.

What bothers me isn't that seventy or eighty years later, advertisers are still aping Caples. These "lifts" are examples of the touchstone technique, and well-structured touchstones work. No, I'm bothered by the ambience in which they appeared.

Seeing them, I riffled through the magazine. I'm glad I did, because here was a choice that hung the carpets out to dry:

"I Made Over $1 Million Cleaning Dirty Mini-Blinds!"

I'd hate to inspect this fellow's hands. He can make even more money starring in a Lava Soap commercial. (Do they still make Lava Soap?)

His space ad says "There are well over 600 million dirty mini-blinds on the market already." That's about four for every man, woman, and child in America. And the ad says the infestation is growing at the rate of over 100 million per year. We're up to our eyeballs in dirty mini-blinds, and thank God somebody is finally doing something about it, before it's too late. Twelve families in Poducah, who mistakenly thought the problem was only botulism, closed their blinds and expired.

In the same issue was this old chestnut:

MAKE $500–$1000 WEEKLY!
Or More Stuffing Inquiry Envelopes According to Our Instructions.

The arithmetic is primitive enough: "You will earn $1 for every piece of mail you process according to our simple instructions. If you process 100 pieces . . . times $1 . . . we pay you $100." And so on, up to $1000. The deal seems to be that they mail you a "Guide" listing "the names and addresses of dozens of companies that will pay you to work at home to assemble products and do clerical work."

Assemble products? You mean like sewing up baseballs or cementing model airplanes? Buddy, I'd wind up making $1 per week. But I'll never know, because the coupon asks for "$20 plus $3 for 1st class S&H for a total of only $23. Thank you." Uh—no, thank you.

Yet another *in the same issue*—and this is just one of a dozen or so magazines of its type—a headline in 72-point type:

FREE MONEY!

Text is fascinating:

NEW money-making concept makes all others obsolete. This 'FREE MONEY' is generated automatically and must be given away. I cannot keep it. Someone has to get it. It might as well be YOU!

Let's make an assumption—that every one of these offers is legitimate. Let's assume that hundreds of millions of mini-blinds are poisoning the ozone . . . that lettershops are closing their doors because people are outstuffing them at home . . . that somebody has so much money he has to run ads because it's overflowing his house and office and he's suffocating under a mound of money and is desperate to find takers so he can get rid of it all.

Aren't you bothered by ads like this? No, I don't mean because you didn't think of them first. No, I don't mean because we all could be making huge fortunes on carpets and mini-blinds, or sitting around counting free money instead of working in an office whose carpets and blinds are making millions for brighter entrepreneurs.

I mean this: The great unwashed public, with their great unwashed mini-blinds, lumps all of us into one cauldron. Direct marketing, direct response, direct mail, mail order, telemarketing—it's like that line from the defunct comic strip *Pogo*: "We have seen the enemy and it is us."

Our credibility is on the line. We're regarded as sharpies, as highbinders, as fast-buck artists.

So what can we do about it?

Our options are limited. We can't make a public stink, because to outsiders the smell would saturate our own marketing garments. We can't politely or impolitely ask these people to stop, because every facet of marketing today is shot through with puffery, and we'd be even more hypocritical than we already are (if that's possible).

What can we do? We can laugh.

We can laugh when somebody shows us one of those ads. We can say, "Yeah, go ahead . . . and call us when that first million is in the bank."

Then we can write our own ad:

"We laughed when they said, 'They laughed when I said. . . .'"

But I have an even better one, the Caples original: "They laughed when I sat down at the piano." This ad would be for a company making zippers.

Standing on Our Heads, Riding the Tsunami

I still remember taking an advertising course in school (Northwestern Class of 1906) . . . just about the only advertising course I had, as I remember.

One of the students handed in an ad for his father's dry-cleaning business. It showed his father, standing on his head. The headline: "We'll stand on our heads to please you." He was awarded a "D" accompanied by a stick drawing of a tombstone lettered "R.I.P."

More than half a century ago, an adman named Frederick Wakeman wrote a novel, "The Hucksters." (Ancient recall: I think the book became a movie with Clark Gable and, oddly, Sidney Greenstreet.) The book was a ridicule of "We'll stand on our heads . . ." messages. One example was, "I'm tossing my hat into the ring," showing—gee, what a surprise—a guy tossing his hat into a ring. We laughed the practice out of existence.

Ha! Fifty-year locusts! The computer age, which has dragged more unqualified practitioners into its ranks than any field other than politics, seems to have spawned a revival of the huckster-plague. I can't pick up a magazine without seeing the hucksterish creative excrescence of an IQ-70 writer/artist team.

Here's an ad for IBM: "Indiana manager rides tsunami (of information)!" Illustration: a guy on a surfboard atop a tidal wave. The same picture would work for "Idiot drowns, surfing tidal waves miles from shore." Body copy tries desperately to tie the picture to a concept—a CIO at an Indiana company has an IBM computer which "takes care of just about anything the Internet happens to throw his way." Yeah, right.

Full page, color and bleed (naturally, for a marketer who feels safer with form than with substance): "ProMark One Scores Again!" It's a picture of two football players fighting for a pass. The only problem is, the one with "ProMark" on his jersey seems to be fumbling the ball.

Here's one: "Running A Business Has Its Hurdles." Okay, guess what the photo is. Aw, you peeked. It's a man in a business suit and track shoes (an odd outfit), jumping over one hurdle but about to smash into the next one, which some lunatic placed only about three feet from the first one. What's it for? Dun & Bradstreet's "Business Solutions in a Box."

More full color and bleed: An orchestra conductor in a computer monitor screen, against a background of sheet music (it's a Mozart piano sonata, which doesn't usually require a conductor): "Orchestrate solutions . . ." What solutions? Well, it's hard to say, because the first sentence of text is, "with variable data printing from Scitex."

Oh, here's an upbeat message: "You're in the business of capturing big-time spenders." Under this heading is a picture of a sad sack in a jail cell. Then a follow-up subhead: "Not two-time losers." Zen and the art of obfuscation! It's for a telemarketing company.

Omnipresent Hucksterisms

Look, I didn't have to start a month-long search to find these. They're everywhere. "Are you covered?" It's a guy with an umbrella. Product is business insurance. "At L&H we have what it takes to get you to the top." Here's a woman struggling to climb a mountain, bare-handed without pitons. Product is speech recognition software. "The world's Easiest way to make a Splash in Business." A smug male model with big hair and an ill-fitting suit standing barefoot on the beach, holding an upright surfboard. Product is business software. (Surfboards seem to be generic to hucksterism; strange use of capital letters, as this heading exemplifies, is generic to small brainpans.)

From surfboard to toy boat—a full-page ad by Sprint Promotions in an advertising publication, headed, "Want a promotion that leaves competitors in its wake?" Come on, what kind of wake would a toy boat leave, except the kind of wake you'd hold for a dead ad?

My two favorites feature heavyweight boxing champions. One identifies the fighter as "Larry Holmes—Heavyweight champion for

7 straight years." The headline: "Think Fast! Get Performance ADSL
. . . or you'll be knocked out by your competition." This has to be
the strangest matchup since Mike Tyson chomped on Evander Holy-
field. A portly Larry Holmes is gently caressing the eyeglasses of a
bespectacled businessman with his boxing glove, while at the edge
of the ring a girl in swimsuit and high heels holds up a sign, "ADSL
7 Mbps."

Almost coincidentally, here's George Foreman—*not* in boxing
trunks but dressed in mufti, whee!—with the headline, "High Quality Dependable Brakes, All At a Great Meineke Price!" George is
holding a sign labeled "Lifetime Warranty Brake Pads & Shoes—
Meineke Discount Mufflers." Hey, George, unfair. Even though the
word "All" suggests the heading was intended for other items as
well as brakes, we understand the message. You're not playing the
game.

We're back to normal with this one: "Like a Hammer and Nails
. . ."—and, naturally, a full-color shot of a hammer and three roof-
ing nails. The explanation of the ellipsis can be misleading—"NEBS
checks and forms are *guaranteed* to work with *your* software."
Okay, how do a hammer and nails work with my software? Oh, I get
it. You put the nail on top of your hard disk and you . . . Well, why
not? My ellipsis is as valid as theirs.

Obviously, sitting in front of a computer screen all day causes
some dendrite-damage. Here's another one—full color and bleed, of
course. It's a scuba diver hanging onto a rope that wanders down
and away, not up. Under the picture is the heading: "The Best Way
to Retrace Your Steps." Yeah, if you're looking for your buddies in
the Suicide Club. What are they selling? "Don't get lost in a sea of
calls! *[Get it?]* If you need to retrace your steps, NICE Systems offers
a direct route to the surface." Direct? Yeah, if you go through the
center of the earth.

Here's an elephant jamming its head into the stomach of a hapless man stuck in a phone booth. The comforting headline: "Our massive new hard drive comfortably fits you and your customers." Doesn't look all that comfortable, buddy.

Here's an out-of-focus shot of a racing bike, just the pedals and gears: "HP & Cheyenne *together*. The new force driving tape storage." You mean they can't even afford a car? What if it rains? (I know, I know . . . they'll slide under that insurance umbrella.)

Getting bored? Me, too, especially since this next one is headed "What's your next move?" How many think it's a chess-board? Nuts. There goes the surprise . . . except with this board you could beat Bobby Fischer, since every piece is black.

"No Worries. For complete Fulfillment, COMAR's The Place!" The photograph is one of a 1940s family, with Dad giving his daughter a piggyback ride in front of an old-fashioned radiator. Junior, on Mom's lap, holds a squirt-gun. State-of-the-art antiques? No, they're pitching *order-fulfillment*.

And so it goes. Want twenty more? Neither do I.

So I have a suggestion, if you're creating a message and are about to succumb to SHS (Stupid Huckster Syndrome): Sign the ad with the name of one of your competitors.

Let's Be More Niggardly with Our Euphemisms

Remember when the one literate guy in the unsurprisingly illiterate District of Columbia government was castigated for using the word "niggardly"? Even before then, we should have become overly sensitive to those who are overly sensitive.

And as communicators, we should direct streams of disgust at those who yell "Foul!" at imagined slights. Those who see the devil in the Procter & Gamble logo or Mr. Ed's theme song played backward can target us, too, because our dedication is to *information op-timizing* . . . creating the most positive word-images possible within our command of the lexicon. We have to pre-empt those cretins.

We Aren't "Afraid." We're Just "Cautious."

Do you get the feeling we're operating in fear? The Kosovo mess was and is about *ethnic Albanians*. We swallow the term without chewing on it. Just what are *ethnic* Albanians, anyway? And why do we sanitize extermination by calling it *ethnic cleansing*? Nothing clean about it.

Manufacturers who want to sell direct refer to *disintermediation* instead of *cutting out the middleman*. Suddenly *gambling* doesn't exist any more—it's too declassé. The word is *gaming*.

Those of us in the force-communications business have long since denied that used cars exist. No such thing as a *used* car: It's *pre-owned*. Computer *programs* are what people installed in their computers ten years ago. Today any self-respecting program isn't a program, it's an *application*. And here's an oversized comic book. Comic book? That's what our grandparents read. Today it's a *graphic novel*. Since adding some snazzy new 777s, Continental Airlines doesn't have any machinists. They're *engine shop technicians*.

Then of course we have a whole new lexicon the current wide-open world of sexual information has brought to us. These aren't *porno* or *smutty* videos; they're *adult* videos. They aren't *dirty movies*; they have *mature themes*.

Some historian or anthropologist, a couple of centuries from now, might trace the origins of political correctness to Ronald Reagan or George Bush the First. Their administrations replaced *rebel* with *freedom fighter*. Clever! The euphemism eliminates any possibility of mistaking who the heroes are. Bill Clinton didn't have an affair (or whatever) with Monica Lewinsky; he had an *improper relationship*. Hell, I've had improper relationships with my publishers for years, and now because of Bill Clinton I have to find another term for it or draw stares.

Rosalynn Carter joined the club by objecting to Nestle's taffy bars, Psycho Sam and Loony Larry, as being insensitive to the mentally ill. Uh . . . Rosalynn, before you go too far hark back to the giant rabbit. And take a look at some of the fearless flavors from Ben & Jerry's.

Remember when department stores had Complaint Departments? That wasn't smart of them, so they became Adjustment Departments. Now they're Information Desks . . . closed during store hours.

Drug addicts don't exist any more. They're persons suffering from substance abuse. A janitor who asks for a raise won't get it; instead, he gets a new title: *Sanitation engineer*. And *fireman* has disappeared through the gender gap. It's *firefighter*, which combines sexual equality with Ramboism.

At colleges, we can't call new entries *freshmen*. They have to be *freshpersons*, probably more accurate in contemporary ambience. And *full professor* has too many negative connotations, leading us to realize what they're full of. If we're afraid of *niggardly*, what repercussions might we expect when a student *matriculates*? They'll call out June Allyson (who always seems to be about to cry) with whatever that absorber is she's hawking, and instead of dry eyes there won't be a dry pair of pants in the house.

GENDER EQUALITY

The clamor for equality—unnecessary, as my own household can witness—leads to some strange word combinations. *The International Herald-Tribune* reported on a tennis match in which Venus Williams "woman-handled" her opponent, Anna Kournikova.

Gloria Steinem has resurrected *Ms.* Magazine. But the magazine's philosophy, like its founder, is somewhat more sedate than it was in Ms. Steinem's *Playboy* bunny-bashing years. Then *Ms.* might have attacked terms such as "manhole cover" as being sexist. What might the replacement be? "His/Ms.-hole cover" seems mildly salacious, and "personhole cover" suggests a defective blanket. I guess we've come a long way, baby, but in what direction?

Who would attack *canola oil?* Certainly it's less vicious-sounding at the checkout counter than rape-seed oil (although rape seed is the descendant of the Latin word *rapa,* which, placidly, means *turnip*).

Beauty contests aren't beauty contests any more. They're *pageants.* (The scientific name: *orthodontia vulgaris.*) Wrestling matches have become a little more honest. They're now wrestling *exhibitions.*

And no one has a defect. Short people are *vertically challenged.* Daisy Fuentes and Keanu Reeves aren't untalented; they're *talent-impaired.* The producers who hire them aren't stupid; they're *intellectually challenged.* People don't die; they *pass on.* Their doctors, whose patients *fail to achieve their wellness potential,* haven't misdiagnosed; they just were mild witnesses to *negative patient outcomes.* I guess that means that drunks are *bourbonically oversufficient.*

BACK TO CLARITY?

But a backlash is under way. I actually heard a doctor refer to *older folks* and not *senior citizens* or *chronologically challenged.* I saw an ad—online, naturally—referring to a video offering not as an adult movie but as *pure porn.* And weight reduction plans have given up on euphemisms such as *take off inches* and gone back to the more graphic, ergo more dynamic, *melt away fat.* So maybe we're in a renaissance of candor. Maybe being politically correct isn't the Kingdom of Heaven it was even a year or two ago. Well, thank heaven.

(Or to be correct, should that be Heaven? The Great Beyond? That Great Response Device in the Sky? Or just plain Lewis's Follies?)

New and Improved: A Good Old-fashioned Home-made Original

How big a house do you need to make "home-made" ice cream?

If you have one of those electric gadgets that can turn out a pint of mushy ice cream for about eleven dollars' worth of ingredients, you can prepare that pint in a studio apartment. But you'd need every room in a mansion to supply a chain of stores.

My son Bob (*InfoWorld* columnist) took his two little daughters out for some ice cream. He chuckled when he told me about it:

"It's called 'Kemp's Home-Made ice cream,'" he said. "They sell it in a couple of hundred stores. I'd like to go to their house and watch Mrs. Kemp wrestling with half a ton of chocolate syrup."

The "home-made"conceit set me to thinking about all the phrases we in the force-communication universe corrupt in our mindless grappling for attention and sales.

One of the most obvious . . . and it also applies to ice cream . . . is "old-fashioned." Curious, isn't it, in the rocket-speed Internet era, that we venerate the past when we're describing a space-age pistachio-nut concoction. Oh, we understand the sales pitch behind the label: Contemporary products, they tell us, are loaded with ersatz ingredients such as sawdust and iron filings and camel dung; theirs come from cows whose udders are massaged with Jergen's Lotion.

So okay, "old-fashioned" can be a smart (if semi-subliminal) marketing ploy. But please, please, refuse to buy any item advertising itself as "old-fashion." Truncating the phrase is the work of semi-literates, and if you patronize them what does that say about *you*?

Two curious descriptions are "original" and "new and improved."

Even more curious is the oxymoron resulting from combining them—a symbol of copywriting desperation. (My old friend Don Logay points out that the two terms are mutually exclusive—something can't be both "new" and "improved.")

What benefit does the word "original" transmit? In one of its purer interpretations, the word means *unchanged*. First (original) definition, American Heritage Dictionary: "Preceding all others in time." Would you want to be writing or handling a layout or doing a spreadsheet with your *original* computer, which in 1986 was the wonder of its time with 20 megabytes of memory and 4 megabytes of RAM? Would you want to submit yourself to the *original* treatment for many illnesses—heated cups stuck onto your back by the local barber?

"New and improved" is a nondescript non-description. In what way? I remember without any particular fondness reading that phrase on containers of the semi-tasteless orange drink Tang. Oh, yeah, I had to admire the honesty behind it—"The previous formulation wasn't very good but we marketed it anyway."

"New and improved" somehow parallels a sign on a failed business: "Under new management." So what? Those of us whose incomes depend on success in driving customers or clients through the door certainly ought to know that *benefit* outsells thin chest-thumping. In what way is it new? In what way is it improved? Or is the claim a hope that dissatisfied buyers will ignore their previous disgruntlement?

Yeah, I'm being wry, but the conclusion isn't wry: Whatever use we make of "original" and "new and improved," we have better expressions at our command; or, at least, as professionals we *should* have better expressions at our command.

ADDING TO THE LIST

Let's add two massive entries to our list: "heavy duty" and "heavy-weight." I admit to being a sometime patron of "heavy duty";

but after buying some "heavy duty" AA batteries at Walgreens, I no longer can accept the term without challenging it as puffery. Wouldn't it be nice if our bureau-crazed government added one more: The Department of Heavy Duty Evaluation?

"Heavyweight" doesn't carry as heavy a burden as "heavy duty," so let's consider this just a preliminary warning, a caution: If you describe something as a heavyweight, meaning anything other than avoirdupois, accompany that claim with an explanation.

Which brings us to "discount." Living in Florida, I've become immunized to the word, which attaches itself leechlike to stores and space ads and mailings and Web offerings, often mindlessly and often duplicitously. Oh, it still works on the unaware. For those of us whose skepticism it regularly feeds, the word needs validation. Who has been responsible for the latter-day rash of unbacked claims of"discount"? Wal-Mart? No, Wal-Mart's prices actually are discounted. A simple demand: Discounted from *what*?

What else? "King-size." For beds and bedding, it's a measurable absolute. For a claim from the clouds, it conjures up the image of getting something bigger and/or more intense than we're paying for. We see the intensification at work in "King-size discount." The Mother of all discounts? Based on the typical shouter of the phrase, it should only be.

A recent addition—in fact, I'd place it from 1998 upward—is "Enterprise." Now, this isn't the original *enterprise* as we've always known it; nor is it the starship. No, no, it's the new and improved *Enterprise* with a capital "E," grasped to the bosom of electron-lovers. We see magazine columns and entire books with the "Enterprise Computing" title. What does it mean? I've asked several who inhabit that half-world to explain the term; invariably the answer is something like, "It's the whole thing . . . the entire . . . well, the entire enterprise." Oh. Thanks.

One more for now: "World class." I have no idea whence this phrase came; somehow I associate it with that marvel of corruption, the Olympic Games. But maybe I'm wrong. Our shrunken globe, rubber-banded into a tight little ball by jet aircraft and discounted (for real) fares, has eliminated many of the peaks and valleys we used to assume were there, between Texas and Tajikistan. So "world class" already may be on the route to join "23 skiddoo" and "hooch inspector" and "cuspidor" as a once-active expression.

Aw, enough already. Are these the only candidates? Even as you read this, you undoubtedly have others to contribute. If you have some favorites, tell me so and we might immortalize them and you in another book of harangues. But don't give me "ultimate" or "your partner in. . . ." I'm saving those.

Customer Abuse

You may be gathering, by this point in the text, that the divisions are somewhat artificial. Some comments might easily have migrated from one section to another.

No matter. If you've read this far, you're as determined a curmudgeon as I am. That means you're as disgusted with smug, in-your-face advertising as I am, as revolted by advertising copy laced with asterisks as I am, as sickened by marketing messages constructed by an in-group for an in-group and foisted on us, the out-group, as I am.

The marketing murderers turn loose all those smug spokespeople who can't quite conceal the sneers underlying their smiles. We're supposed to not only react to those spokespeople but adore them. Hey, guys, the days of we'll-follow-you-anywhere spokespeople such as Arthur Godfrey and Dinah Shore are over. We're in the Age of Skepticism, remember? Get out of my face!

One of the most common symbols of customer abuse is the asterisk. That little demon has done more to destroy customer and prospect confidence than any element since Ponzi. And from its humble beginnings as a footnote (often hidden in mice-type) in insurance and financial offers, the asterisk has migrated to a position of unpleasant prominence in letters.

Hasn't anyone told these asteriskers that an asterisk in a letter not only brings the message to a dead stop but also is an instant negative-generator? We know . . . we *know* . . . bad news is about to strike. Equally bad, we lose any momentum the letter may have initiated, because we have to hunt for the bad news. Where is it? Is it at the bottom of the page, where our tired eye has to hunt it out and then, sadder and wiser, come back to the promise it belies? Oh, it isn't there? Then we'd better look at the end of the message. Yes, there it squats, together with double asterisks and daggers and other disclaimers. Ugh.

Whatever happened to sincerity? Whatever happened to clear, forthright messages, which didn't leave us shaking our heads or reluctantly responding *in spite of* our misgivings?

Now, don't get me wrong. Puffery is part of our game, and we all love being in this game. But can you see the direction so much advertising and marketing is taking, in which marketers who have a genuine and undiluted offer feel they have to descend into duplicity to match competitors whose motives aren't as pure? And the whole universe becomes contaminated.

Warning signs are all over the place. The phrase "public confidence" has become an oxymoron.

Every now and then we see a religious fanatic carrying a sign worded "The end is near." Those of us who toil in the furnaces of force-communication could do well to heed those signs, hoisted subliminally but with increasing visibility inside our own vulnerable universe. It's like global warming: We don't have a lot of time left.

Certainly there's advertising clutter. Certainly it's more and more difficult to break out of that clutter. Certainly the clamor for attention has brought panic and frenzy to our ranks.

True, true. But yielding to panic by sticking it to our prospects is—your choice: a) cowardly; b) unprofessional; c) thoughtless; d) con-artist; d) conscienceless; e) tunnel-visioned; f) all of the above.

As this next group of marketing mayhem examples shows, these peccadilloes don't pass unnoticed. Wouldn't it be beneficial for the entire world of marketing if our targets joined the ranks of conscientious objectors and said to those who perpetuate the transgressions: The end is near. Wouldn't it?

With that imprecation, take a look at some case histories:

Service with a Snile

You're reading right: The word is "snile," my invented word for the combination of smile and sneer.

We seem to be getting a lot of sniles in the mail and online these days. It's the marriage of "Lucky you" and "Who, me?" . . . liberally doused with *caveat emptor* (just in case: "Let the buyer beware").

I've reached the point of looking for a catch. Usually it's there. By not being disappointed because I've found duplicity, I save myself the disappointment of falling for duplicity.

Here's an offer for "The Card That's Miles Above The Rest." Suspicion is implicit, because the heading is caps and lower case (a great way to keep score!). Okay, in what way is this card miles above the rest? A grid compares it with American Airlines' Aadvantage, Delta Skymiles, and United's Mileage Plus First. Looks pretty good, even with the mice-type warning, "Capital One has the right to change or cancel this Miles*One* program at any time." So why is my e.s.p. bristling?

Well, here's one hidden gem: I can't combine these miles with any others. So if I want a free round-trip *economy* ticket to Asia, I have to spend $75,000 with this credit card, to get 75,000 miles. But hold it: There's a monthly limit on the number of miles, and every mile expires in five years. And if the published rate is higher than $1500 these miles don't qualify. For that matter, the basic pitch—"a free round-trip coach ticket to anywhere within a zone*" for 18,000 miles—applies only if the published fare is $360 or less. Even without that accursed asterisk, I'm wondering about paying an annual fee for this card. Oh . . . here's an explanation: "Complete information on this Miles*one* program will be sent to you after your account is opened." Gee, thanks. Who can resist this sniling offer?

A communication that sniles even wider is a fax—a *fax*, damn it—that's one of the contemporary descendants of those fake Wall Street Journal pages with a stick-on note saying, "Herschell, this will interest you. J." This fax is a fake bylined news story headed, "Homeowners Beware—'Wow! Was I being ripped off!'"

The subhead says a local lender "reveals how to save thousands on Mortgage and Credit Card interest charges." Handwritten in the margin is "Thought you might find this interesting," with illegible initials. The pitch is, on analysis, funny, winding up, "As a very experienced financial analyst, I give this service my highest recommendation." Y'know, I have to tip my hat to this promotion, because it almost smacks of integrity. Just the last two words of this supposed news story, "Call Now!" tosses it back into the Snile Pit.

An Internet provider sent me a check for $3.50. I admit, I'm intrigued by the amount. And I could see the sender sniling as he/she/it structured the legend on the back of the check: "Endorsement and deposit constitute agreement of desire to utilize service and agreement pursuant to terms attached. NOTICE: Payee agrees to terms of $29.95 monthly, due and payable in advance." Snile when you say that, podner. Anyway, I have a personal vow to avoid doing business with anybody who uses the word *utilize*.

Moving on into the sniling labyrinth, I have a "Voucher Certificate" for $41,750.00. Now, *that's* more like it, and it brings a smile to my face. It's a loan offer, with a lovely asterisk that says "Actual loan amount may vary. See reverse for details." Well, of course: "This offer is contingent upon receiving a valid first or second lien on your owner-occupied, one-to-four family residence or condominium. . . ." Sigh.

LET A SNILE BE YOUR UMBRELLA.

Lisa von Freiberg of Omaha Steaks sent me a dilly of a sniling message from Who's Who in Canine America, Ltd. The envelope says, "Your Dog Has Been Awarded An Honor Money Can't Buy." Aside from the caps/l.c. giveaway, the concept boggles the mind.

Here is "an honor offered to less than 1% of all dogs and their owners in America." No charge for inclusion, but a copy of this strange and exotic volume is $49.95. How did they get their mailing list? Lisa guesses that her vet would be sniling at this very moment, except that she never has owned a dog and is, in fact, allergic to them. She's willing, though, to consider a volume titled "Who's Who Among Non-Pet Owners." Okay, Rover, Spot, and Buster. We'll include your photograph in this extraordinary use of wood-pulp, gobbling up trees you otherwise might have used for more appropriate purposes. Snile!

P.R. whiz Grace Cohen sent me a sniler from—who else—American Express, that master of obfuscation and MBA-speak. The envelope says, "Presenting your new monthly statement. It's simply better." Yeah, for a team of accountants. Inside is a six-point "Cliff Notes" primer, with callouts directing me to a form that rivals the IRS for complexity. Some of those callouts can turn a snile into a belly-laugh. Example: "We've made it easier to pay your balance, including Sign & Travel charges, in full." Oh? You've made it easier? Does that mean a discount? Or does it mean a uniformed attendant will arrive to pick up the payment?

Hey, here's an envelope that says, "Automatic insurance protection—paid in <u>full</u> for you." Sure, why not? Well, by gum, the letter, addressed to my wife and me, begins, "At Washington Mutual, we're concerned about your financial security. That's why we're giving you $1,000 in insurance coverage <u>at no cost to you whatsoever.</u> We pay the premiums—just sign and return the enclosed form."

What nice guys they are! Now, where's that enclosed form? Uh-oh. No sniles here. Sure enough, it's $1,000 in Accidental Death and Dismemberment Insurance. I have the option of buying more, but it doesn't seem to be mandatory. So what's to lose, except my question: What's a legitimate offer doing in the snile-house?

Maybe this: Maybe it's like Pandora's Box, where the last factor to escape is Hope. Maybe if enough marketers actually deliver what they promise, sniles will turn into smiles. Grins, even.

Get Out of My Face!

I don't like smugness. I don't like smug advertising messages. I don't like smug people who smugly deliver smug advertising messages.

So I admit, with no shame whatever: I don't like Dennis Miller as a spokesman for *anything*.

Dennis Miller typifies the in-your-face smugness that's too common in today's TV-dominated marketing ambience: Celebrities are allowed to glorify themselves more than what they're supposed to be hawking. A few years ago, for reasons known only to some obscure deity, he became spokesman for a chain of pizza restaurants. I've forgotten (mercifully for both me and the pizza chain) which one; I do remember eliminating that brand from any buying consideration.

Now Dennis Miller is pitching a long distance phone service. While I can't blame him for the execrable copy, I certainly can blame him for the know-it-all delivery. He hasn't mellowed. Neither have I.

Oh, Dennis Miller is a flea in the ear, and I really can't justify on logical grounds devoting such negative attention to him. But you see, it isn't Dennis Miller who's the target. It's what he represents.

We're seeing an epidemic of advertising that even a couple of years ago wouldn't even have been accepted by the media in which the ads run. A whiskey refers to itself as "The best damned Scotch . . .": Analyze the shift in marketing philosophy behind this in-your-face verbalism for what traditionally has been the most sedate of all drunken libations.

SOCIETAL DEVOLUTION

A societal change? So what? Let movies, not ads and mailers, be the mirrors. (Had my friend John Waters produced a movie titled "Pecker" even a few years ago, most newspapers would have rejected the ads . . . which today causes not even a stir).

How many ads have you seen lately that proudly tout a product as the one that "kicks butt"? See my point? This isn't dumbing-down; it's devolving-down, an early indicator of social deterioration.

Miller Lite beer suffered—deservedly—because of a totally stupid and ineffective campaign centered around a troglodytic nerd named Dick. Sales plummeted, as they certainly deserved to do. The advertising agency took the blame, although *somebody* at Miller had approved the asinine concept.

The Miller campaign is peripheral to the next example. I may be giving more credit than is actually due to PointCast, which in a series of full-page ads, had this as the selling copy:

They gave you Dick.
We give you Richard.

The subhead: "That's the Senior V.P. Richard who lives in L.A., drives a BMW and wants to buy a DVD player and a kayak."

Oh, we understand the demographic intention. But if you aren't jarred by that first line, I salute you for having been insulated from low-level schoolyard epithets. If you are jarred, you may wonder, as I do, not only about both this marketer's degenerated dignity, but also about the damage to all our futures as force-communicators if in-your-face messages become total replacements for salesmanship.

PointCast isn't alone in schoolyard smirk-humor. Director-Search, a company in the peculiar business of supplying directors for tv commercials, had this huge heading on its full-page ad:

Is that a hard drive in your pocket or are you just happy to see us?

An ad for Glenfiddich Scotch has this heading:

Made the same damn way since 1887.

I can envision a bartender saying that; as an ad in *The New Yorker*, it may be a stopper . . . today, but probably not two years from now if it's indicative of future in-your-face messages.

Glenfiddich is mild (at last it's message is comparatively mild) compared with Smirnoff vodka:

"This Himalayan vodka is supposed to make me fashionable, hip and on the cutting edge. What does your Smirnoff make you?"

"A kick-ass martini."

So we're unsurprised on two levels by:

"I've played so much guitar it'd make your ass hurt."

Why two levels? First, it's for Winston cigarettes; second, it's in *Yahoo* magazine, which also has a semi-impenetrable ad for an on-line company called Bluefly.com:

Your fly is open

A space ad in a computer magazine:

Should we call it E*TRADE 98? E-TRADE 2.0? Or E-TRADE kicks butt?

The posterior seems to be the current target as this type of ad bottoms out and its exponents ass-ess its effectiveness. <u>www.movi-ola.com</u> has a full-color, full-page bleed ad with this heading:

Get off your ass.

National Telecommunications Services says:

Democrats! If you want to kick some Republican butt, we're your phone firm.

Dataman Group says:

Kick butt and take names . . . we've got the names.

How clever can you get?

Lincoln, one of the more sober automobile advertisers, shows a full-page photograph of its SUV with this heading:

Kick derrière.

Okay, Lincoln's ad is mildly charming. But it's mildly charming only because we can relate it to the other ads we're now seeing. Would it have appeared at all if we weren't midway through a transition?

That last question isn't as rhetorical as it might seem at first glance. If you listen to radio talk-show hosts you may be hearing language that would have had them kicked off the air even five years ago. Heck, make that three.

And what sea-change have we witnessed over the last three years? Emergence of an Internet "kultur," that's what.

You might say, "If we can accept "architect" as a verb we can accept butt-kicking as an advertising exercise." Okay, we're doubly infected.

It's your call, whether you think the Internet deserves a large part of the responsibility or a large part of the credit for these ads. Are they advances or aberrations? Please, though: Think carefully before embracing them as "New Age." The last two cultures to enjoy a New Age were the Roman Empire and Nazi Germany, and look what happened to them.

Yes, we're the logical and designated mirrors of society. And here are our professional representatives, playing a game of "Mirror, Mirror on the Wall, Who's the Fairest One of All?" . . . without considering that what the mirror shows might be warts.

Your Call Is Important to Us. Please Rot on the Line.

One of the great lies of our time: The recorded voice saying,"Your call is important to us."

I've come to believe this statement was created by sadistic customer-haters who sit by their phones, laughing and scratching, saying to themselves, "Let the suckers suffer."

Hearing "Your call is important to us. Stay on the line and one of our representatives will be with you shortly," is an order-losing indication of vendor naïveté and stupidity when hooked to a phone line dedicated to original orders. It becomes a fib when used as a way of avoiding ample post-sale service.

My most recent run-in with this inducement to high blood pressure came when the hard disk on one of my computers froze. I had bought the thing, loyal subject that I am to the buy-direct crown, from a mail order source. The transaction was less than three months old, which meant the warranty was still in place. So I called the toll-free service number. And please note, when evaluating this adventure: I called about one pm Eastern time.

The phone rang. It rang a second time. It kept ringing. Doggedly I hung on; after all, it was the middle of the business day. After 18 rings—no kidding, 18 rings (I know because I called this number four separate times, with identical results)—*click/click* . . . and this recording, in a neither friendly nor unfriendly woman's voice, word-for-word:

> Thank you for calling Comtrade's customer service and technical support department. Customer service hours of operation are seven am to twelve-thirty pm, and one-thirty p.m. to seven p.m. Pacific time, Monday through Friday. On Saturday, customer service hours are eight a.m. to five p.m. Pacific time. Currently all of our representatives are on the line. Please try your call again later. For 24 hour response, fax your inquiry to 818-330-1829. That number again is 818-330-1829. Remember to include both your invoice number and fax number. Thank you again for your patience. Thank you for calling. Good-bye.
> *Click. Dial tone.*

Now, what?

A PERFECT CATCH-22:

Eventually, for those hardy souls who hang in there, an answer exists . . . only it isn't an answer, it's a connection with a device that spouts without accepting input. And this one—clever devils!—doesn't give the caller the option of hanging on the line until hunger, exhaustion, or a change of seasons defeats him or her. It ends not with a bang, but with the caller's whimper.

In this instance, after four traumatic experiences the first day and two the second, I faxed that area 818 number. Three days went by. I know—the dog ate my fax.

So, defeated, I called the company's regular line, another area 818 number. (What the hell—it's only a toll call. My hard disk is frozen and I'm on a backup computer.)

Oh, they answer *this* line on the second ring. It might be an order coming through, not an existing customer struggling with a defective component.

This time, tee-hee, *they* were the ones who were nonplused. I turned down the invitation to call the toll-free service line, explaining I had been that route. While I was in the neighborhood, I rid myself of a couple of aggressions by asking whether they had one, one-half, or no actual service representatives on staff and, if they actually did have one, whether he or she had a phone or was simply a bemused observer of the human scene.

Some of these companies have no sense of humor. I had to call that 818 number yet another time and ask for a supervisor. "We don't have supervisors." Well, that was self-evident. Eventually I actually reached someone with a brain-pan, who asked me to send back the hard drive.

"Can I depend on you to send me a replacement today? I'll send the original hard drive back by overnight courier today."

Customer service is an oxymoron: "We can only ship by UPS ground unless you give us a FedEx number to charge it to." So I gave her my FedEx number, and with mutual mumblings of dissatisfaction, the conversation ended.

So okay, I had to call in my computer guru to open the box and take out the hard disk. Out it went that same day.

Wait, the story hasn't ended.

Naturally, the next day came and went. No new hard drive. So once again I went through the drill of trying the service number, waiting through the 18 rings, and getting a "Thank you again for your patience. Thank you for calling. Good-bye."

Back to the toll call. When I asked for the person I had talked to, nobody—and I mean *nobody*—had ever heard of her. Resorting to the role of Hellraiser, I rousted out another service person. He said, "We can't do a thing until you return the other hard drive." I explained that I had and gave him the airbill number. "Hold on."

Hold on? I didn't dare disconnect, because he hadn't identified himself, and I knew if I called again, he wouldn't exist. Eventually he came back on the line: "We don't have another gig drive of that capacity. We can send you one with a smaller capacity."

I won't bore you with the eventual non-resolution; this individual episode now is an anecdote. What *isn't* funny is the cavalier attitude so many direct marketers take toward post-sale relations.

You know, as I do: The person or company that has bought from you before is *seven* times more likely to respond to your next offer than a cold-list name. Walking away after the sale, undermanning service and technical support—these are deadly corporate doctrines that damage other mail order companies whose business philosophy is a little more benevolent and a little more sensible.

If you're in the marketing end of your company and have even a one percent influence over post-sale relations, try this experiment: Call your own company's service or tech-support line as though you were a customer.

If you get the same treatment I did in this instance, roll some heads. Not to worry: They're probably empty anyway.

"And How Are You Today?" "Terrible, Thanks."

"Hello, Mrs. Lewis? How are you today?"

What a deadly dead-giveaway! Some infernal machine is stamping out robots who write this boiler-plate opening . . . then turning the scripts over to other robots who read it.

Ever since I hung up on one of those "Hi, how are you today?" calls and found out later it was a tennis buddy calling me for a game, I've listened to certify the call's phoniness. My wife isn't so benevolent.

Depending on her mood of the moment, she'll either remind the caller of Florida's new law which imposes a fine of $5,000 on those who call "don't-call-us" numbers listed with the Direct Marketing Association (ours isn't), or she'll actually answer the question:

> Not so good, I'm afraid, since the dog died. You see, the dog was in the garage when it caught fire. We really hadn't expected the fire to spread from the house, but hadn't realized one of the cars was parked right next to the house. Our housekeeper did, but she wasn't able to get out of the car before the gas-tank exploded . . ."

And on she goes, until the befuddled caller either mumbles "I'm sorry" and hangs up, or until she gets bored and hangs up herself.

Now, look: I'm not railing against telemarketing. I'm absolutely denouncing *mindless* telemarketing and *invasive* telemarketing.

Three relevant opinions:

1. No question about it—the telemarketing industry is in hot water.

2. No question about it—many of the criticisms and crackdowns are deserved.

3. No question about it—many telemarketers are victims of a bleed-over effect of criticism generated by their less-ethical counterparts.

State after state has passed anti-telemarketing legislation, some strangling-restrictive and some more a warning than a legal move. What has (or should have) all telemarketers worried is the threat of national legislation—the Telephone Consumer Protection Act, which would award $500 to $1,000 in damages if repeated recorded calls were made to a number.

The Omens Are There.

The Supreme Court ruled that a Minnesota ban on pre-recorded au-
todialed messages is *not* a violation of the first amendment. You
know who attacked that ban? A company that had made more than
800 calls to one number—a hospital.

Now, why would a state ban or restrict autodialing, which only
a few years ago was a pleasant novelty?

You know the answer: user abuse. So 42 states already have
statutes . . . which wouldn't be there if the industry kept its head.
You also know the drill: One company pushes the limit *and increases response*; to be competitive, others do the same. It's like
those airline fare wars, where everybody loses.

And here's the core of the problem: How many telemarketing
companies exist? What the heck, it's a $400 billion business, involv-
ing 3.4 million people. How can I, calling Mrs. Sample to sell a subscription (in the guise of a "market survey"), know you just called
trying to sell her oil leases (in the guise of a market survey)? How
do I know my pre-recorded message doesn't ring hard on the heels
of yours

Whose fraud is it, anyway? The Federal Trade Commission has
emerged from its cocoon of the golden days in which it was tele-
marketer-friendly . . . or at least, not telemarketer-antagonistic.

According to the FTC, victims of telemarketing fraud—and a
"victim" seems to be anybody who decides he or she is a victim—
recouped only 25 cents on the dollar of money judges ordered telemarketers to repay.

In fact, the FBI says when that bureau successfully nailed 100
fraudulent telemarketers (in 12 different states) in a sting called
"Operation Disconnect," sure enough some smart cookie was con-
tacting victims, claiming to represent Operation Disconnect, and offering to get individual restitution for a $424 fee. How was this
contact made? By phone.

The late Gerald Arenberg, who headed two non-profit organizations—the American Federation of Police and the National Association of Chiefs of Police—once pointed out two problems for the telemarketer trying to comply with the crazy quilt of state regulations:

"Every state has its own peculiarities. For a while Florida prohibited us from saying we're a charitable organization and Illinois demanded we say we're a charitable organization. Imagine having to change the approach in every state.

"Our contract with various telemarketers demands complete compliance. But unless we're sitting in the room with them, they tend to get greedy. Unless that telemarketer has the soul of a saint, the commercial telemarketer can get a client in hot water."

Arenberg added to the stew another problem unique to telemarketers: Competing organizations, he said, sometimes make calls using your name, making outrageous statements and claims designed to get states attorneys rushing for their writs.

Ugh, what an image! In one seminal year, the FBI said it made 202 arrests for wire fraud at 123 telemarketing "boiler rooms." The principal transgression: promising something over the phone, then delivering something worth much less . . . or nothing at all.

A bylined newspaper story that same month quoted FTC documents: Judges ordered phone marketers to repay $197 million in 80 fraud lawsuits. How much has been repaid? About $50 million, with $30 million more being held in frozen accounts or by receivers.

The nature of the story was to isolate telemarketers as scoundrels for not paying judgments. In fact, FTC officials said many phone marketers declare bankruptcy to avoid making refunds.

Come on! Lots of companies declare bankruptcy; Johns-Manville did it to avoid paying claims, and nobody singled out that company as being shady. If telemarketers were airlines, the FTC wouldn't be so vocal. The Commission has a natural target, one so loaded with abuses they can make a generic accusation.

Therein lies the peril for all of us. Telemarketing not only is part of marketing; it's an integral part. The jackals already are baying at our heels, with that black, greasy word "Fraud."

Hey, kids, we're all playing in the same sandbox. I have three suggestions to restore just a glimmer of telemarketing's luster, which in the public mind—even though not in our own—is pitted with tarnish:

1. For the rest of your life, plus six months, never again open a pitch with "How are you today?"

2. Have an ombudsman whose income doesn't depend on sales volume monitor scripts for integrity . . . and calls for accuracy.

3. Fire any telemarketer whose ad libs change the thrust of the sales argument.

Do we have a deal? If we do, when direct marketers call each other to ask, "How are you today?" we'll be able to answer, "Just fine."

The Decline and Fall of Telephone Manners

Maybe it's the fault of e-mail, which has condensed communication into a tight ball. The niceties of conversation have been squeezed out.

That isn't necessarily bad. Effective force-communication tends to be in direct ratio to getting to the point.

But e-mail and telemarketing are two different sales procedures. Society hasn't yet devolved into total chaos, and manners still have some position when we analyze or respond to a pitch originating with a human voice.

So when the phone rings, and a voice of questionable humanity demands harshly, "Lewis, please," recognition of two factors is swift:

1. The caller doesn't know me.

2. The word "please" has no significance to either party.

Despite what I just said in the previous section, some telemarketing companies still provide their unwitting pitchpeople with antediluvian scripts that begin, "How are you today?" As pitiable as this approach has become, it's preferable to the latest anti-rapport approach in which the caller seems to have been instructed to assume a position of dominance: "Achtung! Der Feuhrer calling."

Assuming dominance is easy. All one does is emphasize "I" instead of "You." Nothing to it. Thump your chest and you're dominant . . . assuming the person you're calling lets you get away with it.

Sure. Just limit your calls to wimps. List companies probably have them categorized, and you can cross-match them with Mylanta-swallowers.

One More Crack in the Veneer

Well, yes, the "Bowl 'em over" approach probably does work on some people. But aside from generating post-call Buyer's Remorse, isn't this another crack in what once was smooth telemarketing veneer?

My business phone rings. My wife answers it. The caller's voice is rough and demanding: "I have to talk to Herschell Gordon Lewis."

Our end: "May I ask who is calling?"

His end: "Huh?"

Our end: "May I ask who is calling?"

His end: "Marsden."

Our end: "With what company?"

His end: "What difference does that make?"

Oh, it makes a difference. The call didn't go through.

Now, suppose (and it's possible) the call wasn't from a telemarketer. Instead, it was from a potential client, eager to shower me with money for writing copy or criticizing his creative work. Who is the loser?

Don't tell me I'm the loser by avoiding a possible business relationship with a bully. Everybody in our business knows the pitfalls attending a no-respect beginning. No matter how well, how professionally, how effectively a job is completed, the bully has to justify his position by finding fault.

Perfect timing! The phone just rang.

Our end: "Lewis Enterprises."

His end: "Do y'all take credit cards for payment?"

Our end: "For what?"

His end: "I'm calling Lewis Enterprises. I'm doing a survey. Do you accept credit cards?"

Notice, please: If this guy actually was doing a survey, he and whoever scripted him both need help. Why couldn't he have said, "Good morning. My name is Joe Glutz. My company, International Research, has been hired to do a survey of businesses. Can you tell me: Do you accept credit cards for payment?"

In another episode this very day, our third business line rang. The first two lines weren't in use. Now, that in itself is a giveaway: Somebody is dialing numbers automatically, unaware and unconcerned. So it's the middle of the business day. So what? So the call is instantly recognizable as an unsolicited pitch, even before the first word comes tumbling out. So what? They deal in bulk selection, in both their employees and their targets.

The call: "Who is in charge of health insurance?"

Any number of wry answers come to mind: "The president of the United States, but he seems to have run into a roadblock"; "Oh, that person is in the hospital"; "Health insurance? What's that?"; "Who the hell wants to know?"

That last one is visceral, not usually spoken. But what causes the viscera to be in an uproar? The substitution of *demand* for *request*. That's the infernal development we seem to be witnessing.

WHO IS APPROVING THESE SCRIPTS?

If today's society offered a kinder, gentler business ambience, one would expect telemarketing scripts to be subject to a final pass/no-pass inspection by somebody—*anybody*—who has a nodding acquaintanceship with primitive sales psychology. You'd think they'd know a telephone pitch is dead in the water unless it makes at least a feeble attempt to establish rapport. But rapport has given way to its sworn enemy, arrogance. Who advises these people, anyway?

If you're old enough, you remember when we used to feel guilty, turning down an unsolicited (but politely offered) proposition on the phone. These days, when we hang up on an unsolicited call or a semi-literate voice or the computerized demand, "Please stay on the line for an important message," we feel a flash of satisfaction: That'll show 'em who's in charge here.

The relationships have changed, and not for the better. Proof is that we're willing to risk alienating a caller who actually wants to do business with us if it means alienating a caller who doesn't care about our sensibilities. As Jimmy Durante used to say, "What a revoltin' development!"

Au Revoir to an Old . . .
but ex . . . Friend.

What do you do when an old friend, whom you've nurtured and defended through tough times, sneers at your friendship?

If you have any self-respect, you walk away in dignity. And that's what I'm doing with WordPerfect, the word processing program (or "application," as current terminology describes it).

My relationship with WordPerfect goes way, way back to version 3.0. I touted WordPerfect when WordStar was king. I applauded WordPerfect when it introduced innovation after innovation. I stood astutely at its shoulder during the strange and lean period when Novell owned it and opened the gates for MSWord to achieve dominance. Even after installing MSWord, I used Word only when I had to send or read a disk or e-mail in that format.

Then Corel, a company headquartered in Ottawa, bought WordPerfect. Wow! Great times were ahead. And out came version 7, which closed the gap with MSWord and even made it possible to send communications in both formats. Nice recovery, guys.

One reason it made sense to stay with WordPerfect was the company's legendary technical support. One could call toll-free at almost any hour and reach a helpful technician who would stay with us until the problem was solved.

An invitation came in the mail: I was invited to a demonstration of WordPerfect Office 2000, which includes WordPerfect 9. Off I went. The silver-tongued demonstrator showed a batch of improvements, ranging from being able to place the cursor anywhere on the page and start typing there, to improved speech-to-text capability. The sales pitch promised free tech support for 30 days. Oh, well, I'd either conquer new challenges in 30 days or not at all. I ordered version 9 on the spot.

In it came, a whole bunch of CD-ROMS and the strangest User

Guide I've ever come across. I installed the whole shebang. Unlike previous versions, some components, such as macros, seemed to be empty files; the "save" feature seemed to go nowhere; and other unexplained changes challenged my non-technie user skills.

HELP, HELP

When I went into the "Help" menu, it became the Hell menu. I wanted to know what had happened to the macros. Nothing there. I wanted to know what the "save" options are. Nothing there. All the references to tech support were for version 8, not version 9, and a nasty message said that "Classic Support will be discontinued as of April 1." Hey, old friends, this version came to me long after April 1.

So okay, I called the number, even knowing that number might not be apt. After the usual interminable "Press one," "press two," "press three," and a substantial wait, I reached a live voice who listened to my problems, asked a bunch of personal questions, and then said, "To get help will cost you twenty-five dollars." I explained that the sales pitch had included a promise of 30 days' tech support, of which two days had elapsed. He wasn't impressed. "To take advantage of that system, call area 716-871-2325. That's all I can do for you." I asked if he'd give me the number of the Corel executive offices. "This is just tech support. We don't have those numbers." So I was discarded, like a squeezed lemon.

Naïf that I am, I called that area 716 number. Again, considerable time spent wading through various menus. Then, pressing what was supposed to be the right set of keys, a series of "Thank you for your patience," followed by huge gaps of times. After 18 minutes, I hung up, still informationless.

Like the guy who was bitten by a shark and then jumped back into the water just to be sure it was a shark who bit him, I dialed the number again, determined to enrich the phone company until somebody answered. After 21 fruitless minutes, guess what: Corel disconnected me.

ONE MORE SHOT

One more interminable and fruitless wait. Sure, I'd have been better off paying the twenty-five bucks, but who knew how disgusting the proletarian version would be?

So I reached what is too standard a conclusion in this Information Age. Corporate think is: It's our information, not yours, and if you want it you'll have to sweat for it. Here is supposed tech support for a new program, and it's probably manned by one guy who's on coffee break, walking to Denny's half a mile away.

In the quiet rage that follows betrayal, I wasted two calls: One to Ottawa information and one to Corel, to get the name of the CEO: Grudgingly—Dr. Michael Cowpland. Off went a letter to Dr. Michael Cowpland, explaining in clear English-language prose what the circumstances were and suggesting that he might try to reach somebody on that area 716 number.

Lots of luck. I could send a communication to the Dead Letter Office and get more satisfaction.

Well, minor satisfaction. Corporate reversals at Corel. Cowpland is long gone and I'm still here.

So, Dr. Cowpland, your hapless successor, and whoever remains of your misguided minions, au revoir. I'm off to Microsoft-Land, where at least the perils are known. As a disgruntled and disillusioned alumnus of WordPerfect, I leave with both regret and relief.

So why am I inflicting this annoying tale on the readers of this book, who undoubtedly have software horror stories of their own to share?

I'll tell you why:

If there be a moral to this tale of commercial immorality, it's this: Force-communication—getting someone to respond—is a one-way street. But loyalty is a two-way street. Vendors complain and complain about the lack of customer loyalty. Hey, fellows, show us a little and we'll show you a lot. But the "Me" generation has penetrated to the core of business, and that's why customers and clients don't even consider loyalty when making their next buying decision.

Like so many other marketing writers, I've created letters and brochures and question/answer forms and response devices and envelope copy and of course ads, all of which make a promise (based on what we ourselves have been told). That's what *we* do. What the originators of these applications are supposed to do is *implement* these promises.

We wallow in the Age of Skepticism. Wouldn't it make sense for those who have the power to nibble away at public skepticism— whether in government, in business, or in interpersonal relations— to assume just a little responsibility as a complement to their natural ego and greed?

What's the most discouraging is that WordPerfect and Corel aren't isolated examples. No, no, they're *typical* examples. What a sad commentary on our society: We're surprised when a product performs the way it's been advertised to perform.

I've used MSWord enough to know that I shouldn't expect any miracles. But then, Word didn't have the running start WordPerfect did, so I can't be as annoyed or disappointed. Tomorrow will be brighter. See how right Shakespeare was when he wrote, "Sweet are the uses of adversity"? But on the other hand, he also wrote, "It is a tale told by an idiot, full of sound and fury, signifying nothing."

Latest Online Service: Customer Elimination Department

By now we're pretty much used to being ignored when we send an e-mail inquiry to a Web company. "Customer service" isn't part of the deal. If you can't put up with whatever happens based on a quick in-and-out, stay out.

But Priceline, as part of its inevitable entropy, moved this concept to a wonderful new plateau: the Customer *Elimination* Department.

The story is a hoot. It's too silly to make anyone angry. After all, how seriously can I report that I have been shat upon by William Shatner?

Oh, I don't mind William Shatner, or what's left of him. He seems to be a decent guy, although he had to feel pretty silly playing the part of a superannuated rap "artist" on Priceline's television commercial losers.

What the heck—he got paid, and handsomely, I understand. So if he can't carry a tune, he's no less talented than most other rap "artists." (That word "artist" *has* to be in quotation marks or somebody might take what these guys do seriously.)

Priceline Almost Made It.

As Priceline faded in the brutally competitive world of discount travel, its star seemed to be rising again for a few magical months in the newly-discovered worlds of discount groceries and gasoline. I admit to having shifted a considerable amount of supermarket haunting to a different store, based on Priceline's deals. And I had begun to explore the possibilities of buying gasoline at Priceline-connected gas stations.

Thereby hangs a tale.

Dealing with Priceline was an adventure. In a perverted way, I miss it. It was one of the most sophisticated Web sites anyone could come across. So who would question Priceline's direction to fill the tank at "Oakland Park Amoco, 7191 S.W. 8th Street, Plantation, Florida 33317"?

Now, I certainly admit I thought it was strange that Oakland Park Amoco would be located in Plantation instead of Oakland Park, but questioning Priceline struck me as parallel to questioning the Deity.

Uh . . . minor problem. The address is in the middle of a residential section. No gas station there. No phone number for any gas station with the name "Oakland Park" in Plantation.

The next step was to call an actual Amoco Station. There *is* an Oakland Park Amoco at 2091 W. Oakland Park Boulevard, in Oakland Park. Logical enough. This was the phone call:

"Amoco."

"Do you have a branch in Plantation?"

"Huh?"

"Is there an Oakland Park Amoco in Plantation?"

"In Plantation? This is Oakland Park Amoco on Oakland Park, in Oakland Park. If we were in Plantation, we'd probably call it Plantation Amoco. We're on Oakland Park, in Oakland Park."

The next step was to contact Priceline, because a charge for 20 gallons already was on my credit card. But getting an answer from Priceline is about as easy as getting an answer from the Deity. I sent seven e-mails on consecutive days, figuring somebody there would get tired of a full mailbox and send an answer.

My messages were consistent. A typical one:

I'm still waiting for an answer to a previous message to you:
I can't use my card to get the 20 gallons at:
Oakland Park Amoco
7191 S.W. 8th Street

Plantation, FL 33317.
Why? Because this station does not exist.
Please reply.

From my seven e-mails, I got one answer:

Thank you for your e-mail. If you already locked in your Re-
quest price, you cannot change the gas stations you selected.
You already prepaid for a specific number of gallons at a spe-
cific gas station. If you experience a problem with a gas
station, please contact our Customer Service Center at Gas-
Generalinfo@webhouse.priceline.com.

Catch-22: That online address brought me to the grocery page.

(Disclaimer: I have to temper my frustration with the realization that my wife, who had the same problem with the phantom gas
station, got an acknowledgment and a cancellation of charges for
gas at that nonexistent station. But then, she's a bigger fan of
William Shatner than I am.)

So, masochist that I am, I sent my eighth e-mail to Priceline.
Aha! This time I got an answer:

Thank you for your e-mail.
We cancelled your Priceline for Gasoline membership.
We have received your e-mail to cancel your Gasoline Request
and refund your credit card on file for any unpumped gaso-
line. We have submitted your request to our Refunds Depart-
ment for cancellation. Your refund will be posted within 7–10
business days and, depending on your credit card company,
the refund will appear on your statement within the next two
billing cycles.
We hope that you will continue to use Priceline for Gasoline
to help you save money on your gas. If you have any further
questions, please feel free to reply to this e-mail.

Sincerely,

S. Gruber

Priceline for Gasoline Customer Care

Uh—what?

Isn't that the ultimate indignity—being kicked out of Priceline? But why, after kicking me out, did S. Gruber add, "We hope you will continue to use Priceline for Gasoline"?

So, to that representative of Priceline's Customer Elimination Department, I sent one final e-mail:

I don't understand your communication.

I had no intention of canceling my membership. I simply want to cancel billing for a service station that doesn't exist.

May I still use my card at other (existing) stations?

S. Gruber, as well-trained as he/she/it may be in Customer Elimination, didn't reply. William Shatner was busy practicing his rap lyrics. Jay Walker hasn't taken my calls since Priceline went public. Oh, the h— . . . hold it!

Eureka! Three days later, "Matthew G" e-mailed me to say, "Your request was cancelled in error when we were unable to locate the station, which you were supposed to go to in order to get your gas. You are able to make a new Request for gasoline on our Web site at your convenience."

Whee! Beam me up, Scotty. (Too bad. They cancelled the whole deal.)

Retail Riddance

Cynics that we are, we no longer are surprised by exclusions to what the advertiser tells us is a terrific offer. But a Macy's—well, charitably, let's call it "offer"—in a newspaper space ad, reinforced by the identical offer in a free-standing insert, sets a new standard for exclusions.

The heading proclaims, in big bold type:

TAKE AN EXTRA 15% OFF
A SINGLE PURCHASE STOREWIDE!
(10% OFF THE CELLAR, TABLETOP,
LUGGAGE, HOUSEWARES, BED & BATH)

Hey, Macy's, nice promotion! It isn't often we get a storewide discount.

In fact, we don't get a storewide discount *here* either. Immediately following this heading is this body copy (I've reproduced every word):

> *Excludes DEPARTMENTS: Candy, Cosmetics, Fragrances, Designer Handbags, Small Electrics, Women's Shoes, Furniture, Floor Covering, Mattresses. DESIGNERS: Tommy Hilfiger, Nautica, Calvin Klein, Polo, Lauren, Claiborne for Men, Guess, Tumi, Hartmann, Seiko. COLLECTIONS: INC., Levi's, Swiss Watches, Fashion Watches, Fashion Jewelry, Waterford, Villeroy & Boch, Lalique, Kosta Boda, Baccarat, Lladro, Wedgwood, Lenox, Orrefors, Swarovski, Portmeirion, Gorham, Noritake, Denby, Arthur Court, Nambé, Christofle, Calphalon, Henckels, Krups, Royal Doulton, Spode china, Godiva. Not valid on Grinch plush, Super Buys, Best Values, prior purchases, services, Gift Bonds/Certificates, Leased Departments or phone orders. Macy's coupons cannot be combined.*

Storewide, huh? The Macy's giveth and the Macy's taketh away. Did you notice one of the exclusions is Grinch? How apt. They probably would have used less space if they'd listed the *in*clusions.

While we're laughing and smirking, we also might ponder why this offer deliberately shoots itself in the foot. How easy it would have been to reverse the thrust, asking us to look for specially-tagged merchandise or bargains within a department. Gimbel's, where are you now that we need you?

Now that Macy's has learned the route, they trod it heavily. Their newspaper ad says, "30%-50% off ALL† sweaters, ALL chenille, ALL cottons, ALL textures, for misses, petites and women."

Clever. Note the symbol following "ALL." Instead of an asterisk, "Is this a dagger I see before me?" (Lady Macbeth, Macy's legal advisor). Yup. "†Excludes designers and Best Values." Well, what the hell, "ALL" certainly can't be interpreted as meaning "ALL."

Penney's doesn't want to be left behind in advertising stuff they won't let us buy. The Penney free-standing insert offers "30% Off the regular price." Let's look at the women's wear coupon. Uh-oh: "Applies to regular-priced items only and excludes Special Buy & Value-Right items, items sold every day in multiples of 2 or more, Cosmetics Dept. Aerosoles®, Easy Spirit®, Gucci® watches & Catalog (Catalog Desks, Catalog Phone, Catalog Outlets), No Fear® sportswear, JNCO®, Nike® Team License Apparel, Starter® outerwear, Limited to stock on hand." Coupon copy ends, "Cash value 1/20¢." Yeah, that's about right.

At that, these FSIs have less duplicity than the "reader" space ad headed, "Used cars to be sold for $75.00." Subhead: "Local Honda dealer is overstocked and is forced to sell cars and trucks for as low as seventy-five dollars."

All those who believe this dealer, who obviously is overstocked with guile, will sell for $75 any car that doesn't have to be carried off the lot in pieces, please raise your hands so I can sell you a bridge for your car to stall on. I'm waiting.

Aw, you're as cynical as I am. Text of the ad points out, "In fact, cars that normally sell for eight to ten thousand dollars will be sold for six to seven thousand." That suggests a discount of about 25%. Okay, no problem: My $75 Stanley Steamer normally would sell for $100. And get this quote: "Since we are a local business we would like to give back to the community." An eye for an eye, eh? Sure . . . in this community if your ad isn't larded with "discount" and "wholesale" you can be driven out of the corps. Get out the tow-truck.

PLEASE TURN OVER.

And where is an ombudsman to yell and scream at whoever sent the two-page letter with the imperative "Please turn over" at the bottom of the first page? I can testify that "Please turn over" doesn't work. I turned over, and all I saw was an upside-down message.

Which brings me to one of the nastiest upside-down messages I've had the aggravation of opening lately. Here's an envelope from the U.S. Department of Commerce. On the face of the envelope is 'YOUR RESPONSE IS REQUIRED BY LAW." Gee, what warm, friendly envelope copy. Who's your writer, Heinrich Himmler?

Inside is a questionnaire about our business. The disclaimer, obviously written by F. Lee Bailey, says, "Your Census Report is confidential. It may be seen only by Census Bureau employees." Yeah, I got that word "may." And it may not. Oh, how many Census Bureau employees are there? I know, I know, none of my business.

Some of the questions suggest the Census Bureau thinks businesses have the same level of mentality their own staff has:

Is this establishment physically located inside the legal boundaries of the city, town, village, etc.?

1❑ Yes 2❑ No 3❑ No legal boundaries 4❑ Do not know

An indication of the specificity of Census Bureau questions is that "etc.," about as specific as "some." Nah, I don't know where I am. But coward that I am, I resisted checking "Do not know" and adding "due to sudden urban sprawl." I had our bookkeeper enter some numbers, and off it went.

So if you work at the Census Bureau and you're reading this, remember: You promised you wouldn't show our response to Jay Leno.

High Tech, Low Tech, No Tech.
How Badly Do I Need the Web?
The Breitling Chronicles

I admit it. I'm a sucker for wristwatches. My wife Margo buys me a watch whenever she senses I've seen one I like. I've long since crossed the Rolex border into Patek Philippe territory. I have so many watches I sometimes wear two, just to keep them running.

Margo saw an ad in *The Wall Street Journal*:

FINE SWISS WATCHES
WORLD'S BEST VALUES
AMERICA'S 1ST DISCOUNTER

We had been to Paris a few weeks earlier; in a little store in a flea market I saw a Breitling watch and made the mistake of admiring it. She wanted to buy it on the spot, but I was convinced that we'd be able to drive a better bargain closer to home. And, after all, I wasn't exactly watchless.

She called me over to her computer. There, on the screen, was a Breitling watch. "It wasn't easy finding this," she said. "I entered the .com address and got page after page of 'How great we are.' Then, when I finally was able to click to actual offers, I had to wade through about a hundred watches before I found this one."

I looked at the picture on the screen: Nice-looking Breitling.

"Wellll"—this is my standard semi-guilty reaction to seeing something I like but certainly don't need.

Ordering wasn't easy. She had to call a toll-free number and wait forever to get attention. She ordered the watch.

Within a few weeks, the watch showed up on her AmEx bill, but not in our house. After about six weeks, she called. "Oh, Breitling was refurbishing the watch and left out a seal. We'll ship within 10 days."

Two weeks later, Margo called the company again. "It hasn't come in yet." Hell hath no fury! "Are you aware you're in violation of the FTC 30-Day Rule?" Margo snapped. With some promoting from me, she canceled the order, demanding a credit on her AmEx bill.

That afternoon she went to a local jewelry store and picked up the identical watch . . . for about a hundred dollars less, even after state sales tax. I'm wearing it as I write this, although when we go to a dinner party tonight I'll switch back to the Patek Philippe.

THE REAL POINT

Now, the point of the story isn't that the online marketer lost an easy sale. It's that the online marketer acted unprofessionally in *every* aspect of its business. The home page has zero information and just one link. Click on it and you get a letter to the owner from a 30-year customer. (The first sentence is a hoot: "I have just learned that our relationship goes back over thirty years." Wow, what an unexpected revelation!)

Again, only one link. Click: a copy of the company's trademark. I'm not kidding. And again one link. Click: a page of puffery with a picture of the owner. And again just one link.

Click on that one and options appear. But nowhere is the opportunity to select or specify what you want. So that's Dereliction "A."

Dereliction "B" is considerably more serious, tied to the company's arrogance rather than to its Web site. What does *any* direct marketer do when a shipment is going to be late? Right! He communicates with the customer. Not this company. Every follow-up call came from us.

And Dereliction "C" follows right in line. When you have an irritated customer, you soothe the irritation, right? Nope, not here. Since canceling the order we've heard nothing, even though the company had not only our street address, phone, and fax but also Margo's online address. Yes, we did get an AmEx credit; but light-years of difference exist between what the result of this transaction is—the words you're reading, for example—and what it might have been—an ongoing customer.

That company isn't alone in its assumption that the medium is the message. Here's an ad in *The New Yorker*. I'll quote the entire text:

Brand Name Closeouts

Over $200 million worth of brand name Closeouts & Liquidations of consumer products from hundreds of bankrupt and overstocked wholesalers, retailers and distributors. Thousands of products are posted weekly at up to 90% off original wholesale prices.

www.productdiscounts.com

You might want to check it out; before you do, jot down what you expect to find.

Lots of luck.

Then there's a strange entry whose URL is www.5thavenuechannel.com. If you're a genuine card-carrying masochist, try buying something from that source.

A research company called Jupiter Communications says that during one recent holiday season 14 percent fewer shoppers were satisfied with Internet retailers than they were before the holidays:

slow-w-w-w-w sites and out of stock were two of the common gripes. Hey, there's no reason whatever for a Web marketer to be out of stock, when the webmaster (how I had that word!) can knock an out-of-stock item off the listings as fast as the item disappears from inventory. For first-time users, the Web should be like Caesar's wife.

What burns me, as one of the fifty million certified Web experts, is that those who misuse what's going to be the most dynamic medium in the history of communications are killing off its best buying prospects.

Sigh. I know it isn't possible to dump the dumb. But from now on I'm going to measure the amount of time I waste on those marketing neanderthals . . . on my new Breitling.

The Large Type Giveth and The Small Type Taketh Away: That *$%#@* Asterisk Strikes Again

As I get older and more crotchety, I'm becoming less and less tolerant of The Asterisk Exception.

Lawyers hired to cripple copy for financial institutions love asterisks. They demand that attention be drawn to an exception the reader would slide past . . . or, better yet, *accept* . . . if the same information were in parentheses as an ongoing line, instead of a "Fish for the bad news" asterisk after a promise-line.

Ever try arguing with a lawyer who thinks asterisks and legal briefs are wonderful ways to sell, and "whereas" is on a par with "free"? So okay, our logic falls on barren ground. So okay, the old saying, "Painters and lawyers can change white to black, including their souls," still lives. It's their turf, by fiat.

What's more puzzling and more exasperating is the use of asterisks to obfuscate. Intolerable! For some masochistic reason I was reading a funeral chapel ad in my local paper. They're giving me three choices:

- Northern Burial* $1995.00
- Classic Chapel Service** $25.00 per month per person
- S. Fla. Cemetery Ground Burial, Marker Included***
  $25.08 per month per person

Now, don't go rushing off to see Dr. Kevorkian because that last strange entry includes a free marker. Those asterisks, ferreted out at the bottom of the ad, let us know we're a long way from resting in peace. The $1995 price: "*Based on $244.95 down and 59 monthly payments of $39.95; total payments $2,357.05. Prices subject to change in air fare." The second one is $117 down and 59 payments of $25; the third is $221.74 down and 84 monthly payments of $25.08. (Who wrote this ad, an accountant?) As a pre-calculator student, I know 84 months = 7 years. What if . . .? Aw, I'll let my survivors worry about it.

DESPICABLY PICKABLE

Throughout much of this book I've picked on cellular phone ads, but that's because they're so despicably pickable. Here's an ad that crows, "360 Minutes of Free Long Distance.*"

Actually, it isn't so bad: Asterisk copy, when deciphered with a microscope: "360 minutes of residential long distance based on joint offer of 30 minutes per month for 12 months. Requires integrated billing. O.A.C."

All right, what's integrated billing? Something to do with affirmative action, I suppose. And O.A.C.? Probably means "Obfuscatory Asterisk Con."

Here's one for an "All inclusive vacation" at the Radisson Cable

Beach Resort. Nice—includes airfare, meals, drinks, free golf*,—whoops. Now, what do you suppose that asterisk is doing there?

"*Mandatory cart not included with free golf." Yuck, that word "mandatory" suggests it's a barracks, not a hotel. Say, Radisson, ever hear of the word "rapport"? I'm perfectly willing to pay for a golf cart, assuming you don't gouge me; but that nasty turnoff word suggests that's what you plan to do.

Remember that Gilbert & Sullivan gem in which one singer says, "I'm never, never sick at sea." Chorus: "What, never?" His reply: "Well, hardly ever."

That had to be in the mind of whoever concocted this one:

*Upgrade Your Cellular Phone With Any New Motorola Cellular Phone For Only $49.88!***

Wow, a <u>double</u> asterisk! And what happy message is connected to its sibling?

*** Offer excludes the Motorola 6000E.*

Oh. Well, "Almost Any" is almost as any as "Any."

That double asterisk suggests another earlier one is lurking somewhere. Having resigned from the Masochist Society, I didn't look for it.

But I couldn't avoid the double asterisk in a mailing from Citibank touting its Platinum VISA card. It hit me in the eye after two references: warranty extension and protection against damage or theft of something bought with the card. The bottom reference: "See back of Citibank Platinum Select Invitation for pricing and program details."

Program details? Sorry I looked.

The back of that form lists "Warranty Manager"; "Buyers SecurityK"; "Automatic Travel Accident Insurance"; and "Auto Rental Insurance." For all but Buyers Security, "Certain restrictions, limitations, and exclusions apply. For Buyers Security, "Certain conditions and exclusions apply." And the Warranty Manager gives a double dose: "Details provided when you become a cardmember." You're saying, "Trust me" after making me dig for details and then coyly saying you won't give me those details until after we're married? Wow, what a way to inspire loyalty and confidence!

Bloomingdale's is a sedate asterisk-user. A full-page ad headed (lower case is theirs) "take 25%–50%* off" refers us to this puzzle: "*Savings may not be based on actual sales." Oh. Thanks. But shouldn't it be, "*Savings may not be based on actual sales.**" . . . with yet another reference: "**Whatever that means."

My favorite is an annual report sent to me as a stockholder of a company called FSI International. (What does FSI stand for? Not free-standing insert, so it's probably something obscene, but I'm just guessing. This heavily produced gem, which referred to "a challenging year" (read: sales declined 17%), had this statement on page 2:

> While this down cycle in purchasing semiconductor fabrication equipment put pressure on our financial performance, our investments in infrastructure, technology and globalization provide us with significant leverage for an improved fiscal year.*

Out of sheer cussedness, I decided to track down the mate to that asterisk. Some 32 pages later, I conceded defeat: None existed. So it wasn't just a challenging year; it was a challenging annual report.

YES MEANS NO.

Here's a gem—if you consider a rhinestone a gem—in a computer reseller magazine:

Includes 1 Year On-Site Service*

At the bottom of the ad:

*On-site service may not be available in some areas.

See how jaded we are? We not only aren't startled by this non-revelation; we expected it.

Speaking of expectations, here's an offer that's typical of what you can expect from me: *Mention this chapter to a decision-making executive today* and receive $10,000 from the nearest bank.***

Pretty good deal, huh?

* Blackout dates may apply.

** Not valid from January 1 through December 31.

A MARRIAGE MADE IN HELL

Oh, yes. The cursed asterisk, is flourishing like a weed in a petunia patch. Perfectly matched to three-point type, it's a cancer growing—and, damn it, thriving—as it eats away at the credibility of advertising messages.

For years I've railed against this "Asterisk Exception," the standardized use of an asterisk to mask the truth. Hey, guys, that's cheating. For example, Sprint says in a big newspaper ad, "Get 1500 minutes for $34.99 a month. That's 250 Anytime Minutes plus 1250 Night & Weekend Minutes, all including nationwide long distance with a one-year Sprint PCS Advantage Agreement.K"

Clear enough, right? Straightforward enough, right? And no asterisk, although there's a "K." Well, lookee here: At the bottom of the page, in type so small I had to use a magnifying glass to read it, are eight tiny lines of "explanation." First, this offer is available only if I buy a Sprint PCS phone. Nothing in the ad—*nothing*, even here—tells me how much that phone costs.

But wait, there's more. A nonrefundable $29.95 "phone activation fee" applies. Roaming calls are charged at "$0.69 a minute or $0.39 cents per minute, depending on specific local-market offers. [Doesn't Sprint know where they've placed their ads?] Domestic long distance calls made while roaming on the Spring PCS Network are charged at an additional $0.25 per minute. Additional minutes charged at $0.35 per minute." And on it goes, chipping away at the promise of "nationwide long distance" made in a typesize four or five times bigger than the disclaimers.

HERE'S JAMIE LEE, HER ASTER AT RISK.

I have to pick on Jamie Lee Curtis again. Here she is, next to an outline of the state of Florida, snickering at us out of a space ad in my local paper, hawking "VoiceStream" long distance service: "500 statewide anytime minutes, includes long distance and digital roaming within Florida*, plus 2000 nationwide weekend minutes only $39.95 per month." Hold it. There's an asterisk lurking in the bowels of this offer. And at the bottom of this ad, somehow VoiceStream has managed to reduce type to a size even smaller than Sprint's. Good thing, too, because in five lines of teeny tiny type is a catalog of exclusions. It begins, "*Coverage not available in all areas. Map is not a representation of coverage"—and gets steadily worse. Weekends don't begin until midnight Friday; "Our digital PCS system is not compatible with analog TTY which may delay or prevent emergency calls." And then the standard asterisk *coup de grace*: "Additional restrictions may apply."

AT&T offers "Free installation* and $29.99 per month (first 3 months). Now, I have to hand it to AT&T. Their ad tells me straight out that the $29.99 is for three months only. The mice-type at the bottom doesn't tell me what the rate is afterward, only that the "current" rate is $39.95, but I as emptor am caveatized by the warning in readable type. Still, AT&T's asterisk doesn't disappoint the implicit cynicism that little mark generates: "Separately priced additional equipment and Service packages may be required . . . In addition, prices do not include equipment changes, franchise fees or taxes which may vary from area to area . . . Additional local taxes, fees or changes may apply . . . Certain restrictions may apply." Well, they hit that last one right on the nose.

BANK ON THIS ONE.

BankAtlantic gets into the spirit of advertisers making as-terisks of themselves with one of those "7.49% APR*, Prime for Life" ads. On their behalf, some of the unreadable type is immediately adjacent: "Introductory Rate for 6 months." But that doesn't relate to the asterisk.

Oh, no. Lots of goodies at the bottom of this ad. Just a few: "There is no limit to the amount the rate may increase or decrease monthly, except it will never exceed 18% APR. Property insurance is required. Flood insurance may be required. Checking account is required."

THE COMPUSERVE EFFECT

Aren't you getting tired of those ads that giveth, then taketh away, by linking what seems to be a bottom-end price to a three-year linkup with CompuServe? Office Depot says on the front page of an FSI, "Save $400 Instantly with 36-Month CompuServe Subscription**."

As impressed as I am by the double asterisk, it makes me wonder where the first asterisk might have been. Can't find it. So let's see what we're in for. Well, the only reference is "See other details on inside pages.**" Come on, guys, that's cheating. *Which* inside pages? I look more closely at this page and see that Compuserve will cost $21.95 a month. Oh, will it? "Long distance charges and hourly surcharges may apply." Yeah, *may*. And $21.95 a month for 36 months totals $898. Intel may be inside your computer, but Show-and-tell is lurking outside.

Now, look: I'm perfectly aware that complete disclosure not only is preferable to incomplete disclosure; in some cases, especially financial, it's mandatory. What I'm attacking isn't the deal, it's the deliberate obfuscation. That's what leads to nasty calls to the bookkeeping departments of these companies . . . or worse, to the Better Business Bureau.

Is It Any Wonder They're Skeptical?

If you wonder why the people to whom we aim our messages are increasingly skeptical, all you have to do is take a look at your own mail.

For example. . .

My friend Bob Dunhill of Dunhill International Lists sent me two mailings, both of them sporting first class postage. The return address of one was "Disbursements Division." Above the window on the envelope is the legend, "Addressee: Sweepstakes simulated check enclosed."

Pretty good, huh? A lot of people, who don't have the foggiest notion what the word "simulated" means, will rip open the envelope to get at the check from "Disbursements Division."

The first sentence of the letter, below my favorite device (an official-looking rubber stamp):

Dear Robert Dunhill:

You have just been declared fully vested with guaranteed eligibility for the $7,500.00 Grand Prize in our national sweepstakes.

They're asking for a call to a 900 number. Uh-oh. They admit to $3.98 per minute, with an average call-time of six minutes. Even by their optimistic estimate, a call will cost $23.88.

(Infuriating? Try calling some of the new 900 numbers for computer software technical support, spending two minutes wading through the voice-mail menu, then having a recorded voice tell you, "All of our representatives are busy. Please wait." *That's* infuriating.)

I used the "Disbursements Division" envelope in a book titled "Open Me Now." Does that mean I embrace the concept of misleading mailings? Hell, no. It means I admire the craftiness behind this mailing, even as I detest the damage it inflicts on the image of direct response.

The second letter was from "Assessment and Search Commission." As any reader of this book easily can guess, what's inside is a cunningly worded and totally obfuscatory letter. The bottom line—actually, an official-looking form at the bottom of the letter—is a monthly "membership" which authorizes the mailer to "automatically enter me in the numerous cash sweepstakes you have identified. . . ." Memberships are $5 for one month, $10 for three months. I assume renewal mailings are equally high-powered.

The reaction to mailings like this depends on who the recipient is. Bob Dunhill, a sophisticated direct marketing expert, was outraged by these mailings; Joe Doakes, seeing the "Assessment and Search Commission" letter as one of three pieces of mail arriving at his home in Ottumwa, is likely to say to his wife, "Martha, look at this! We may be getting half a million dollars. And it only costs us five bucks."

So the skepticism this mailing generates is due to a standard error of list selection: mailing to the wrong target, in this case a knowledgeable list compiler who's aware of what induces skepticism in the first place. I'm assuming, of course, the offers are legally sound.

NEXT EXAMPLE: THE COATTAIL-RIDERS WILL MAIM US ALL.

Sweepstakes creating skepticism? Aw, come on.

Sweepstakes are as American as apple pie and Abe Lincoln and Michael Milken and Hillary Rodham Clinton and Leona Helmsley.

But legislation aimed at other targets, such as some of the less-benevolent 900-number operators, can gather in its catch-all net legitimate sweepstakers. American Family Publishers already has thrown in the towel, and Publishers Clearing House is a shadow of its former self, bolstering flagging mail response by forming a new company, PCH.com, to give online users access to contests and sweepstakes tied to magazine subscriptions as well as merchandise. It's like catching dolphins in a tuna net, and I'll tell you why:

The very legitimacy of the big sweepstakes (and despite the hue and cry of people who interpreted wording to imply they'd pre-won, the big national sweepstakes are totally legitimate) brings success to the coattail-riding peripheral operators. Misleading promotions invariably are the illegitimate and unadopted children of authentic promotions.

There's zero logic in attacking an entire phylum because of real or imagined abuses by some hangers-on.

NEXT EXAMPLE: PHONY STROKING

They send us e-mail or snail-mail loaded with phony stroking. They tell us we're titans when we know we're pygmies. They promise thrilling satisfaction and eventually leave us frustrated. They play fast and loose with our emotions. They're *emotional sweepstakes* operators, building us up for an artificial ego-boost by giving us (Wow!) our names in print. In *print*! And in a big, bound book!

Aren't they as culpable—in terms of deceptive illusion which eventually engenders a skeptical attitude aimed blindly at all our wares—as the peripheral sweepstakes operators?

Suppose *you* got a letter from Who's Who Worldwide. The one that came to me begins:

Dear Mr. Lewis:

You were recently nominated by our Editorial Office for possible inclusion in the WHO'S WHO REGISTRY.

Okay, that makes sense. What took them so long?

But what's the action, Jackson? The letter makes two points clear: 1) No cost is involved for inclusion. 2) This "Who's Who" "is not affiliated with any other 'Who's Who' publication other than our own."

The third point, implicit if unspoken, is the logic of buying a book with your name in it.

So this isn't the venerable "Who's Who"; so what?

Well, two other points just might trigger the skepticism-glands: First, the "Registry" form is, to say the least, Spartan. I have just one line each to name my type of business, my personal expertise, and my "major product line." I did considerably better than that with the old Marquis "Who's Who."

Second, they sent me two of these, one at my post office box and one at my street address. They're identical, and I wonder about the redundancy-factor. I can envision a meeting of this publication's editors:

"Oh, my God, we don't have Lewis in the book."

"We can't publish without him. I'll put him on the list."

"No, we'd better be sure. *I'll* put him on the list too."

Merge-purge doesn't work when one has multiple addresses; skepticism does.

AND MOST INFURIATING OF ALL . . .

It's my curmudgeonly temperament coming to the fore, I know, but what bothers me most isn't the wiliness of sweepstakes sharpshooters nor the elephantine subtlety of ego-publications. No, it's more basic than wiliness or subtlety, both of which show some intellectuality.

Nor does my fury stem from an "I wish I'd written that" envy . . . nor blue-nose morality . . . nor even contempt for those who denigrate the dignity of advertising and marketing. Oh, no, it's more primitive than that. It's a knee-jerk "anti-stupid" reaction.

Want some examples?

Here's an envelope that just has to be the result of listening to two consultants, neither of whom knows the other exists. One says, "Stamp the word 'PERSONAL' in big red letters. That'll get their attention. 'Personal' always works."

The other consultant says, "Hey, don't spend the extra half-cent to have the lettershop put a third-class stamp on the envelope. That's a waste of money. Just imprint postal indicia."

So out comes an envelope with a big red "PERSONAL" on it . . . and, in the upper right corner, the betraying word "BULK."

(Inside is a "Sweepstakes CASH VERIFICATION" pointing out: "Total cash to be awarded: $3,525,000.00, $117,500.00 annually." Huh? That's 30 years. By that time I'll be deep into Alzheimer's and will have forgotten your promise. Or maybe my embalmer will remember to collect.)

ETHICS AND MORALS AND BEARS, OH MY!

Professional organizations such as the American Association of Advertising Agencies and the Direct Marketing Association for years have wrestled with questions of ethics and morals. The inability of even these august organizations to come up with a definitive solution proves the complexity of the issue. Legislation that would murder legitimate businesses and fund raisers along with fringe operators—dolphins along with tuna—is on the docket or already has become law in a number of states. Members of Congress are making pious speeches. One person's skepticism-generator is another person's apparent good fortune.

All those storm clouds gathering on the marketing horizon verify: The apparition of good fortune is becoming rarer and rarer; public awareness is gradually becoming public skepticism.

I don't object to skepticism. Nor should you. Public skepticism is our insecticide, our weed-spray, our water-purifier. Skepticism is far more effective than any legislation which drives the fringe operators to more and more artful deceptions. We'll survive skepticism; they won't.

So to television shows such as *Extra* and *Hard Copy* and *Inside Edition* . . . to publicity-seeking attorneys general . . . to members of Congress desperate for a re-election hook . . . I offer this suggestion:

Go ahead and attack those who deserve to be attacked. Go ahead and pontificate against those who deserve to be pontificated against. Cast your nets, even though some of them are pre-loaded with phony morality. But be sure you don't snare the dolphins of legitimacy while you're catching the sharks of duplicity.

(Too deep an allegory? Oh, well, I'm out of patience anyway.)

Where Is Ed McMahon
Now That We Need Him?

When I quit laughing I'll share this magnificent exercise in duplicity with you.

Okay. Saliva is all dried up, so here we go.

Over the past months I've been bombarded with phone calls by a won't-take-no stockbrokerage. Sometimes it's a man's voice and sometimes it's a woman's voice, but the calls always come during the dinner hour. They always tell me the company has a red-hot issue with limited availability, and I'd better give them the okay right now if I don't want to miss out on a million dollar scam—uh, deal.

My wife usually answers the phone. She's wise to "I want to talk to Herschell. It's a personal call." (Half of them say, "I'm a friend of Gordon's.") But she knows I like to test the waters, to see what the next slimy pitch will be, to occasionally throw a loaded question that derails the "How are you today?" boiler-plate.

This call was different. Margo looked at me with some puzzlement: "He says it's the Russian Mint calling."

Now, how often are *you* called by the Russian Mint? Not that the ruble is worth anything these days, but by golly this is an exotic diversion.

Picking up an extension, I resisted the urge to say something like "Dos vedanya, Tovarisch," or "Shostakovich's Fifth Symphony is my favorite," or even "Da." Instead, I asked a question: "Hello?"

The voice on the other end was a shocker: Pure Americana, slightly Noo Yawk. He at least could have rolled a few "r"s.

"Hi, Herschell."

A letdown. Eastern Europe had to be at least a generation or two removed. Red flags—not the old USSR type—started to wave. "Who is this?"

"I'm calling from the Russian Mint."

Come on, buddy, you're about as Russian as George M. Cohan. I had to ask the next question: "Just what is the Russian Mint?"

Long pause. Then, "Before I answer that question, I have to ask you one."

"And that question is?"

"Do you ever invest in I.P.O.'s?"

Laugh? I was convulsed. "Wrong question," I said and hung up. I was on an extension that didn't have Caller I.D., but one of the ones that did betrayed the ruble-rouser: It was that same brokerage firm.

INVENTIVENESS OR DECEIT?

Do we applaud them for inventiveness or damn them for deceit? Before I degenerated into a grizzled cynic I'd have had some admiration—one percent or so—for the cunning behind the Russian Mint ploy. But that was a kinder, gentler time. Now we who sell with words get heat from every quarter, and I'm not about to applaud dishonesty. Ingenuity, yes. Dishonesty, no.

So when I get a "No purchase is necessary" card telling me I'm "eligible for the Grand Prize totaling $125,000.00 in cash," and in addition I may also win a new car (I'm to check: ❏ Chrysler Voyager ❏ Chevrolet Blazer ❏ Ford Mustang GT Convertible) I'm torn between admiring the ingenuity behind the check-the-car-you-expect-to-win ploy, plus a marvelously obfuscatory line in the Rules, "Entries must be received by May 31 in the next year ending with an even number"—and disdain for the clinker I know I'll find if I read carefully.

Ah, there it is: "At the same time, you are invited to try a special introductory offer one-year *[NAME OF MAGAZINE]* subscription for only $14.97. Send no money—you'll be billed later."

Oh, yeah, I know I can still enter the sweepstakes by printing my name and address on a 3"×5" card and mailing it. But I'm weary. I'm tired of the battle. I'm worn down from looking for the gimmick I know is there.

So here's a card with 72-point type telling me, "Here is your **free $5 calling card**." Yeah, sure.

I have an 800 number to call for "instant activation." Yeah, sure. "It's yours to use, with no obligation." Yeah, sure. So how come, when I call, I hear a recording saying, "Please have your name, address, and a major credit card ready"?

How come I sigh instead of chortling at this headline on a space ad: "Computer Warehouse Wants to Give You A Free *$3,000 Laptop Computer!" I don't know what that damned asterisk refers to, because I can't find a matching one in the solid four-point text on the page. I do know I'm not surprised to see this in the coupon:

> *Requests must be accompanied with a $20 fee for the complete information pack and application info. All requests received without this $20 one-time fee will be shredded. Sorry—we cannot ship your "Free Laptop Computer" package without this non-refundable fee."*

And, oh, for another three bucks they'll send the "info" by special rush delivery.

Sigh.

Somebody in Houston wants to make me an "Instant Millionaire." A genuine altruist, he tells me "I only want people who seriously want to be in business for themselves requesting the Information Kit, so I'm charging a nominal $10 fee to receive the Kit." Statesman that he is, he says he'll "even apply the $10 to the cost of your distributorship package." And thank goodness: "We accept all major credit cards." Gee, I was afraid you'd reject them.

And on we go. I've "been selected" to receive a free trial issue of Internet Shopper. Yeah, if I like what I see I can save 17 percent off the newsstand price—a curiously small saving. Into the pile it goes with the worn-out "Good news!" mailings and e-mails and double postcards from 1,785 different magazines offering me free issues and the absolute right to write "Cancel" on the invoice. Another pile: Credit cards that offer 0% APR on the envelope but a return to the usual deal after three months on the response device. And here's a company expressing its appreciation for my being "our customer this past year" by offering me a mini boom box provided I send another order within 30 days" (I never heard of this company).

So what a relief it is—no, a surprise—to open an envelope that says, "Receive absolutely free a 30-day supply of high-potency multivitamins" and—well, what do you know! It actually is free! Where did these guys come from? I was so stunned I didn't mail back the coupon.

Except for the vitamins (obviously an aberration) why am I no more disillusioned than I was before looking at these offers? Because I'm already at maximum disillusionment-thrust.

Will the next mail bring relief? You've gotta be kidding. Aw, why wait? Without any free vitamins to gulp down, I guess the million dollars will have to do.

"Ve know Vhere You Liff!"

Even a couple of years ago I wouldn't have reacted to a credit card mailing whose message begins . . .

> "So you're hooked on the fun and excitement of baseball. Now there is a unique way to demonstrate support for your favorite team all year long—the new Florida Marlins Platinum Visa Card."

So why does this annoy me now? Aw, I guess it's because I'm like the wedding guest in the poem "The Rime of the Ancient Mariner"—sadder and wiser.

From an emotional point of view, the sales argument has both feet planted firmly in the clouds. I haven't been hooked on the fun and excitement of baseball since professional baseball quit being fun and exciting. When those overpaid louts went on strike in the mid-1990s, so did I.

Then there's the peculiar South Florida circumstance. I'm supposed to demonstrate support for the Florida Marlins when the owner of the team has announced he has no support for them. He's looking either for a city to build him a stadium or for a buyer who may move the team, whichever comes first.

And then, as a dedicated masochist, I have a different favorite team—the Chicago Cubs.

THE "ASSUMPTIVE" POSITION

But my biggest beef is that this message typifies an approach favored by the latter day non-saints of marketing—the *assumptive* position. It may be because of overdependence on databases that paint their subjects with smeary broad strokes—I live in South Florida, so I'm a Marlins fan. It may be the arrogance we see in messages created by transplants from the world of conventional advertising, in which a television commercial tells us who we are and what we like.

Whatever the cause of any particular assumptive message, my position is that in this Age of Skepticism it's lousy psychology. We can stroke 'em and we can give 'em freebies and we can even preach at 'em. But assumptive loyalties? Assumptive economic circumstances? Assumptive personal tastes? We're on dangerous ground unless our databases are simon-pure. Starting a message with "I know you'll . . ." can be the Kingdom of Hell as often as it's the Kingdom of Heaven, *unless it's one member of an in-group communicating with another member of that same in-group.*

I got a check from a company whose slogan is "Loans you can afford. Service you can rely on.®." That registration symbol makes a statement—in my opinion, a statement of insecurity, because only an insecure marketer would register a slogan as nondescript as that one.

The check had an interesting legend on its face: "The face of this document has a colored background on white paper." Huh? Thanks for clearing that up. The check is for $2,471.23—odd amount. (Is that a prime number? It isn't divisible by 3, 7, 11, or 13. Is that why they chose it, or is this an arithmetic test when I try to balance my account?)

The attached message says the check is "an extra convenience to our customers with good credit records." Assumptive! Hey, buddy, even though this mailing is slickly done and 100 percent professional, with its standard "Personal and Confidential" envelope copy validated by a presorted first class indicium (free suggestion if you do this: add a rubber stamp "First Class Mail" imprint), I ain't your customer. And the interest rate is 27.08% . . . for which *I'll* gladly loan *you* money.

What would *I* have done? I'd have made it non-assumptive, more solicitous—"This is proof that we want you to be our customer."

THEIR CLAIRVOYANCE IS FAULTY.

Another credit card says to me, "I know you're concerned about being able to pay off your high-interest credit cards. I know you'd like to get rid of all those nagging bills that keep you awake at night, worrying about tomorrow."

Here we go—another "Ve know vhere you liff" clairvoyant with a pebble inside his crystal ball. What keeps me awake at night is the fear that tomorrow another assumptive (and mildly insulting) message such as this might darken my mailbox.

That mailing was an aberration. Most of the mailings and e-mails still tell me I've been pre-approved for something or other, although the "pre-approved" pitch now is old enough to have mold growing on it.

So by now I know the drill, and (aha! *My* assumption!) probably so do you. The names come from one of the credit bureaus—Equifax or Trans Union or Experian. So they're reasonably safe with a "pre-approved" offer. The only trouble is, every credit card company uses those same credit bureaus, so even a well-written assumptive message runs afoul of a marketing truism:

> *Those who represent your best assumptive targets are those who get the greatest number of similar offers from your competitors.*

That truism generates a type of mailing too many recipients regard as the most objectionable of all direct mail and e-mail "offers"—the unexpected negative option assumption.

A mailing has this theme:

> *Because you've shown an interest in the arts and literature, you can expect a real treat in the next few days. Your personal copy of "Mastering the Zone" is on its way to you. . . .*

What follows? A coattail-riding assumption: You bought that, so you're fair game for this whether you've shown an interest or not. Oh, you can send it back "if you're not delighted"; but gee, fellows, couldn't your assumption be a little more benevolent, giving the recipient the privilege of original selection?

THE FUND-RAISING SNAKEPIT

How about fund raisers? Yeah, I know, criticizing them parallels bushwhacking Abe Lincoln and motherhood, but come on! Fund raisers can be so assumptive they raise my gorge instead of my dollars.

One fund raising mailing begins with a consummate annoyance:

Sit by your phone, because you're going to get a call.

Oof! Please let somebody else answer the phone when it rings with this call. The opening sentence is precursor to a bald warning that the organization is going to pitch for a contribution, in exchange for which I'll get (Wow!) a Donor's Certificate. *Ve know vhere you liff!*

Another fund raiser doesn't even bother sheathing the mailed fist inside a velvet glove:

> *I know you can. The <u>question</u> is, <u>will you</u>?*
> *In plain English: You won't sleep tonight if you don't support this most worthy cause . . . and I know you can, if you want to, certainly to the extent of $350.*

Yeah, that's plain English. In fact, it's a classic example of candor—telling somebody something unpleasant. Why couldn't you, dear dilettante fund raiser, have put this in question form instead of whanging me over the head with an assumption? (Note, please: I used the euphemism "dilettante" for the creator of this letter and worded my reaction as a question, so I'm more sensitive to my message recipient than the copywriter was.)

So it goes. And so will response go, if we don't consider that it's tough enough making an assumption stick when communicating with your spouse, let alone with a "cold list" name.

"Here's Your Official Survey: We Need Your Opinion on Latvian Flag Design."

How many "official" surveys have come to your desk over the past few months?

This device is like those yellow stick-on notes with "Herschell—this will interest you. J." It was clever the first time.

The first time an "official" survey came to me (in the year 1827, as I recall) it was from a fund raiser. It was a clever ploy the first time a fund raiser used it. It was recognizable the third time a fund raiser used it. It became obnoxious when political parties and artificial "research companies" began using it.

You know what? I have a dream. I have a dream that one day somebody will mail out one of these "surveys" and not include some sort of transparent self-serving reason for sending it. I have a dream that one day somebody will ask for my opinion and actually will read my opinion. I have a dream that one day somebody will read my opinion and say, "You know what? That's a good idea. I'm glad we asked for his opinion."

An impossible dream.

Under less clichéd conditions I'd be flattered to get an "Official Survey" from both major political parties. (I suppose in 1992 Ross Perot also mailed one, but only to himself.) Both of these told me I was among (don't they know the word "among" damages exclusivity?) a select group of voters who are receiving this National Survey Document. One had this profound question as number one:

Which of the following do you think is most important for Congress to do?
  ❏ *Lower taxes*
  ❏ *Cut federal spending*
  ❏ *Both are equally important*

Gee, I don't know, fellas. That's a tough one. What isn't so tough is moving on to the spot where you ask for $15 to $100. $15 "pays to contact 33 more voters"; if I send $100, "this amount enables us to contact 222 more voters." No quantity-economies here:

It's 45 cents per voter, so I might as well choose the ultimate exhilaration or put-down, "Other."

Another "Confidential Survey" not only tells me my opinions on health care are "very important" but offers me a free *Guide to Healthy Living* as a premium. And oh, by the way, "past surveys have revealed, for example, that many people did not know about the comprehensive benefits of the Humana Gold Plus Plan." Golly, how ignorant can people be?

BIG MISTAKE: BUYING A RANGE ROVER

Okay, I'm used to that kind of phony "you're important" stroking, encased in a bulk-mail envelope. But I made a mistake: I bought a Range Rover. The dealer—quite a decent chap—said to me, "The U.S. distributor will contact you. I'd appreciate it if you'd tell them you enjoy doing business with us."

No problem. I *do* enjoy doing business with them. They pour coffee. They pick up and deliver. Their vehicle is King of the Road.

Did I say no problem? The U.S. distributor didn't call. Instead, I got a huge questionnaire from some sort of "Research Bureau," with my car as a thin blind, asking me a ton of questions including my income and lifestyle.

Huh? Hey, guys, I paid cash for that car. I don't owe you a batch of personal information, especially if you don't tell me the truth about why you want it. You want me to spend half an hour with your blasted questionnaire? Then tell me the real reason behind it. Your accompanying letter—ice-cold—was more of a demand than a request.

That'll show those turkeys: I traded the Range Rover for a Lincoln Navigator.

PAY ME AND I'LL TALK.

A far shrewder approach was the one a business magazine used. They sent me a four-page questionnaire . . . together with a crisp new one-dollar bill. Aha! Now one of the great motivators, Guilt, kicks in. The questionnaire will take about twenty minutes. I have three options:

1. Pocket the buck and pitch the questionnaire.

2. Return the buck in their envelope, with the blank questionnaire.

3. Fill out the questionnaire and legitimize the buck.

As you already have guessed, I filled out the questionnaire, justifying being a yokel by rationalizing that a dollar for twenty minutes was equivalent to three dollars an hour . . . which isn't bad pay, is it?

Over the past few years I've encountered surveys ranging from whether I think whales are worth saving to whether, "if you were considering to buy," I'd prefer Norman Rockwell plates to fuzzy animals. Each of these has a thin coating of varnish over a purpose other than gathering data.

That doesn't bother me. Marketers have to market, and I'm part of this desperate universe. What does bother me are two variations on this theme:

1. You owe us information because you're out there.

2. We're clever and you're not.

I can't yell and scream about phony telephone "surveys." I did that in earlier pages. But, as part of this overall harangue, I'll point out that whether by phone or by mail, or now, damn it, by fax, if you want information don't smear goo all over your communication by saying you want my opinion.

I'll go one step further: If you're really a smart marketer, acknowledge my response with a "Thank you," plus a discount coupon or another salesworthy tie. You can't do that with the original "blind" questionnaire; you can serve both God and Mammon by following up with a commercial mailing identifying yourself as the sponsor of the survey, making me privy to the results (assuming those results are beneficial to you), and giving me the well-deserved reward of an apparent discount—which, if used, also will be beneficial to you.

See? I'm not the "heavy." *You* are. That'll be one dollar, please.

Post Mortem: How Do You Avoid the Mayhem?

So how does a marketer avoid all the mayhem . . . the mindless murder of customer loyalty and accompanying slaughter of profitability?

First, notice which companies aren't in the rogue's gallery that has just been presented. Chances are, successful companies follow the five mandates listed below and reflected in this book. If you decide to join the marketers who think like marketers, you'll be difficult to beat.

- Work to build customer rapport. In every phase of your marketing and business operations, let your customers know you consider *their* interests first.
- Communicate eye-to-eye. Don't talk down to prospects and don't toady to them. If you really need a spate of acronyms to establish a sense of congeniality, conviviality, and rapport with your target-group, okay. If you have to use technical jargon, okay. But don't bully. Don't confuse. Don't beg.
- Use all your rhetorical tools, your electronic tools, and your production tools. Use them without fear, but use them properly. New technology and processes are the hammer and nails of our world. Wield that hammer and smack those nails square-on.
- Test. Take nothing for granted about your selling arguments, your customers, or your product. Don't let your own opinions

rule. What matters is the reaction of those who see or hear your message. As old-time journalists were fond of saying, "If your mother says she loves you, prove it. If someone of the other gender says he or she loves you, ask him or her to prove it."

- Don't sell in clichés. Everything you market—every product and service presentation—can be unique to the right prospect for it. A cliché destroys uniqueness. That means destruction of competitive effectiveness.

See how simple? See how basic? See how often "professional" marketers ignore these little principles? Don't let the word "professional" in quotation marks apply to you. Genuine professionalism means customers and clients.

Of course we all know the venerable definition of "customer": someone who automatically buys from us . . . again and again. Nope. Sorry, that might have been true before the Age of Skepticism. That kind of loyalty doesn't exist anymore. Our prospects have too many choices, *and they know it*. As has been documented throughout this book, too many of our fellow marketers have broken faith with too many people too often. Skepticism is the unpleasant but natural result.

Want to keep yourself solidly in customers' and prospects' field of vision? Easy enough: Make sure they trust you. And they *will* trust you . . . if you've worked intelligently, sincerely, and coherently to build rapport . . . if you've communicated with them in an "information optimizing" way . . . if you've stood behind your offers . . . and if you haven't insulted them with irrelevant sales pitches for products that have nothing to do with what they want or can use.

Marketing Magic instead of Marketing Mayhem? Hardly. Nothing magical about it. A better word is sensible. What's more uncommon than common sense?

What a bonanza is there to be picked up! Without spending all that time and money on integrated marketing and one-to-one and CRM and branding seminars, you'll be able to avoid the present-day marketing mayhem plaguing so many of your competitors. Even better, you'll be able to make a happy leap back in time and re-create the too-often lost *real* . . . and profitable . . . one-to-one marketing environment. How? Why, just by establishing genuine sterling silver customer relationships.

Index

A

Acronyms, 92–95, 150–52
Ads, purpose, 37–39, 40–41, 55
Appeals, 53–55
Assumptive presentations, 258–61, 264
Asterisk Exception, 241, 245
Asterisks, 124–25, 140–42, 145,
  146–49, 154–56, 164–67, 206, 207,
  236, 241–45, 256

B

Basic Law of Database Parallels, 88
Benefits, 49, 54, 69–70
Brand, 177
Broadcast, 44
Bulk rate, 47
Business-to-business, 91–94, 96–99,
  182–84
Buying decisions, 28

C

Campaigns, 36, 40–49
Cable, 27, 44
Celebrity, 18, 20, 71–74, 214–20
CEOs, 24–25
Checks, 167–70, 210–11, 258
Clarity Commandment, 98
Cliches, 171–73, 200–2, 203–6
Commercial overload, 29
Commercial sponsorships, 21, 22, 23
Commercial time allotments, 27–29
Comparative ads, 142–46
Continuity program, 121–22
Cost-per-thousand, 74–75
Creativity, *See* Ten Creative Myths
Credibility, 185, 190, 194–95, 20
Cultures 23
Customer relationship, 109

Customer relationship management,
  79–81, 104–10
Customers, 207–65
Customer Service, 209–12, 226, 231–34
Cynicism, 24, 53

D

Database, 74–75, 85–90, 104, 104–5,
  108, 175–77, 258–61
Direct mail, 28, 33
Direct response, purpose, 40–41
Disgust Factor, 30, 32, 33

E

Endorsements, 17, 18, 19, 20, 71
Ecommerce, 37, 39, 113
Email, 39, 57, 75–76, 110, 223–24
Envelope, 68–70, 69–70, 249, 252

F

Fake Importance Syndrome, 163
Features, 69–71
Financial mailings, 29, 161–63
Force-communication, First Law of, 56

G

Generalization, 185
Generic Determination, 187–89

H

Hit-and-Run appeals, 56, 162–65,
  168–70

I

Illustration, 54, 78–79, 187, 188, 202–3
Illustration Agreement Rule, 55, 56, 187
Image, 182, 184, 185
Incredible Shrinking Universe Rule, 94

Infomercial/DRTV, 34, 77–78
Information optimizing, 163–62,
    193–95, 204–6
Inquirers, 81, 82
Integrated marketing, 110–11, 181

L
Lists, 57–59, 71–72, 81–82
Loyalty, 86, 116, 117, 119, 138, 149–52,
    161–62, 234

M
Management, 110–16
Manuals , 89–92
Messages, 43, 183
Motivators, 56–58, 60, 117, 137–43,
    186, 187, 190, 194–95

N
Network TV, 39
Non-profits, 64–65
Numbness Factor, 41

O
Obfuscation, 45, 54, 95, 97, 128, 136,
    145–49, 151–53, 155–57, 170–72 ,
    186, 187, 194, 202–4, 215, 246,
    249–51, 252–55
Offer, 122, 178–80, 210–11, 213, 238–39

P
Presenter, 23
Price, 117–23, 174–75
Production values, 41, 42, 73–74,
    183–85, 202–5
Promises, 127–33, 245
Prospects, 209–11
Psychographics, 83–88
Puffery, 201, 211–13

R
Radio, 33
Rapport, 23–24, 31, 83, 86, 111–12, 114,
    147, 228, 230

Relationship and procedure, 115–16
Relevance, 55, 149–60, 187
Response rates, 71–72, 73–74, 95

S
Sales letters, 75–77
Salesmanship, 17, 33, 46, 49–50, 51,
    80, 108, 143, 165, 179, 212–15
Salesperson, 32
Scripts, 30, 31, 219–22, 224, 228
Selling arguments, 68–69, 80–81,
    73–74, 76–77, 99, 111, 117, 121,
    157–59, 171–74, 175, 177–78, 203–8,
    221–23, 225, 258–6
Service, 209–12, 216–19, 227–30,
    231–34
Shipping and handling, 129–33
Skepticism, 248–51
Slogans, 42–44
Space ads, 17
Specifics, 185, 186
Spokesperson, 26
Stick rate, 33
Sweepstakes, 35–36, 52, 112, 250, 252,
    253–56
Stroking, 250
Surveys, 32, 158–59, 221–23, 225, 237,
    261–64

T
Telemarketing, 30, 32, 33
Ten Creative Myths, 64–78
Term-throwers, 79, 86–99
Testing, 37, 77, 120, 193–94
Touchstone advertising, 192–95
Trade advertising, 44–48
TV ads 17

U
Unique Selling Proposition, 49

W
Web, 20, 44, 108, 150–51